Women's Money®
Guide Book

Fourth Edition

Women's Money®

is a program of

The International Association of Working Mothers

A 501c3 tax-exempt non-profit organization

This Women's Money® Guidebook and Action Plan are the Proud Property of: _Anne Ann Gardner_

If you find this book, please send it to Women's Money Council on behalf of the owner.

Please mail it to the Women's Money Council P.O. Box 50008 Henderson, NV 89016

Table of Contents

About Women's Money® Program

The Women's Money Council®, a national council of community, financial industry, and policy leaders, conducts research and provides women programs for advocacy, education, and mentorship in order to foster financial independence, social and economic justice.

84% of women say they are not understanding or receiving information from financial and investment institutions1. Currently, 1 in 3 women lives in or on the brink of poverty2. 90% of women say they are completely or mostly unprepared for retirement3. As a result, 3 out of 5 women in the U.S. will retire in poverty. Why is that?

Most financial experts believe that college savings and retirement planning are put off because women say, "Oh, I have time to figure that out later" - then years have gone by and they've run out of time. We don't believe that is true. We believe that this procrastination mindset is a small part of a bigger picture. It is not the cause. It is the effect.

Women's Money® has developed a unique proprietary system to close the three gaps women experience in understanding and managing money concepts.

Clearly there is a communication gap – a big one, and reducing the Communication Gap is the first space in which Women's Money® sets out to make a difference. We are developing the tools and methods to reduce that gap. However, it's more than just a **Communication Gap**. There's also a **Confidence Gap** and **Action Gap**. The old adage, "you'd do better if you knew better" doesn't hold true when fear, confusion or insecurity are involved. Women's Money® is developing and implementing methods that reduce the gaps in **Communication, Confidence and Action** and support women into taking achieving measurable results in their path to financial wellness.

Women's Money® has been able to successfully pilot its unique and innovative financial education program in Nevada and has now expanded to several locations nationwide. Program ONE, the foundation building phase of the process includes mentoring events, personal mentoring, and conferences.

Program ONE focuses on three core concepts to build a strong foundation:

- <u>Financial Management</u> (Budgeting/ Debt/ Spending/ Money Triggers / Financial Goals and Organization)
- <u>Financial Safeguards</u> (Savings/ Income Development/ Credit)
- <u>Financial Protection</u> (Insurance/ Taxes/ Retirement)

Some of the women in Program ONE are ready for us to launch the next level with Program TWO and attend the Women's Money® Wealth Building Bootcamp.

What makes **Program TWO** so exciting is that women can be ready for Program TWO after only 6-18 months in Program ONE. When you realize that some of these women haven't been able to get to this point with existing resources in the last 20-40 years, this makes their achievement even more outstanding and exciting.

2/3rds of American household breadwinners and co-breadwinners are women (The Shriver Report)

90% of women are mostly or completely unprepared for retirement. (Sheconomy)

3 of 5 Women age 65 and older (married and single) cannot pay for their basic daily expenses. (Wowonline.org)

1 out of 3 women live in poverty or on the brink of poverty. (The Shriver Report)

84% feel misunderstood by investment and financial companies. (Sheconomy)

Dan Schwartz
State Treasurer

STATE OF NEVADA
OFFICE OF THE STATE TREASURER

Dear Women's Money Conference Attendees:

It is my great pleasure and honor to welcome you to the 4th Annual Women's Money® Conference for Nevada, sponsored by my office and the Nevada College Savings Board in cooperation with the International Association of Working Mothers. You are to be congratulated for your decision to make a positive difference in your life and that of your family's by attending this conference.

My appreciation to Gina Robison-Billups, Executive Director of the National Women's Money® Council, and her staff, as well as our fellow sponsors - Direct Selling Education Foundation, Intuit®, Carol's Daughter®, and NV Energy® - for their dedication to this initiative.

As your State Treasurer, I firmly believe that having control of your own finances is a key step to opening the door to economic opportunity and security. While today many women control the majority of household spending, some feel they lack sufficient knowledge of financial products and tools. As a result, they may find themselves less able to save for their children's college education or for future financial needs, and may feel more helpless in avoiding fraudulent or abusive financial practices.

It is my sincere hope that this Women's Money® Conference will provide you with education regarding the many financial issues faced by today's women, as well as the confidence in addressing them.

With Warm Regards,

Dan Schwartz
Nevada State Treasurer

STATE TREASURER PROGRAMS
Governor Guinn Millennium Scholarship Program
Nevada Prepaid Tuition Program
Unclaimed Property
College Savings Plans of Nevada
Nevada College Kick Start Program

CARSON CITY OFFICE
101 N. Carson Street, Suite 4
Carson City, Nevada 89701-4786
(775) 684-5600 Telephone
(775) 684-5623 Fax

LAS VEGAS OFFICE
555 E. Washington Avenue, Suite 4600
Las Vegas, Nevada 89101-1074
(702) 486-2025 Telephone
(702) 486-3246 Fax

Website: NevadaTreasurer.gov   E-mail: StateTreasurer@NevadaTreasurer.gov

Introduction to Your Money

These days, everyone thinks about money and worries about their financial well being. These can be difficult times for many families and households, resulting in the need for and awareness of the importance of stretching dollars and planning for the future. As America recovers from the most severe financial crisis since the Great Depression, developing the financial health and wellness of every American woman and girl will be vital to ensuring that families are more secure for their financial future. This Guidebook is one tool you can use to create financial independence and stability.

- Only 41 percent of parents have set aside money for their children's college education.
- The majority of Americans do not have a "rainy day" fund for unanticipated financial emergencies and are not adequately preparing for their children's college education and their own retirement.
- More than one in five survey respondents use high-cost, alternative borrowing methods, such as payday loans or pawnshops.
- Fewer than half (46 percent) of correctly answered two basic questions about how interest rates and inflation work.

The U. S. Department of Labor's latest data on women illustrate important facts:

Women are more likely to work in part-time jobs that do not qualify for a retirement plan. And working women are more likely than men to interrupt their careers to take care of family members. Therefore, they work fewer years and contribute less toward their retirement, resulting in lower lifetime savings.

Of the 62 million wage and salaried women (age 21 to 64) working in the United States, just 45 percent participated in a retirement plan.

The good news and the bad news is that you are not alone. Many families are experiencing financial tragedies that are devastating – even the families you would never think have problems. Most of them are "putting on a good face" in hopes that something will happen to them. After reading the findings of The National Financial Capability Study we hope that you become one of the women who is no longer "waiting for a solution" and become a woman who is creating her own solutions.

Like many today, perhaps you face new financial challenges. Maybe you are employed and searching for work. Maybe you are going to school or have a new job. Maybe you are a newlywed, a new parent, or suddenly single. Perhaps you have an established career or are an entrepreneur, a community volunteer, or a "soccer Mom." You may wonder if you are handling your money as wisely as possible. No matter what your situation, one thing stands out.

You work hard for your money, and you want it to work hard for you!

You would like to have more money, or at least make the money you have go further. You want to be more "money-savvy" because managing money wisely is challenging stuff. Your busy days are filled with many decisions related to money: how to pay the bills, what to buy or not to buy, how to pay down debt, how much and where to save, what to put on credit, how to save for future emergencies, how to invest for the future, what to teach your children about money, how to decide about insurance, how to understand employee benefits, how to afford college for your children, how to have a secure retirement for yourself, and a thousand other things that ultimately affect your financial security.

As part of a comprehensive financial education program, this Women's Money Guidebook is designed for women and girls from age 11 to 95years old, but your age doesn't really matter! Survey results from past Women's Money participants have demonstrated that all age groups of women are benefitting from the program. They have been able to make positive changes in how they manage their finances. Regardless of your present age, Women's Money is reaching you at a good time in your life... a period in which you're ready to make changes.

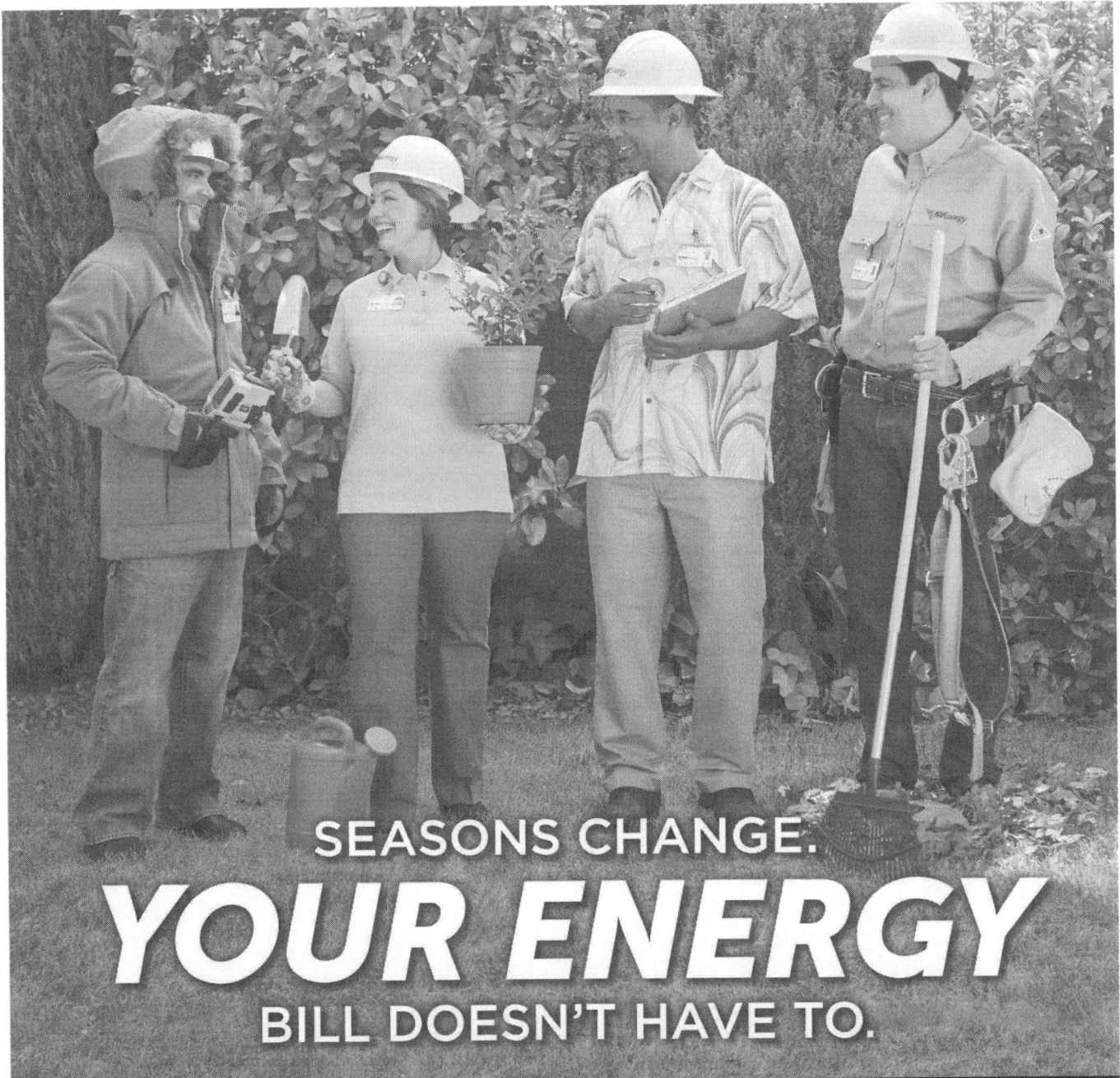

Women's Money® Conference Action Plan

Today you will be inspired to take action toward your goals, and you will be connected to many people who will support you in the achievement of your goals.

While you listen to the speakers and have discussions with the women with your mentor or your Women's Money® Mentoring Group, you will come up with great ideas, questions and Aha! Moments – many of which will guide you to connect with resource providers in the Women's Money® Resource Pavilion.

I need support to do, learn or get...	Questions I need answers to:	My Aha! Moments

Take a Money Break!

• **Share** your Aha! Moments. • **Discuss** your needs and questions with your mentor.
• **Decide** on what resources you need.
• **Visit** professionals in the Pavilion, online or in person that can help you achieve what you want.

Financial Action Ideas

Select one or more action step(s) or create your own:

Develop a Spending and Debt Reduction Plan:

- Track your spending for 30 days. Whenever you spend money, write down how much you spent and what you spent it on.
- Make a commitment and set goals to become debt free.
- Decide not to incur any more debt.
- Never carry your credit card unless you plan to use it.
- Accelerate your credit card payments. Make more than the minimum payment on your credit cards.
- Call your creditors to request a lower interest rate.
- Get a credit card with no annual fee and a low interest rate.
- Request your creditor waive any annual fees.
- Consider transferring balances from higher-interest rate accounts to lower-interest rate accounts.
- Read the fine print on your credit card accounts.

Develop a Savings and Investment Plan:

- Always pay yourself first.
- If you pay more than $500 or receive more than $500 in a tax refund, review your W-4 form and adjust to keep more of the money you earn.
- Set aside a percentage of each paycheck for savings.
- Open an emergency account.
- Open a contingency account for your unexpected or irregular expenses. For example, car repairs, home repairs, vet bills, etc.
- Make your savings and investments automatic. Use payroll deduction or have the money regularly withheld from your bank account.
- Save your change each day. At the end of a month, open a savings account.
- Reduce your mortgage payments by refinancing.
- Educate yourself on mutual funds and open an account.

Learn More About Social Security and Plan for Your Retirement:

- Complete the online calculator to estimate your potential Social Security retirement benefit. Visit **www.socialsecurity.gov**.
- Review your Social Security Statement for accuracy and make any corrections.
- Request your Social Security Statement (if you don't have it)
- online at www.socialsecurity.gov or call 800-772-1213.
- If you change your name, complete the necessary paperwork with the Social Security Administration.
- Participate in your employer's pension plan. If you can't afford to contribute the maximum, start small, but participate!
- Review all pension options available to you when your spouses retire. For more information, visit the Women's Institute for a Secure Retirement at **www.wiserwomen.org**.
- Make an appointment with a financial advisor or certified financial planner.
- Open and fund an Individual Retirement Account (IRA).
- If you don't work outside the home, have your husband open and contribute to a Spousal IRA for you.

WealthClinic is a global educational community developed to help people improve their relationship with money through private mentoring, online interactive workshops and in-person retreats.

WealthClinic shows you how to identify, then break free of limiting money behaviors so you can open the door to money and wealth building at a whole new level.

By bringing together the inner and outer work of wealth building, our programs help you live with less stress, greater empowerment, and more financial abundance.

To learn more, you can reach Leisa Peterson, CFP® at 530-448-7081, via email at lpeterson@wealthclinic.com or go to our website www.wealthclinic.com.

Request Your Credit Report and Credit Score:

- Request your free credit report annually from all three credit-reporting agencies at **www.annualcreditreport.com**.
- Request your credit score for free from credit.com or creditkarma.com
- Review your credit report for errors and report errors in writing to both the creditor and the credit-reporting agency.
- Understand what your liability for joint accounts will be at the time of divorce or death.
- Pay your bills consistently on time.

Minimize Your Risk of Identity Theft:

- Only give your Social Security number to those who need it.
- Questions to ask: "Why do you need it? How will it be used? How do you protect it from being stolen? What will happen if I don't give it to you?"
- Don't carry your Social Security card in your purse or wallet.
- Never have your Social Security number or driver's license pre-printed on your checks.
- Make a photocopy of the contents of your wallet.
- If your bills and bank statements don't arrive on time, follow-up with creditors.
- Don't leave unwanted blank credit applications in your mailbox.
- Keep unsolicited, pre-approved credit card applications out of your mail by exercising your opt-out rights. Call 888-567-8688 or visit www.optoutprescreen.com. You'll need to provide your Social Security number.
- Reduce your junk mail by registering at the Direct Marketing Association website at www.dmachoice.org
- Reduce the number of unsolicited telemarketing phone calls by registering your phone number at www.donotcall.gov.
- Password protect your computer to prevent access by unauthorized persons.
- Install a firewall to limit uninvited access to your computer.
- Stop opening email attachments from people you don't know.
- If you think you are a victim of identity theft, call the Identity Theft Hotline at 877-438-4388.

Protect Yourself and the People and Things you Love:

- Review your automobile and homeowners insurance deductibles. Raising deductibles can reduce your premiums by up to 20%.
- Review your life and disability insurance to ensure you have adequate coverage.
- Investigate and consider purchasing long-term care insurance.
- Make an appointment with an attorney to write a will to protect your family.
- Prepare a durable power of attorney and advance health care directive.
- Write a letter to your family providing them with all the information they will need if you die or become incapacitated.
- Complete the funeral planning forms found online at www.peoples-memorial.org
- Review your non-probate assets (life insurance, pension plans, IRAs, etc.) to ensure you have named the appropriate beneficiary.
- Talk to your family about being prepared for a disaster.
- Make Emergency Contact Cards for everyone in your family.
- Get an evacuation box to protect your financial paperwork.

Why 5% Succeed

Wednesdays at 1 pm Pacific time.

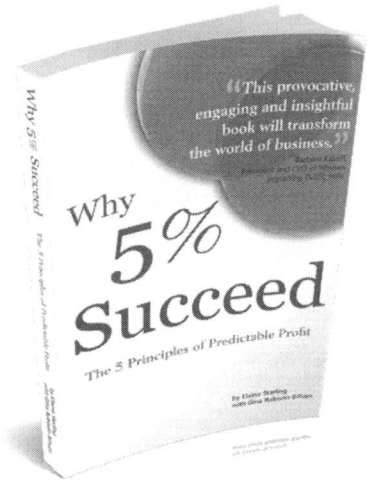

Watch "Why 5% Succeed," to discover how business owners are increasing return-on-investment - and you can too!

Each week reveals the tips, tricks, tools, and techniques business owners use for consistent business growth. You'll learn the four ways your business generates a return-on-investment for your clients.

To learn more or apply to be a guest on the show visit :
www.Why5PercentSucceedMembers.com

Vi
VESTED INTEREST
INVESTING
for beginners
Curious about investing?
We help you get started.
InvestWithVi.com

Chapter One: Money, Communication, & Happiness

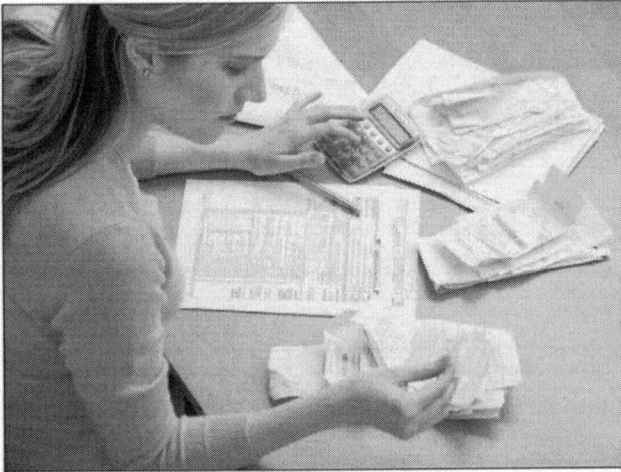

The main money challenge in life is to make our money last as long as we do, or longer and without giving up enjoyment along the way! That's a tall order, but it's not impossible to achieve. It all starts with awareness.

The mistake most people make is that they don't take the long-range view about life...much of their energy goes to worrying about current problems and issues. That's a normal response. After all, the bills have to be paid. But without taking a long-range view of our lives and doing the best job possible of planning for the future, we are likely to experience some unpleasant money surprises along the way. This is lesson number one. Money is for life, not just for now!

Does Control Over Your Money Equal Happiness?

In her research on happiness and financial security, financial author Jean Chatzsky found that good money control is a matter of cultivating certain money control habits. She says that there is a difference between families who are in control of their money and those who are not. Successful families don't necessarily earn a lot of money. In fact, her book explores how it is not how much money people have that makes them happy. Rather, poor money management can make them miserable - even if they have a lot of money. Look at the differences in financial behavior between families IN CONTROL of their finances and families with LESS CONTROL.

Families in control of their finances have adopted at least four of these practices:	Families with less control of their finances have at least two of these habits:
They balance their checkbook at least once a month.	They don't balance their checkbook every month.
They have some sort of filing system in place.	Their financial records and paperwork are disorganized, so they have to scramble to find what they're looking for.
They pay their bills as they come in rather than once a month.	They pay all of their bills once a month rather than as those bills come in.
They don't spend more than they can afford on three or more things (though they may bust the budget on one or two).	They spend more than they can afford on three or more items.
They don't often buy things they don't need.	They often buy things they don't need.
They don't find money evaporating out of their wallets.	They find money evaporates out of their wallets, *and they don't know where it has gone.*

Communications within the Family

Communicating with others about money can be an emotional experience. Talking about money can lead to arguments. Hidden agendas and relationship pitfalls can keep money talks from being successful. Attorneys and therapists have identified unresolved money problems or differences as the primary causes of divorce.

The conversations that occur within the family will depend on who is part of your financial life at the moment. Think to the future, too, about changes that may occur in your life or in the lives of people who are closest to you.

Consider the nature of money talks that critical documents are kept. You can probably think of many other issues that range in severity from financial problems associated with substance abuse to which brand of a certain product to buy.

Everyone has a "money personality". Good communication will help your family be financially successful. It will help you determine joint goals, develop a shared vision, and reach an agreement on how to spend, save, invest, or donate your family's money. Try to create a stress-free environment for discussing money if there are other people in your life with whom you must discuss financial matters. Money issues that can arise include who pays the bills, what to buy, how much to spend, how children's allowances are set, or how to ask a parent where you have had or will have with the people in your life. Remember that there is less room for argument and conflict when financial matters are well organized and under control. Try to focus on the facts, not the emotions.

Conflicts over money or difficult conversations about money can be eased if a few recommendations from conflict resolution counselors are heeded. Choosing a good time and place for discussion, perhaps away from home, can help. Remaining calm and practicing self- awareness, acknowledging emotions, listening carefully to the other person, and focusing on the problem and not the person are all helpful strategies. Avoid blaming and raising your voice. Each person should be encouraged to suggest potential solutions, without judgment or criticism. With a list of solutions in hand, ideas can be reviewed and evaluated together, in a less emotional or confrontational manner.

Personal and family financial decisions are influenced by attitudes, personality types, past experiences, and family dynamics. When you understand yourself and others, you can make financial decisions more effectively. You may also reduce conflict. As you change, so do your needs and abilities for flexible money practices. Awareness and self-analysis can. With clarity and balance come a sense of control and well-being.

Think about and **list the people** and **the issues** you need to discuss:

Your spouse or significant other _____

Your children: _____

Your parents: _____

Your grandparents or other older relatives: _____

Your siblings: _____

Members of your spouse's family: _____

Your ex-spouse: _____

Financial/Legal professionals: _____

"My Money Story" is where it all starts.

Do you ever wonder why you manage your money in a certain way? Maybe you spend money on this or that when you know you shouldn't, you don't need it or you even know that it is harmful? Do you ever wonder why you continue to do it over and over again? Most likely the answer is hidden in a life episode you don't even remember – a subconscious connection that was made to money in the early years of your life. These become "money triggers" that can lead us to spend in the wrong ways, ignore debt, and lead us into money dangers with our eyes wide open to the potential catastrophe that lies ahead and we are left feeling guilty, stupid, and desperate….we feel like a victim of our own money behaviours. You can't stop the money-trigger merry-go-round unless you can slow it down enough to jump off. This exercise provides you with a jumping off point.

This next exercise is about you and your money story. Write down what you know or feel about money (the good the bad and the ugly) and why you feel that way about money…what brought you to this "fact". Don't edit yourself. Just write from the heart.

After you have written it down, read it and ask yourself:

1. Does this attitude/belief system serve me?
2. Is this accurate and absolutely truth? Does it serve me? If it doesn't serve you, do you need to continue acting as if you do believe it?
3. How do I act out my money story in my daily life?

My Money Story

_____

_____

_____

_____

_____

_____

_____

_____

_____

_____

_____

_____

_____

_____

_____

_____

Financial Organization

Before you can move forward with a new financial strategy for your life, you need to be financially organized. Sometimes the roadblock to making financial change is a lack of organization. Everyone's financial life consists of giant paper trails and e-records.

You might wonder why financial organization is under the topic of Emotions and Money. The reason is that many times having unorganized or under-organized financial information is often caused from fear. It's easier to avoid the situation if you don't take a look at it. Ignorance is not bliss in this situation. Financial ignorance actually causes you more stress.

Financial organization is not budgeting, and because so many people are afraid or don't like budgets, they choose to avoid all types of financial organization. In this chapter, we've given you tools to easily get organized.

Being organized gives you freedom!

It cuts down on stress so you can focus on actual financial management.

Two types of organization are required:

1) the physical organization of papers and electronic records, and

2) the organization of your financial data and information.

The physical organization of papers and electronic records.

These are the paper or electronic records we find at home or work, in our bags and briefcases, on our computers, and in our billfolds. They include a listing of your vital documents as well as your account numbers, passwords, and personal identification   numbers (PINs). These statements and records are the sources of our core financial data, and they demand a simple filing system.

> We need simple ways to file and retrieve financial records without wasting valuable time looking for critical statements and money papers. We also need a safe way to keep personal information, so that it does not make its way into the hands of unauthorized people!

A word about the electronic world: In recent years, new technology has transformed how we conduct our personal financial affairs. As you opt to do more of your financial transactions on-line, a new need has emerged:

- how/ where to record and
- keep all of those website
- account numbers and PINs.

Think carefully about how to protect the privacy of this information, but at the same time, think about how the information might be needed by someone else should something happen to you. You need an electronic reference list, but you should be cautious about where you keep it and with whom you share it. Since this is very new territory, be sure that the information will not be open to snoopers. Keep up-to-date firewalls on your personal computer, and be very cautious about how you share sensitive financial information with others.

Remember to keep track of all the types of electronic accounts that you use: checking accounts, brokerage accounts, retirement accounts, credit card accounts, bill-paying services, creditors, on-line stores you order from (yes, even eBay!), free subscriptions to financial newsletters, frequent flyer accounts, and other types of accounts. Sooner or later, you will forget an account number, log-in name, password, or PIN, which will be frustrating and cause you to lose a lot of time recovering from your memory lapse if you haven't kept the information in an easily-accessible but secure mode. You may wish to investigate secure, web-based sites that specialize in storing log-in names, passwords, and PINs in a safe, encrypted manner. These sites require you to remember only one log-in name and password. And always select passwords/PINs that are considered "strong," that is, not easily figured out by others.

For the most effective organization of your financial information, you need all of your financial data and information to know how to make sense of the money in your life and how you want it to be directed and used.

7 Simple Steps to Getting Financially Organized

The information you compile is vital to your future!   It won't take you as long as you may think.

Step 1.   Complete the Credit and Debit Card Safety Record.

This is an easy step and an important one. Much of the information is in your billfold already, but you may have to find information from your credit card issuers to fill in addresses and telephone numbers. (Never keep PINs in your billfold.) Try to keep this record up to date. But be careful where you store the information.

Tools to use:

- Download the preformatted excel form from womensmoney.org called "Credit and Debit Card Safety Record" to print and file in a locked file drawer or safe or save as a password protected document on your computer.
- Use an app! There are several apps that secure your passwords, pins and credit information such as *My Wallet, Password ABC, Save it Save, eWallet and Safe!*

Sample Credit and Debit Card Safety Record		
Name of Card	Visa	
Account Number	1234567-89	
PIN	xxxx	
Users	Cindy, Joe	
Lost Card Telephone Number	1-800-111-2222	
Lost Card Company Address	234 Street City, ST 00000	
Card Expiration	4/12	

Step 2. Complete the Vital Documents Inventory.

Not all components of this inventory will apply to you, and some elements of your financial life may not be listed. Be sure to add them. You can complete this task fairly quickly if you know where your documents are located. Use a pencil, because you are likely to make location changes as you organize yourself.

Tools to use:

- Download the preformatted excel form from womensmoney.org called "Vital Documents Inventory" to print and file in a locked file drawer or safe or save as a password protected document on your computer.

Sample Vital Documents Inventory		
Name:		**Date:**
Type of Document		
Emergency and Estate-Related		**Document Location**
List of Key Names, Addresses, Phone Numbers		
My Letter of Last Instruction		
Wills/Trusts		
Other (could include vital information about parents)		

- Shoeboxed.com can store scanned documents in a safe online support platform. You can scan receipts, business cards and documents safely. Scan your documents and upload them to shoeboxed.com. If you prefer to scan and keep them on your own computer. Password protect each document and have an online backup tool like Carbonite.com that backs up your documents in case your computer is lost, stolen or your computer crashes.

Step 3. Complete the form, My Electronic Accounts, Passwords, and PINs.

Be sure you keep this information in a safe place. Do NOT keep this information in your purse or billfold where it could easily be stolen.

Tools to use:
- Download the preformatted excel form from womensmoney.org called "Electronic Accounts Recorder" to print and file in a locked file drawer or safe or save as a password protected document on your computer.
- Use an app! There are several apps that secure your passwords, pins and credit information such as *My Wallet, Password ABC, Save it Save, eWallet and Safe!*

My Electronic Accounts, Passwords, and PINS			
Account Name/Type	Website	Account Number	Log-in or User Name, Password or PIN
ABC Checking 1-800-111-2222	www.xxx.III/U	12345sp	gigi-v Xxxxxx

Step 4. Create a Financial Center at home (or as the Feng Shui advocates like to call it, a Wealth Center).

The Financial Center will be where you keep your financial records and conduct your financial affairs. If you use a computer, provide adequate space for it. Invest in a filing system (metal filing cabinet, baskets, or bins) and plenty of file folders. Some people prefer hanging files to non-hanging; let your own preference prevail. If you do not have the money to buy such equipment for your Financial Center, paper storage boxes will work just fine. Determine whether you want to make your filing system lockable or not.

Step 5. Establish a filing system.

In Step 2 above, you jotted down where you keep your vital documents. Now it is time to file them systematically. Develop a filing system. You may wish to use the file categories in the Vital Documents Inventory or create your own. Some people merely file everything alphabetically, and it seems to work for them. Label each file folder so you can easily find what you are looking for. Only file your documents in a password protected computer file, a locked safe or a locked metal file cabinet (best if bolted to the floor).

Step 6. Decide how to organize your electronic files.

With many financial institutions now providing only electronic copies of statements, decide how you will keep these records. One option is to organize "file folders" on your computer that match the categories in your filing cabinet. You must also decide if you plan to print paper copies of your electronic statements as back-up. You may wish to scan some of your paper documents to eliminate bulk. Consider what would happen if your computer crashes. You need a system for backing up your electronic files, or you may elect to store them on an external hard drive or flash drive. If you do not back up your computer files regularly, you may decide it is better to print off vital records. Make sure your firewalls are always up to date, and when you replace your computer, make sure that the hard disk on the old computer is completely disabled and destroyed.

Step 7. Shred paper copies with personal information.

It is strongly recommended that you purchase a paper shredder if you do not already have one, shredding all old hard-copy documents that you no longer need that include your identity and/or account numbers rather than just placing these documents in the trash. Even incoming credit card solicitation offers should be carefully discarded by shredding. Ask your financial institution if they provide free shredding services.

Electronic Accounts Recorder

Social Media Site	Password Clue	Username (Clue)	Email attached to Account	Security Question Answer(s)

Websites	Password Clue	Username	Email attached to Account	Security Question Answer(s)

Email Host/Address	Password Clue	Username	Email attached to Account	Security Question Answer(s)

Bank(s) & Credit Cards	Password Clue	Username	Email attached to Account	Security Question Answer(s)

BUSINESS SERVICES	Password Clue	Username	Email attached to Account	Security Question Answer(s)

Other Accounts	Password Clue	Username	Email attached to Account	Security Question Answer(s)

Vital Records Inventory

Everyone has vital documents. This inventory can help you organize your basic information. Not all components of the inventory will apply to you. Some elements of your financial life may be missing, so be sure to add them. You can complete the inventory fairly easily if you know where your documents are located. Use a pencil, because you are likely to make location changes as you organize yourself. Make sure you keep this information in a safe place "away from prying eyes." Developed by Nancy L. Granovsky, CFP®, Professor and Extension Family Economics Specialist, Texas Modified for excel by Women's Money®

Emergency and Estate Related	Location of Document
Key Names, Addresses, Phone Numbers	
Letter of Last Instruction	
Wills/Trusts	
Other: could include vital information about parents	

Insurance Related	Location of Document
Auto	
Disability	
Health	
Life	
Long Term Care	
Other:	

Certificates and Deeds	Location of Document
Automobile Titles	
Birth Certificates	
Death Certificates	
Divorce Decrees	
Marriage Certificates	
Military Service and Discharge Documents	
Passports	
Real Estate Deeds	
Other:	

Investments and Savings (non-retirement)	Location of Document
Certificates of Deposit	
Mutual Fund Records	
Savings Passbooks or Statements	
Stock Certificates	
Other: could include brokerage account records and	
real estate investment records	

Retirement Accounts	Location of Document
IRA Account Records	
Roth IRA Account Records	
Retirement Account Records (401[k], 403[b], etc.)	
Other: include all retirement accounts	

Checking Accounts	Location of Document
Primary Checking Account Records	
Secondary Checking Account Records	
Other: locations may be paper or electronic or on-line	

Loans and Credit Cards	Location of Document
Credit Card Safety Record	
Loans and Mortgages Outstanding	
Other:	

Tax Records	Location of Document
Last Year's Tax Return	
Past Tax Returns (last seven years)	
Other: Could include permanent records for home	
improvements that affect real estate basis/value	

Other Records	Location of Document
List of my websites, account numbers, and PINs	

Chapter One: Record Your Accomplishments!

Possible Action Items for this Chapter:

☐ Found some money triggers.

☐ Shared Money Story exercise with my spouse/children/group to launch a conversation about how our money beliefs add to our behaviours and our stress.

☐ Made a list of who you need to talk to about financial issues.

☐ Completed the *What's Important to You?* Exercise. Shared with my spouse/children to launch a conversation about what is important to all of us.

☐ Filled out *Vital Documents Inventory* Form (Document is available online for Program ONE members).

☐ Put it in a safe place

☐ Downloaded or Printed the Electronic Accounts, Passwords and PINS Form

☐ Put it in a safe place

Accomplishment Tracker

Date _____Year____ My Name_____ My Mentor is_____

Results from last month's action step(s) or Where I'm at right now...

_____

_____

_____

_____

_____

Challenge(s) I overcame to achieve these results

_____

_____

_____

_____

This is what I would like to accomplish in the next 30 days.

_____

_____

_____

Thoughts and Inspirations:

Chapter Notes and Questions

Chapter Two: Your Financial Goals!

Money for All the Stages in Your Life

Today's women span all age ranges. Some are new college graduates, and some have daughters and granddaughters in college right now. Some have a new baby, while others have grandchildren! It's hard to describe the life stages through which women may pass because of the enormous diversity that characterizes any large population group. But from a financial perspective, it is important to anticipate at least some life stages to prepare financially for those stages when they do happen.

Real Life, Real Money

"All I could think about was landing my first job. I wouldn't have to worry about money! I could finally buy what I wanted, when I wanted, so I did. I filled my apartment with all the things I had been dreaming of, including a to-die-for new wardrobe. I wasn't prepared when my apartment building burned down one day when I was at work, and I lost everything. Did I have renter's insurance? No, .I didn't think it could happen in a million years! Now I tell everybody, "Don't just think about today. Think about tomorrow."

Women's financial lives are impacted by their relationships to others: spouses, children, grandchildren, parents, grandparents, former spouses, partners, or siblings. Traditional family lifecycle patterns are marked by marriage, the birth or adoption of children, children leaving home or the "empty nest," retirement, the death of a spouse, widowhood, declining health, and the eventual death of the surviving spouse. But these traditional patterns have many variations. Other patterns or stages may include: married without children, divorced, single-parent family, remarriage, and stepfamily. Still other patterns might include multi-generational families, adult children returning home, grandparents raising grandchildren, working women caring for elderly parents or in-laws, or becoming disabled at a young age. You may experience (now or in the future) yet other variations from these common patterns.

Choices, Decisions, and Events

The life choices and decisions we make have an enormous impact on financial security throughout the lifespan. Choices and decisions refer to our conscious and deliberate decision- making. Unplanned life events also have a major impact on financial security. These events alter the course of our plans and our economic status when life hands us a curve ball. A few examples are listed in the table below, but you may be able to think of others you have experienced or will experience.

Real Life, Real Money: Mary Thinks about the Future

Mary is 28, the youngest child of older parents. Her Mom just turned 72 and has developed Parkinson's disease. Mary is a single parent of three-year-old Kimberly. She lives in the same town as her mother. Her siblings expect her to be responsible for her mother's growing needs. Mary recently met Jeff, and there is a strong likelihood they will marry, but she's not sure.

Life Choices and Decisions We Make (Conscious decision-making)	Unplanned Life Events (When life hands us a curve ball)
Education and training	

to go to college (or not)
choice of a field of study
to go for an advanced degree
to seek additional training
to choose a field with low-wage potential
	$ no money to go to college or get training
	$ an interruption in studies and failure to complete a Degree
	$ unknowingly choosing a field with low-wage potential
	$ lack of good-paying jobs in the community

Career/job/workplace	

nature and location of jobs
benefits package (or not)
opportunities for advancement
	$ sudden job loss or furlough
	$ long-term unemployment or under-employment
	$ workforce re-entry difficulties
	$ having a job with no retirement benefits

Work and family	

to marry (or not)
to re-marry following a divorce or death
to have children (or not)
how to balance work and family
	$ the costs and benefits of moving from Career Track to Mommy Track
	$ Divorce
	$ illness or death of a spouse
	$ dependent care issues (child or elder care)

Financial choices and decisions	

to set financial goals (or not)
to save for the future (or not)
to carry a large debt load (or not)
to develop financial knowledge and skills (or not)
to purchase insurance (or not)
	$ catastrophic expense due to illness or property Damage
	$ loss of income
	$ income windfall (inheritance)
	$ Bankruptcy

In the table below, we've used Mary as an example.

Mary	Mary in 10 Years	Mary in 20 Years
single	married	married, but divorce could happen
single parent	one more child – college $$ for two	one child out of college, one to go
elder care responsibility?	increasing elder care responsibility?	Mother deceased - thinking about her own retirement in 10

In the table below, write three words or phrases that characterize your present life stage.
How will these descriptions change over the next 10 to 20 years?

Me Today	Me in 10 Years	Me in 20 Years

Each age and stage has unique financial tasks that must be addressed. The earlier you begin to pursue certain financial goals, such as building a retirement portfolio, the better off you will be.

Your Life Levels: Financial Tasks, Common Errors, and Desirable Outcomes

Age Group	18 to 24	25 to 34	35 to 44 and beyond
Unique Financial Tasks	• Establish household • Train for career • Attain financial independence • Purchase insurance • Establish financial identity • Establish a savings plan • Make a spending plan • Develop effective financial recordkeeping system to be maintained throughout life • Develop an effective financial planning system • Make wills when household is established	• Provide for childbearing and rearing costs • Provide for expanding housing needs • Expand career goals • Manage increased need for credit • Provide for training/education funds • Purchase additional protection coverage (insurance) • Make wills, if not done; adjust as responsibilities change • Maximize financial management skills of all members of household	• Upgrade career training • Continue to build education fund • Maximize protection for major income earner(s); purchase insurance • Make will, if not done; adjust as circumstances change • Provide greater income for expanding needs • Establish and work toward retirement goals
Common Financial Errors	• Spending more than you earn • Failure to manage financial Resources • Failure to use professional expertise • Failure to recognize and develop human potential • Emphasis on current needs and failure to anticipate changes in the lifecycle • Failure to start early planning for retirement • Failure to make short- and long-term goals and financial plans	• Over-committed income • Lack plans for children's education expenses • Failure to plan for continuing education expenses • Failure to investigate housing alternatives • Lack of emergency fund and savings • Lack of sufficient long- and short-term protection coverage • Lack realistic family and personal goals • Failure to estimate impact of single or dual income • Failure to view education as investment in one's future • Failure to involve other family members, especially children, in financial matters	• Overuse of credit • Failure to provide funds for major home repairs/ replacements • Failure to provide adequate protection/insurance • Failure to plan for retirement • Failure to increase primary income and seek alternate sources • Failure to manage increased number and complexity of financial needs • Lack of funds for children's higher education and/or training

Desirable Outcomes	• Adequate income to supply basic needs and wants • Financial needs assessed • Consumer knowledge and skills developed • A balanced spending, borrowing, and savings plan • Knowledge of and access to financial and legal records and documents • A balanced view of obtaining, protecting, and using financial resources • Use of professional expertise • Ability to live within income • Short- and long-term economic and social goals determined	• Economic and social goals adjusted • Consumer, legal, and financial knowledge acquired • Financial security program (i.e., savings, protection, investment) expanded • Investment in additional education/training • All family members develop financial skills appropriate for age and role	• Economic goals redefined • Financial security programs continued/strengthened • Primary and secondary income sources diversified as needed • Financial obligations and resources controlled • Retirement income plan established

My Lifeline

Figure out the years in your Lifeline:

- Number of years you expect to live beyond age 60 _____
- Number of years remaining in your Lifeline (expect the longest life you can) _____
- Age you expect to retire _____
- Number of years between now and when you retire _____
- Number of years between when you retire and the end of your life _____

What do you envision retirement to be like for you?

_____

_____

Complete the following sentence:

What worries me most about this picture is _____

Am I at risk? Which of the following factors may put you at risk?

☐ I have no financial goals.

☐ I have no idea of how to calculate how much my future needs will cost along this Lifeline.

☐ I do not know how much money I will need to live on in retirement.

☐ I do not presently contribute to a retirement savings or pension plan.

☐ I am presently in a job that has no retirement benefits.

☐ I do not know my current financial worth.

☐ I have debts that I need to repay.

☐ I have a family history of longevity.

☐ I am married and at risk of becoming widowed one day. (In March 2008, 27 percent of U.S. women ages 55 and older were widowed.)

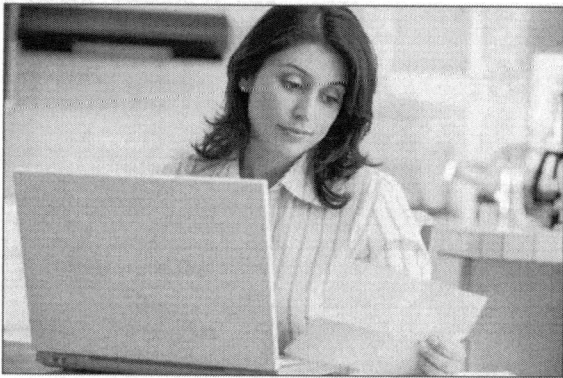

Has this process of assessing future needs and concerns left you feeling stressed, overwhelmed, or even depressed?

Try to see the bright side. Recognizing these potential financial issues early is a huge step in becoming financially secure in the future. Remember the saying, "Rome wasn't built in a day." Taking small steps and actions to address these concerns will help you become more in charge of your financial situation – present and future.

Reducing risks now.... What three actions could you take now to reduce your risk factors?

1. _____

2. _____

3. _____

Setting Goals

Most of us carry around mental images of the life we would like to be living. Whether we achieve the life we want depends on many factors, but the most important element for our "dream fulfillment" is creating concrete financial goals and a process for achieving them. There is a big difference between a dream and an actual financial goal. Dreams have a "some day" quality about them. But financial goals can be our action plans and roadmaps for achieving our dreams. Now is the time to specify those goals and turn them into financial action items.

Good financial planning and money management always begin with goal setting. Goals give direction and purpose to the way money is spent. Goals provide us with motivation and encouragement in working towards what is most important. For the greatest personal satisfaction, our financial goals should reflect our values- our deep-rooted beliefs about what matters most to us.

Financial goals may be short-term, intermediate-range or long-range.

Examples of **short-term goals** are:

        1) Shifting from using credit to using a debit card,

        2) Reducing expenditures for a particular category of spending,

        3) Developing a workable budget, and

        4) Building an emergency fund or set-aside account.

Examples of **intermediate-range goals** are:

        1) Saving for things you want to buy in the near future,

        2) Saving money for a down payment on a house or a new vehicle,

        3) Saving for the college education of a child, and

        4) Becoming debt-free.

Examples of **long-range goals** are:

        1) Building a retirement portfolio,

        2) Saving for a vacation home, and

        3) Developing an estate plan.

There are seven basic steps involved in setting and achieving financial goals.

Goal Setting Systems – Do What Works for You

Basic steps to setting and achieving goals are great to know, but most of us need a system to help us actually achieve those goals. Below is a basic outline of one way to reach a goal.

Steps to Setting and Achieving Financial Goals

Identify the goal, and write it down.

Put a price tag on the goal. How much money will be needed to achieve the goal?

Set a target date for achieving the goal.

Set priorities among your financial goals. It may not be possible to achieve all of them simultaneously.

Develop a plan to achieve your goals. This will mean re- examining how you presently spend your money and working the financial goals into your monthly budget/ spending plan.

Begin to work toward the goal immediately. Procrastination costs money in the long run. If you have a plan in mind for how to accomplish your goal, there is no reason to delay action.

Keep records to monitor your progress and success towards accomplishing your goals.

If you prefer a more structured system, the founder of Women's Money is also the co-author of The Accomplishment Journal for Women series, and we are delighted to share the Accomplishment System with you.

Your Goals, Dreams & Desires for the Year

Chunk those bigger goals into smaller goals that build to the bigger goals.

Take each quarterly goal. Break it down into steps to be accomplished.

Daily tracking of progress steps.

Celebrate daily.

The full Accomplishment System is available for FREE DOWNLOAD through the Women's Money® Program One Online Mentoring Portal. If you are not yet signed up for Program One Mentoring, do it today. It's free. If you'd like the Accomplishment Journal in print, you can purchase it on Amazon.com

What's Important to You? (Part One)

Before you set goals, take a good look at what you value most at this point in your life. Goals that are out of integrity with our values never get fulfilled. After you know your priorities, then you can evaluate which goals fulfil your values.

This is a ranking exercise. Please rank in order of importance, those things that are important to you, in your life with 1 being the most important and 13 being the least important. Think about what you value most in life currently.

_____   Family

_____   Home

_____   Money

_____   Career

_____   Health

_____   Spirit/Mental Wellness/Religion

_____   Community Service/Volunteering

_____   Children

_____   Marriage

_____   Culture/Arts

_____   Friendship/Socializing

_____   Education/Continuous Learning

_____   Self-Improvement

The second half of this exercise is in Chapter 3. Wait to take the second part until after you have working on that chapter.

She Gets RESULTS

Adding Calculations to Your Goals

Figuring costs or making financial projections is easy to do using widely available on-line financial calculators. Many financial websites have embedded a variety of financial calculators to help you answer the "how much" or "what if" questions...including WomensMoney.org.   Be sure to check your bank, credit union, and brokerage firm websites as many financial institutions today provide their customers and members with on-line tools.

You need to realistically see how much a financial goal may cost you. It's quite possible that once you see the price, you may find it is not worth that to you and that realization could leave more money for a goal you really want to achieve.

My Financial Goals			
My Short-Term Goals:	**Cost/Price**	**Target Date to**	**Priority**
New refrigerator	$1200- save $50 per month	in two years	High **#1**
My Intermediate-Range	**Cost/Pri**	**Target Date to**	**Priority**
Become debt-free	Pay off $35,000 in debt – About $500–$600 extra needs to be paid monthly	2012	High **#1**
My Long-Term Goals	**Cost/Pri**	**Target Date to**	**Priority**
Retirement- Roth IRA	$5000 per year, increasing to allowable limits- about $416 per month is needed	Every year so I can retire in 2035	High **#1**

Chapter Two: Record Your Accomplishments!

Possible Action Items for this Chapter:

☐ Determined important goals that I desire and need to achieve (financially and otherwise)

☐ Calculated the cost of my goals.

☐ Completed the *What Is Important to You?* exercise.

☐ Downloaded or purchased goal setting, organizing and tracking system.

Accomplishment Tracker

Date _____ Year _____ My Name _____ My Mentor is _____

Results from last month's action step(s) or Where I'm at right now…

_____

_____

_____

_____

_____

Challenge(s) I overcame to achieve these results

_____

_____

_____

_____

This is what I would like to accomplish in the next 30 days.

_____

_____

_____

Thoughts and Inspirations:

Chapter Notes and Questions

Chapter Three: Where Does All My Money Go?

Follow the Money

The old saying of "follow the money" is usually something you'd hear in spy mystery movie, but the same advice holds true for your own personal finance "mystery". **Knowing your net worth and your budgeting numbers are important, but knowing this alone is not enough.** You need to also know where your money goes on a weekly, monthly and annual, basis. Some people keep very close records and know where every penny goes. Other people rely on their monthly bank statements to give them an idea of where their money has gone. There are several methods to track spending. Over time, you will develop methods that suit your style comfortably without feeling overburdened by the task.

Before you can engage in good financial planning for the future, you have to assess where your money is going today and every day. Keep in mind that how you spend money can vary each day. The ways you spend your money include cash or debit card, check, and credit card. Some people also have electronic accounts, such as Pay Pal, but such accounts are normally associated with a primary checking account.

Why is it important to write down every amount that is spent, even the smallest cash sums? Because it is the only sure-fire way of knowing what you have done with your money. You cannot make successful financial plans for the future without knowing your spending history.

There's an App for That

There are also several free apps to track your spending such as Budget Buddy, My Budget Free, Lumen Trails (free version), and many other money tracking apps are available. Find one that works for you.

More Cool Tools

On the next page you'll find the "Money Finder". You can make copies this page or download and print copies from your computer by getting the document from your Program One Mentee Education Center (accessible through your Online Mentoring Portal).

Also available for free download in your Mentoring Portal's Education Center:

- Money Finder System Calculator – it automatically calculates your weekly and monthly spending totals for you.

- Money Spending and Planning Calculator – this combines the Money Finder System with your Monthly Spending Plan (budget). With this tool you can put in your budget and enter your actual spending to see how they compare. It automatically calculates your weekly and monthly spending totals for you.

MONEY FINDER SYSTEM -- ONE OF THE MOST IMPORTANT STEPS   MONTH _____

The purpose of this tool is to help track of out-of-pocket cash expenses that are often hard to remember. For a total financial "picture", these will need to be added to major expenses such as your utilities, debt payments and so on. Keep this in your wallet. Carry this chart with you each day for at least one month (2-3 months is even better) Put the amount spent each day in the appropriate box. Figure your total at the end of the month. To save space, round off whole dollars. Don't get lost in wondering if you should write something down or not. If in doubt, just fill it out. You'll figure out eventually where it should go.

EXPENSES Days of Month-+	1	2	3	4	5	6	7	total
Gas/Car								
Groceries/Household								
Personal Items								
Alcohol & Tobacco								
Daily Medications								
Medical Costs								
Clothing								
Laundry-Dry Cleaning								
Hair Care								
Food at Work								
Newspapers/Magazines								
Hobbies								
Meals Eaten Out								
Recreation								
Gifts/Cards								
Babysitting								
Travel Food/drinks								

EXPENSES Days of Month-+	8	9	10	11	12	13	14	15	total
Gas/Car									
Groceries/Household									
Personal Items									
Alcohol & Tobacco									
Daily Medications									
Medical Costs									
Clothing									
Laundry-Dry Cleaning									
Hair Care									
Food at Work									
Newspapers/Magazines									
Hobbies									
Meals Eaten Out									
Recreation									
Gifts/Cards									
Babysitting									
Travel Food/drinks									

What are you feeling at the time of purchase?
Jot down your emotions every time you purchase. One-word answers are fine.

MONEY FINDER SYSTEM -- ONE OF THE MOST IMPORTANT STEPS   MONTH _____

EXPENSES Days of Month -+	16	17	18	19	20	21	22	23	total
Gas/Car									
Groceries/Household									
Personal Items									
Alcohol & Tobacco									
Daily Medications									
Medical Costs									
Clothing									
Laundry-Dry Cleaning									
Hair Care									
Food at Work									
Newspapers/Magazines									
Hobbies									
Meals Eaten Out									
Recreation									
Gifts/Cards									
Babysitting									
Travel Food/drinks									

EXPENSES Days of Month -+	24	25	26	27	28	29	30	31	total
Gas/Car									
Groceries/Household									
Personal Items									
Alcohol & Tobacco									
Daily Medications									
Medical Costs									
Clothing									
Laundry-Dry Cleaning									
Hair Care									
Food at Work									
Newspapers/Magazines									
Hobbies									
Meals Eaten Out									
Recreation									
Gifts/Cards									
Babysitting									
Travel Food/drinks									

What are you feeling at the time of purchase?

Jot down your emotions every time you purchase. One-word answers are fine.

Do You Like What You See?

Tracking your spending has no meaning unless you analyze the information you have recorded. You can make your analysis as general or as specific as you wish at this point. The important thing is to do something with the information. In our case study example about Lisa, you saw only a few days' expenses from Lisa's notebook. Lisa discovered some interesting things about herself and her spending habits during the two--month period that she kept records in her notebook - and she didn't like everything she saw. Here were some of her discoveries:

• Household maintenance costs were higher then she thought they would be. During this period, she had several unanticipated expenses for her new house.

• Personal care costs were twice as high as she expected. Having her nails done is important to her, but she had not realized how much money was going for manicures.

• Clothing costs were a surprise to Lisa. She only bought clothes with a credit card, never with a check. Lisa realized that by using her credit card to buy clothes, she was allowing herself to live beyond an affordable amount for clothing; her credit card allowed her to buy what she wanted, not what she could really afford. As she checked her closet, she discovered new articles of clothing that she had forgotten about and didn't even like. She thought she was "saving money" by getting them on sale.

• Debt repayment costs took a lot of Lisa's income each month. In another chapter of Women's Money, you'll learn some important credit guidelines.

• Costs for her child were affordable for Lisa, thanks to the fact that Julie's father made regular child-support payments to Lisa.

> ## Steps to Take:
>
> 1. Write down the spending categories you think you will use when you analyze the entries in your spending notebook. Calculate the total in spending for each category.
>
> 2. Were you able to account for all of your money for the two or three-month period in which you tracked your spending?
>
> 3. Based on your results, what steps do you plan to take to modify what you spend and how you spend it (cash/ check/debit/credit)?

Lisa decided to include a "could have lived without it" category in her analysis of spending because she was not certain how much of the money she was spending ended in regret. Some of the purchases in this category included the purchase of DVDs, items bought on sale, a few of the items she bought on eBay, and about three too many magazine subscriptions. Lisa liked using a "could have lived without it" category when she analyzed her data. It helped her to recognize that thinking before spending could put her financially ahead.

As you analyze your own "Fritter Finder", create categories that make sense for your life such as: work-related spending, children's expenses, personal care, household expenses, food, eating out, entertainment, transportation/car, and "could have lived without it." You can also download the "simplify your taxes" tracking system on womensmoney.org to categorize your expenses according to IRS standard spending categories.

Where the Money Went

Statement of Income and Expense

Hopefully, you have decided to take action by recording how you spend your money for the next two to three months. Later, you will use this information for setting financial goals for the future and for managing the money that flows into your life.

There will be times in your life when you are asked to prepare a Statement of Income and Expense. This statement is sometimes known as a cash flow statement. A lender will likely require you to prepare a Statement of Income and Expense before qualifying you for a loan. **Preparing this statement is easy** if you have records of how your money was spent. You already know some of this information because you use some of it when you prepare your annual income tax returns. If you use a computerized system for tracking your income and expenses, the program will produce a Statement of Income and Expense for you automatically

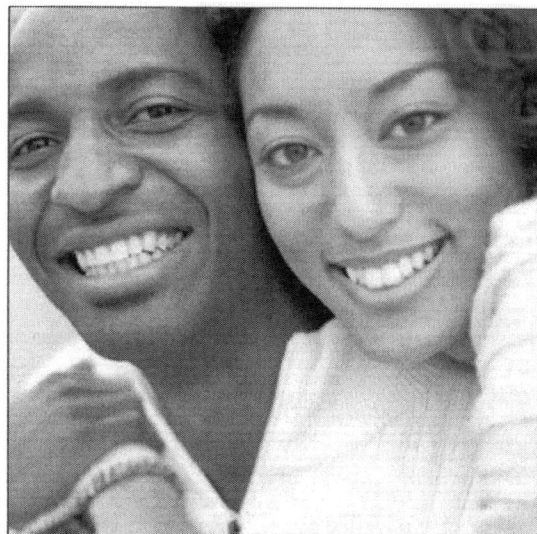

Real Life, Real Money
Cheryl and Rick's Statement of Income and Expense

Cheryl and Rick have been married just over a year. Cheryl asked Rick to help her analyze their income and expenditures, and to develop a Statement of Income and Expense for the past year. They were both committed to "financial harmony" in their marriage and had tried to do a good job keeping records during the year. Because they had developed a good filing system, it wasn't very hard for them to pull out the money facts they needed to prepare the Statement of Income and Expense: payroll statements, monthly bank statements, quarterly earnings reports, annual mortgage statement, and their monthly expenses summaries.

Look at Cheryl and Rick's Statement of Income and Expense on the next page and notice the following:

- It is time specific. It summarizes income received and expenses paid for a full, 12-month year.

- It has a flexible format. You may find other Statements of Income and Expense that look different from this one, use the one that best suits your needs.

- Expenses are categorized as either fixed or variable.

- Fixed expenses include savings and investments retirement contributions, taxes, mortgage or rent, debt payments, and insurance. These are expenses that do not change from month-to-month.

- Variable expenses include food, transportation, clothing, education, medical, utilities, and all other expenses. You may make this form as detailed or as general as you wish.

- It accommodates dual-earning couples or single persons. Notice that the form has three columns, which are labeled "Cheryl," "Rick," and "Total- Both Spouses." If you are not married, you will be able to eliminate two of the columns on the form. If you are married, use the self, spouse, and total columns as needed. It will be easier for you to track income by earner but harder to separate expenses by earner. Separating expenses is not necessary, unless you and your spouse have a clear division of financial responsibility in paying for certain items in your household budget and you wish for your Statement of Income and Expense to reflect this divided financial responsibility.

Cheryl and Rick used only a few categories in making up their statement. One thing they noticed was that the category "All Other" was quite large. They plan to "fine-tune" this category to see how $12,642 was actually spent.

Statement of Income and Expense – Cheryl and Rick's Sample for the Year Ending December 31, 2012			
INCOME	**Cheryl**	**Rick**	**Total – Both Spouses**
Gross Salary/Wages	$34,000	$52,000	$86,000
Dividend Income		$650	$650
Interest Income	$42	$50	$92
Other Income	$800		$800
TOTAL INCOME			$87,542
EXPENSES – FIXED			
Savings/Investments	$1,000	$1,000	$2,000
Retirement	$3,000	$6,000	$9,000
Income Taxes			$16,800
Property Taxes			$2,500
Mortgage/Rent			$12,500
Insurance			$3,000
TOTAL FIXED EXPENSES			$45,800
EXPENSES – VARIABLE			
Food			$10,000
Transportation			$8,000
Clothing/Personal			$3,000
Education			$800
Medical/Dental			$1,500
Utilities			$3,600
Vacation			$2,200
Child Care			
All Other			$12,642
TOTAL VARIABLE EXPENSES			$41,742
TOTAL EXPENSES: FIXED + VARIABLE			$87,542

Your Turn

Study your own completed Statement of Income and Expense. Were there any surprises?

Are there any future changes you want to make in your saving and spending patterns?

Statement of Income and Expense for the Calendar Year Ending:			
INCOME	**Self**	**Spouse**	**Total – Both Spouses**
Gross Salary/Wages			
Dividend Income			
Interest Income			
Other Income			
TOTAL INCOME			
EXPENSES – FIXED			
Savings/Investments			
Retirement			
Income Taxes			
Property Taxes			
Mortgage/Rent			
Insurance			
TOTAL FIXED EXPENSES			
EXPENSES – VARIABLE			
Food			
Transportation			
Clothing/Personal			
Education			
Medical/Dental			
Utilities			
Vacation			
All Other			
TOTAL VARIABLE EXPENSES			
TOTAL EXPENSES: FIXED + VARIABLE			

What's Important to You? (Part Two)

Review your spending and take your best guess to what percentage of your money you spend on the following:
(You can also do this for time spent on each item as well)

This is **not** a math exercise! Enter whatever your best estimate; it does not need to equal 100%.

_____Family

_____Home

_____Money

_____Career

_____Health

_____Spirit/Religion

_____Volunteerism

_____Children

_____Marriage

_____Culture/Arts

_____Friendships

_____Education

_____Self-Improvement

Compare these answers to your Part One of this exercise.
Does your spending match your values?
What matches? What doesn't?

If your priorities and your time don't match, it will be much more difficult to achieve your goals because you will find yourself sabotaging your efforts. If your priorities and your spending don't match, this could be one of the reasons for problem relationships and inability to manage spending and savings.

She Gets RESULTS

Chapter Three: Record Your Accomplishments!

Possible Action Items for this Chapter:

☐ Used the Money Finder or some other spending notebook or app to document daily spending.

☐ Evaluated what you really spend money on

☐ Took my financial snapshot and determined my financial position.

☐ Discussed ways to spend less with your Women's Money Group or Mentor.

☐ Completed the Statement of Income and Expense

☐ Evaluated your Statement of Income and Expense with your Women's Money Group (and spouse) to see what you don't like.

☐ What things would you like to change about your next Statement of Income and Expense?

☐ Completed the *What's Important to You?* Part Two exercise.

Accomplishment Tracker

Date _____ Year____ My Name_____ My Mentor is_____

Results from last month's action step(s) or Where I'm at right now...

_____

_____

_____

_____

Challenge(s) I overcame to achieve these results

_____

_____

_____

This is what I would like to accomplish in the next 30 days.

_____

_____

Thoughts and Inspirations:

Chapter Notes and Questions

Chapter Four: Where Do I WANT My Money to Go?

How to Prepare a Realistic Budget

Many people cringe at the very idea of preparing a budget. It could be that they have a negative reaction to the word. The word budget comes from the French word for wallet, a place to keep money. Other terms used in place of "budget" include "spending plan" and "cash flow plan."

A budget is a self-made tool for directing and controlling our money. Every successful business in America uses a budget to guide operations. Every household should, too, so that families meet their important goals, cover all their expenses, live within their means, and experience the satisfaction that comes from having their finances under control.

A budget is a plan for how you will use your money. Some people shy away from preparing a written budget. They think that having a mental budget is sufficient. They also think that developing a budget is too time-consuming or involved, so they back off. Let's look at a simple, six-step process for budgeting. You should be able to prepare a monthly budget on one page! A handheld calculator will speed the process along.

Building a Realistic Budget

Step 1. Estimate your income. First determine what time period your plan will cover. The planning period may be a month, a year, or any length of time you choose. We will focus on a monthly budget. In figuring income from your earnings, include only your take-home pay or net income. This is different from your gross earnings. Your net income is what you have left after income taxes, Social Security, Medicare, insurance (health, life, disability, etc.), flexible spending plan contributions, retirement savings, and other deductions. Net income is what you have left to spend. You may have other sources of monthly income, too, such as: spouse's earnings, income from self-employment or a second job, interest or dividend income, or child support payments.

Whether you are paid weekly or every two weeks, your monthly income will need to be calculated from the actual amount of your take-home pay, regardless of how frequently you are paid.

Step 2. Estimate your expenses. People who have not tracked their spending find that estimating their expenses is the most difficult aspect of setting up a budget. You've tracked your spending for two to three months. Tracking your spending gave you a fairly good idea of how you spend your money. If you completed a Statement of Income and Expense for the previous year, you also have an additional source of information to use in estimating your future monthly expenses. You may need to consult your records, such as your check register and your receipts, for more details. Expenses may be classified as either fixed expenses or flexible expenses. Fixed expenses, like rent or mortgage payments and loan repayments, are the same each month, while flexible expenses differ each month. Common flexible expense categories are listed in the table, My Monthly Budget Estimates. They are flexible because they vary in amount, such as food; or they are "discretionary," that is, what you spend for them is at your discretion, in contrast to fixed expenses that must be paid and are usually the same amount each month.

You should consider your special financial goals to be fixed expenses. When you do this, you are more likely to fund your future financial goals. This is the idea behind the concept "pay yourself first." The table, My Monthly Budget Estimates, is a tool to help you estimate your expenses and balance your income and expenses.

Step 3. *Make adjustments to balance your budget. In a perfect world, your budget would balance perfectly on the first try. But this is the real world; so don't worry if your outgo exceeds your income on the first go-around.* See how you can bring it into balance.

Is it realistic for you to increase your income? How? Get another job? Get a raise? Hold a garage sale? Check to see if you are over-withholding your federal income taxes and, if so, you may be able to increase your take-home pay by adjusting your exemptions. Or, are you eligible for the Earned Income Tax Credit (EITC) that could increase your monthly take-home pay? The Earned Income Tax Credit is a refundable federal income tax credit for low to moderate income working individuals and families. Information on the EITC can be found on the Internal Revenue Service website at http://www.irs.gov/individuals/article/0,.id=96406,00.html.

If you cannot increase your income, your other choice is to reduce your expenses to bring your budget into balance. Check over each expense category. Are you sure that you are getting the most for your money? Or are you over-paying for things that you could obtain for less? For example: 1) are you sure that your cell phone plan is the best one for the money, or could you find a better plan for less money, or 2) are you paying for a communications package that offers more Internet, cable, and telephone and texting features than you really need or use?

Make the necessary changes to your budget to bring it into balance so that your expenses do not exceed your income. Unless you balance your budget, you will be tempted to use your credit card to finance the difference.

Step 4. Try living within your budget. Until you try to live by your budget, that is, "living within your means," you have no real idea whether it works for you or not. Right now, it is only a tool on paper. Living within your budget is the main challenge of modern living! During this test period, track your spending so that you can compare actual spending to what you had budgeted. Recordkeeping during this phase is vitally important. If you cannot or do not compare what you spent (reality) with what you budgeted (what you thought you would spend), there is no point in budgeting whatsoever. Women like you with important life goals will see the budgeting process as a critical tool for achieving financial success. Getting control of money through effective budgeting is a critically important step in overall financial planning. Live within your budget for a month or two to see if it works.

Step 5. Develop and use a financial recordkeeping system that works for you. The other critical tool in the budgeting process is recordkeeping. You won't know if your budget works until you analyze your real-life spending. In Chapter 2, Money Math, you learned how to create a written record (notebook tool) to track your spending. You can continue with this method if it works for you. Summarize your monthly expenses, and compare them to what you budgeted for each expense category you established. There are many ways to keep financial records, but they all require you to summarize your monthly expenses so you can draw conclusions from the experience and know whether your budget really worked for you during your trial period.

The receipt method is a simple method for tracking spending. Just make sure you obtain a receipt for every transaction you make, whether it is made by cash, debit card, credit card, or check. Mark each receipt with the name of the budget expense category. Each week or at the end of the month, sort your receipts by budget category; tally up the results, and enter the information on a chart. By entering the summaries on a monthly basis, you will immediately see your spending trends and can easily see the times when expenses increase.

The checkbook method works well for people who make most transactions by check or debit card. The checkbook register is the primary data-entry tool. Code each transaction for the budget expense category to which it belong. Each week or at the end of the month, tally up the results by budget category. If you bank on-line, you can access your account readily. You may be able to assign a spending category to each transaction in your on-line account and then download your account information to a spreadsheet or even transmit it to another web-based financial recordkeeping system.

Record book methods work well for people who like to manually record all of their financial transactions on a daily or weekly basis. Many types of household record books are sold commercially at office supply stores, but their income and expense categories may or may not match the categories you use. You can also make your own record book by duplicating the form on the next page, My Monthly Income and Expense Record. Just label the top row with the names of your income and expense categories. At month's end, add the totals for each category. Reserve one page to use as an annual summary. At the end of the year, you will have a complete summary of income and expense. Then you can easily construct a new Statement of Income and Expense.

Computerized financial recordkeeping systems are both useful and popular. People who use these systems are able to tailor their income and expense categories to meet their needs and can effortlessly produce summary reports. Some people prefer the commercial software packages; others who know how to use electronic spreadsheets create their own financial recordkeeping systems. And others keep their financial information at special financial recordkeeping websites. The latest innovations involve web-based systems that bring together all of your financial transactions and allow access by computer, cell phone, or personal digital assistants (PDAs).

Step 6. Adjust your budget to reflect your real life experiences with it. After following your budget for a couple of months, you should be in a position to know if it works for you. Fine-tune your budget categories, and reallocate your income to meet your needs. **A budget is a very flexible tool if you will make the necessary adjustments. A budget is not a strait jacket. If it doesn't work, fix it; don't abandon it!**

Real Life, Real Money

Margaret had just about had it. Sure, she had followed the first three steps of the process: estimating her income and expenses and balancing her budget. But she got stuck when she tried to live on it. She felt like she couldn't have any fun anymore, and she felt guilty whenever she spent money on her favorite hobby. But she persisted. She tried the budget out for six weeks, kept close records, and analyzed them. Finally, she realized the problem was with how she had set up her budget categories. She had actually forgotten to budget for that hobby! So, of course, the budget wasn't working for her. She couldn't believe she'd forgotten it! After readjusting her budget to reflect her lifestyle, her budget worked. It was just the management tool she needed to control her finances.

Where Does My FUN Money Go Each Month?			
	Amount of money I spend each time	Times per month I spend this money	Total amount I spend (Amount x Times per
Beauty Expenses			
Hobbies			
Massages			
Eating out			
Recreation			
Going Out			
Snacks			
Music			
Cigarettes			
Alcohol			
Clothing			
Gifts			
TV			
Movies /Shows			
Lottery/Gambling			
Magazines			

List three ways you will be able to save more money and how much money you expect to save.

1. _____ $_____

2. _____ $_____

3. _____ $_____

Saving 40% of Your Income?

There is a growing movement amongst personal finance "gurus" to try to live on 60% of what you earn. That may seem impossible right now, but many people are working towards that goal. It's not easy, and it's not fast, but it can be very rewarding. So how do you get to the point to save 40% of your income? Budgeting is the key.

1. Make a goal you can feel committed to. If you cannot start with 40%, try 10 or 20%.
2. Know that there are going to be months you miss your goal, so be sure to just save something...anything. Let go of the disappointment and start again.
3. Do your budget (again, and again...most of us forget things the first go around).
4. Adjust your spending habits to save money.
5. Negotiate or change essential services to save money.
6. Calculate: If you adjusted your spending habits and paid off debt, how much would you be able to save? 20%, 30%, 40%?
7. Pay off your debt - add the money you have saved by adjusting spending and bills to your payments.
8. Adjust your mindset to feel as if you only make 60% of your actual paycheck.
9. After you are debt free, split your paycheck to have 40% automatically go into your "untouchable" savings/investing account.

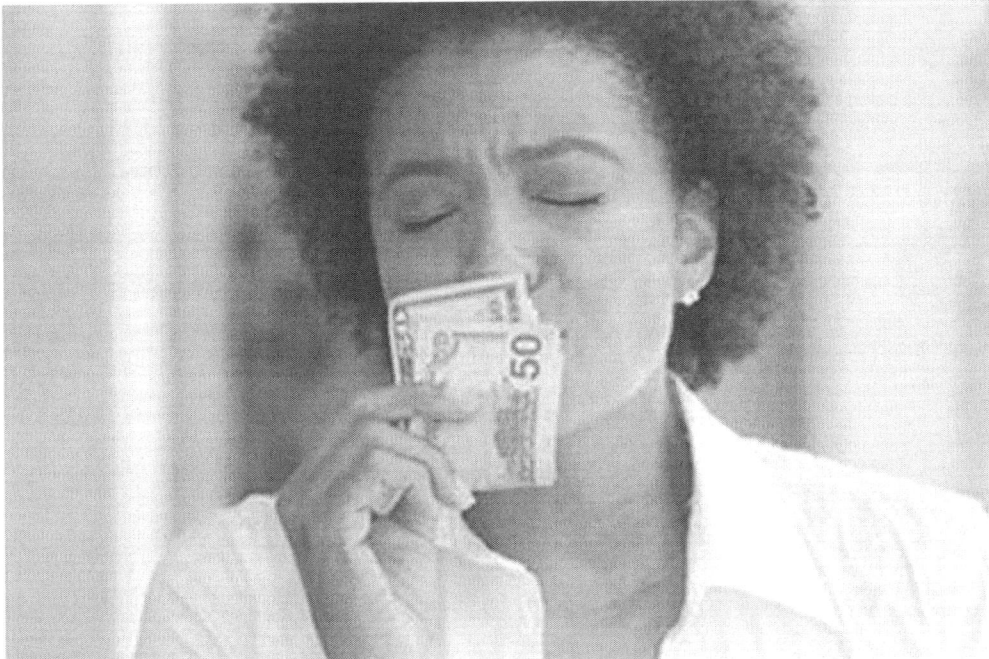

What if you already earn less than your basic living expenses?

This is a very difficult situation and hard choices have to be made. Quite frankly, on some incomes and depending on what part of the country you live in, it's just not possible to save 40%. However, there is hope.

Increasing your income may be the only way. Here are some ways to do that and earn money fairly quickly.

- You can increase your income with a better job. Many of us qualify for scholarships and money for college to train for jobs that pay much more than we make right now.
- Start a side-job or business.
- Move to a home or to a city with substantially lower expenses. Many people are choosing a suburban or rural lifestyle over the hectic city life, and they are finding substantial financial savings.

My Monthly Budget Estimates

1. Circle the categories that correspond to your income and expenses, and add others to meet your needs.
2. Estimate the amount of income and expenses for each category that you will include in your budget.
3. Adjust your estimates until total expenses (fixed + flexible) are in balance with total income.

My Income	$$$	My Fixed Expenses	$$$	My Flexible Expenses	$$$
Salary and wages		Rent/mortgage payment		Food at home	
Self-employment income		Utilities		Food away from home	
Business income		Income taxes (extra payments)		Medical expense	
Bonuses		Real estate taxes		Clothing	
Interest		Property insurance		Dry cleaning	
Dividends		Auto insurance		Personal care	
Rental income		Other insurance coverage		Child/dependent care	
Trust income		Car payments		Personal allowances	
Family contributions		College loan payments		Books, magazines, papers, films	
Gifts		Other loan payments		Entertainment and recreation	
Alimony		Credit card payments		Phones/Internet	
Child support payments		Emergency fund savings		Gifts	
Unemployment benefits		Savings for financial goals		Hobbies	
Disability insurance				Charitable giving	
Earned Income Tax Credit				Household maintenance	
Regular withdrawals from savings				Home furnishings	
Garage sale proceeds				Transportation expense	
On-line sale proceeds				Children's expenses	
Other income				Children's allowances	
				Education expense	
				Job-related expenses	
				Professional memberships	
				Fitness center dues	
				Pets	
Total Monthly Income	$	**Total Monthly Fixed**	$	**Total Monthly Flexible**	$

Discipline to Achieve Your Goals

Sometimes it is necessary to spend less to achieve more. Spending less money can be pain free, fun, and profitable. Economizing can free up money we didn't think we had. We often think that there is "no money" to save, but the truth is, we probably can find at least a few dollars pretty painlessly.

Real Life, Real Money:
Sharon's Family Practices Saving for Disney World

Sharon is a single mom who learned new ways to save money from the newsletter she receives from the University's Cooperative Extension Service (http://extension.org). Sharon has eight-year-old twins, Tommy and Amy. Sometimes she struggles to make ends meet, so she was really ready for a new approach to use with her family. By making small changes in the things they buy, Sharon and her children are setting aside money for a trip to Disney World in three years- their savings goal is $1500. And they're doing it without major sacrifice! They have made just 12 small changes to their buying habits during the year- about one a month. Each time they adopt a new change, they keep it up the rest of the year. Sharon keeps records and actually deposits the money they save into their Disney World savings account. At the end of the year, she had over $500! She had not realized that their old buying habits had a price tag of $60 per month. Here are the 12 changes they made this year:

January	Started using a $1 grocery coupon instead of money every week (52 weeks x $1)	$52.00
February	Stopped drinking two sodas a week (48 weeks x $2)	$96.00
March	Started spending $1 less on candy each week (44 weeks x $1)	$44.00
April	Reduced weekly video rental cost from $2 to $1 (40 weeks x $1)	$40.00
May	Eliminated soft drink with weekly fast food meal (35 weeks x $1.75)	$61.25
June	Started getting a better deal on bottled water (30 weeks x $1)	$30.00
July	Turned off room lights more often (5 months x $2)	$10.00
August	Adjusted the thermostat (20 weeks x $1)	$20.00
	Stopped buying a weekly lottery ticket (16 weeks x $2)	$32.00
October	Eliminated one weekly restaurant lunch (11 weeks x $6)	$66.00
November	Started reading magazines at the library instead of renewing three subscriptions ($15, $18, $12 for 1-year subscriptions)	$45.00
December	Found a great generic cereal (4 weeks x $1.50)	$6.00
	Total Saved by These 12 New Habits	**$502.25**

Careful analysis of common categories of spending by young women like you could yield important savings.

- How much do you spend each month for the items shown in the table?
- Where does your money go each month?
- Approximately how much do you spend each time?
- How many times per month do you spend money this way?
- Could spending adjustments in these categories help out your budget?

Banking Services and Financial Institutions

You probably bank with one or more financial institution currently. But are they right for your present situation? The checklist below has been adapted from The Federal Deposit Insurance Corporation's Money Smart guides (http://www.fdic .gov/consumers/consumer/moneysmart/overview.html). Use the checklist to assess your banking needs and options.

Comparing Your Banking Needs and Options	Bank A	Bank B	Bank C
Name of bank, credit union, or thrift institution			
Type of account			
How much money do I need to open the account?			
How much do I have to keep in my account to			
What are the fees for bounced checks?			
How many checks can I write before extra fees are charged?			
How many withdrawals can I make each month?			
Does this account pay interest?			
Does an ATM or debit card come with this account?			
Will I be charged to use the ATM or debit card at this bank?			
Will I be charged to use the ATM or debit card at another bank?			
Are there any other fees?			
Does this bank offer the services I need?			
Is it close to home?			
Does it have reasonable hours?			
Does it have ATMs? If so, are they located near where I live, work, or shop?			
If I am choosing a credit union, am I eligible?			
Do any employees speak my language?			
Is this bank insured?			
Is on-line banking offered?			

Chapter Four: Record Your Accomplishments!

Possible Action Items for this Chapter:

- ☐ Do you feel you have improved your budgeting know-how?
- ☐ List ways to reduce spending to enhance my budget.
- ☐ Did you prepare a written budget?
- ☐ Are you using a financial record keeping system to track spending?
- ☐ List some ways you are using to live within your budget
- ☐ Looking at ways to live on 60% of what you make and saving 40%.
- ☐ Evaluated current banking needs.
- ☐ Opened checking account or managing the one you already have better.
- ☐ Opened saving account or managing the one you already have better.
- ☐ Check out Money Spending Planner & Calculator in Mentoring Portal (available to Program One Members)

Accomplishment Tracker

Date _____ Year _____ My Name _____ My Mentor is_____

Results from last month's action step(s) or Where I'm at right now...

_____

_____

_____

_____

_____

Challenge(s) I overcame to achieve these results

_____

_____

_____

This is what I would like to accomplish in the next 30 days.

_____

_____

_____

Thoughts and Inspirations:

Chapter Notes and Questions

Chapter Five: Making Credit Work For You

It's hard to imagine a world without credit or credit cards. Credit makes our world go round during good times and bad, as we have discovered in recent times. Credit makes global commerce possible and makes it possible for us to buy "on time." Many college graduates relied on student loans to get through school. Most people, especially first-time homebuyers, cannot pay cash for a home. And now that credit cards have been around for over a half-century, life without them seems almost unthinkable. Access to credit has transformed how consumers make buying decisions.

In this section of the Women's Money® Guidebook you will learn about:

- Determining Your Debt Load,

- Calculating Your Debt-To-Income Ratio,

- Identifying "Good" And "Bad" Debt,

- Managing The Use Of Credit,

- Getting Your Credit Reports Free Of Charge,

- Credit Scores,

- How Finance Charges And Fees Are Determined,

- Ways Of Paying Down Debt,

- How To Establish And Shop For Credit,

- Mortgages,

- Resolving Credit Problems, And

- Protecting Yourself Against Identity Theft.

> ## Real Life, Real Money
>
> Ramona couldn't understand why she was having trouble "making ends meet." She had a good job and had started to furnish her new apartment. The many sales and deep discounts on furniture at stores nearby drew her in like a moth to light. Soon she found herself committing more and more of her monthly income to making payments on the furnishings she was acquiring. Often, she ran out of money for groceries before the end of the month and noticed she was starting to "juggle" when she paid her regular monthly bills. She thought, "Am I carrying too much debt?" But she didn't know how to figure out the answer.

Assessing Your Current Debt Status

How you use credit can make your money management system function smoothly or keep you awake with nightmares. Is your credit use under control? Or is debt controlling you? The amount of debt different people can handle varies. When credit is very easy to obtain, it is easier for people to borrow to meet their financial obligations, but it is also easier to become over-extended. When credit is harder to obtain, it is more difficult for people to finance the things they need, like a home mortgage, a college education, or a vehicle.

Know Your Debt Load and Calculate Your Debt-to-Income Ratio

How much debt is "too much"? How do you know if you are carrying "too much" debt? A good starting point is to list everything you owe. Your list will give you an idea of your total current debt load. Then you can calculate your debt-to-income ratio, which is the percentage of your take-home pay that goes to pay non-mortgage debt.

Step 1. Compute your own debt load by listing all of your debts. Include your mortgage, auto loans, student loans, furniture, personal loans, and credit cards. For credit cards, your current balance is the most important.
For current balances on other types of debt, such as your mortgage, contact your bank or credit union to get your current balances. You can also estimate your mortgage balance using last year's annual statement from the mortgage company. Study this example:

My Debts	Original Debt Amount	Current Balance	What I Pay Monthly
Home mortgage*	$150,000	$120,000	$899*
Car Loan	$18,600	$12,000	$300
Student Loan	$36,000	$34,000	$150
3 Credit Cards		$10,660	$300
My Debt Load >»	Total Debt $176,660	Monthly Debt $1,649

In this example, total debt is $176,660, and monthly debt payments are $1,649.

Step 2. List the amount of each monthly payment you make, except for your mortgage payment. For credit cards, use the amount you usually pay each month. (If you pay your credit card balances in full each month, do not list the balances.)

Example:
Car loan $300
Student loan $150
Credit cards $300 (In this example, $100 is paid to each of three credit accounts.)

Total $750

Step 3. Divide the total amount of your monthly payments by your total net pay (take home pay after taxes and deductions). Suppose your monthly take- home pay is $2,800. For example: $750 7 $2,800 = .27, for a debt-to-income ratio of 27 percent. (After dividing $750 by $2,800, multiply by 100 to get 27 percent.) This example is illustrated in the worksheet below, My Debt-to- Income Ratio.

My Debt-to-Income Ratio				
My Total Monthly Payments (excluding my monthly mortgage payment)	ivided by»	My Monthly Take-home Pay (Net Pay)	Times 100 Equals»	My Debt-to- Income Ratio
$750		$2,800		27%
$		$		___%

In this example, 27 percent of net income (take-home pay) goes to pay off non-mortgage debt each month. An additional 32 percent of net income (take-home pay) goes to make the $899 mortgage payment every month. What remains is 41 percent, or less than half of this individual's take-home pay. From this 41 percent, all other household expenses (food, gasoline, clothing, entertainment, etc.) must be met in addition to setting aside money for regular savings or an emergency fund. Extremely careful budgeting is needed to make it all work out. But what would happen if this person is furloughed, has a reduction in pay, or loses her job altogether? Then how will she meet her debt obligations? Now compute your own debt-to-income ratio in the worksheet, My Debt-to-Income Ratio.

Why does your debt-to-income ratio matter? Financial experts recommend a debt-to-income ratio of less than 15 percent. People with ratios between 15 and 20 percent may experience occasional problems repaying their debts and paying all other bills on time. But once debt- to-income ratios exceed 20 percent, problems with repaying debts and other bills increase dramatically, according to what consumer credit counselors have seen with their clients.   In the example above, a person with a debt-to-income ratio of 27 percent is likely to need professional help from a trained consumer credit counselor. To locate the nearest Consumer Credit Counseling Service office, call the National Foundation for Consumer Credit (NFCC) at 1-800-388-2227, or visit their website at www.nfcc.org. Spanish-language assistance is available at 1-800-682-9832.

Identify "Good" and "Bad" Debt

Another way to assess debt is to look at the type of debt you have. Some financial experts refer to "good" debt and "bad" debt. They regard debt used to buy homes and cars and to pay for education as generally "good" debt. Homes tend to appreciate in value over the long run, and the mortgage interest and property taxes may be tax-deductible, so there are several benefits to going into debt to buy a home. Cars provide transportation to get to work or school, and education loans are an investment that can boost future earning power. Still, even "good" debt can cause difficulties if a job is lost or a home has declined in value at the very time it must be sold. Losing a salary or wages increases the debt-to-income ratio, making it more difficult to repay debt and pay bills on time.

Using credit to pay for things like clothing, food, gasoline, and other goods or services that lose value or are no longer around when the bill comes due are generally put in the "bad" debt category. There is nothing wrong with paying with credit, especially if the consumer is a "convenience user" and pays off the credit card balance in full each month; however, if you only pay the minimum amount due each month to the credit card company and most of your debt is for these types of purchases, your overall cost for the things you buy will be greater than the actual "sticker price."

Lessons from the recession tell us that all workers need a back-up plan. We need to know how we are spending our money and how much debt we have. And we need to think through how we would pay our bills (and our debts) if our income decreased suddenly or simply went away.

Managing the Use of Credit Credit is a convenient financial tool, but it is critical to understand how credit works and know the realities and responsibilities of repaying debt. Using credit creates a financial obligation. You are buying something today with income you will earn in the future. Following the tips below can help you be successful in your use of credit.

• Make a budget, and stick to it. Developing a financial plan (goals, budget, savings plan, etc.) will help you keep your finances in order. Having financial goals will also help you decide how a potential purchase will help or hinder your ability to reach those goals.

Real Life, Real Money
-Susie

Susie shopped around carefully and waited to buy her new wardrobe on sale- in fact, her total cost for the eight garments she bought was less than 70 percent of the original cost.

Susie used her credit card to purchase the garments but "lost" some of the savings when she stretched out her credit card payments. Yes, she was paying for her clothes, but she was also paying extra money for the interest charged on her clothing purchases. She may wind up paying for her clothes longer than she will wear them!

• Set personal and family limits on credit use to keep from charging more than you can afford to pay off at the end of the month. Develop a system for keeping track of the amount of money you have spent so you don't spend more than these limits. Having a credit card can encourage overspending. If you don't keep good records, you may lose track of the amount you have charged and find yourself in financial trouble later.

• If you can't pay the balance in full each month, pay more than the minimum. Paying more than the minimum payment will lower your finance charges and decrease the amount of time it will take to pay off your balance. Paying only the minimum balance increases the cost of the items you purchased and takes forever to pay off! Consider Dora's story in Real Life, Real Money on the following page.

• Recognize the difference between needs and wants. Do you really need to eat restaurant meals most days or to have the latest cell phone model? Will you have the money to make your credit payments and still have enough for regular living expenses? If you charge these items and only pay the minimum, you could be paying for those items months or even years from now.

• Always open your credit card bill, and pay it on time every month. Never be late. Paying on time will help protect you from late fees, sudden increases in the interest rate, decreases in your credit limit, or a drop in your credit score. Keeping up with your bills will lessen the likelihood of identity theft. Read your statement carefully, and follow the procedures outlined on your statement to dispute any charges you did not make. Failing to pay credit card statements on time triggers late-payment fees ranging from $28 to $45 or more. These fees can be avoided by paying on time every month. Some people set up automated bill paying to avoid being late.

• Limit the number of credit cards you have so that you can afford to make payments on time. Most people find they can get along with one or two bank credit cards. You may also decide to keep a gasoline card or department store charge card. Remember, however, that most gas stations and department stores accept major bank credit cards, so your need for special cards may be limited. Having too many cards also increases the temptation to overspend and makes it more difficult to keep track of the total amount you have charged in a month and the dates that payments are due.

• Be wary of anyone who claims they can "fix" your credit. The only thing that can fix a poor credit history is time and a positive payment record. Paying money to someone who claims to "fix" your credit is a needless expense.

• Keep your credit cards secure. Make sure you have completed the Credit and Debit Card Safety Record in Chapter One.

• Think before you close out credit accounts you don't use. If you wish to close a credit card account, cut up the card, and send a letter to the card issuer. Ask them to close your account, and notify the credit bureaus that the account was "closed at the customer's request." In the past, closing out credit card accounts was an advisable practice. Today, however, financial experts suggest keeping your oldest accounts.

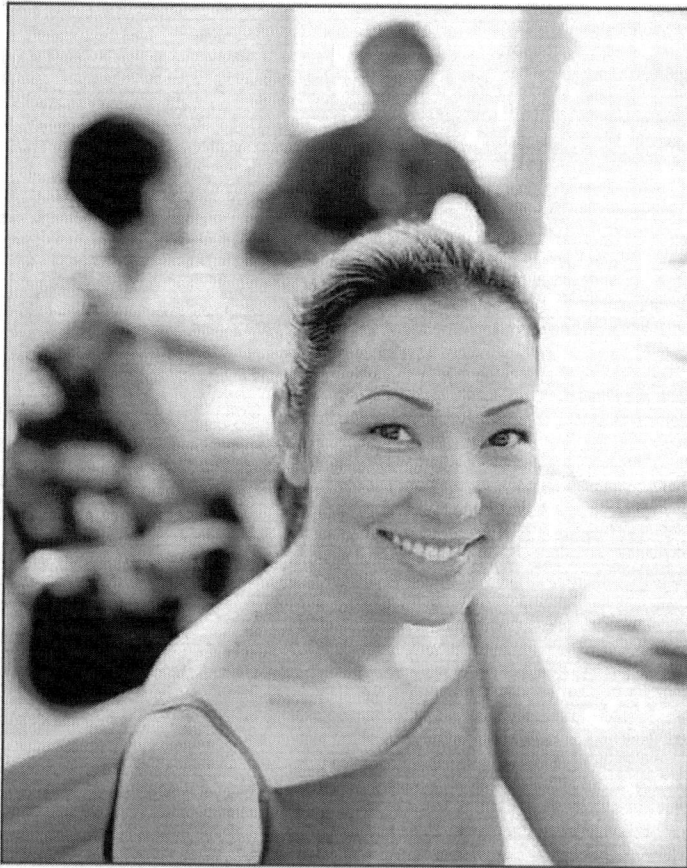

Real Life, Real Money

Alison is 22 and just graduated from college. She will start her first job as a teacher. Her 12-year-old car has been having mechanical problems on a regular basis, and she has decided to replace it. The local car dealership has a three-year-old car that she is interested in. She and the sales person negotiated an acceptable price. When Alison applied for a car loan at her bank, she was turned down because she had no credit history. When she was in college, she avoided getting a credit card. Because she received a major scholarship, she graduated without any student loans, although she did work in a local community center.

Real Life, Real Money – Dora

Dora uses her credit card to charge $50 worth of groceries every week. She also uses her card to buy other things when she runs "short" of money in her checking account. Each month she has been making only the minimum required payment (5 percent of the total outstanding balance or $15, whichever was greater). Her current balance is now $2,500, and the Annual Percentage Rate of interest on unpaid balances is 18 percent.

- Dora wants to compare how long it will take to pay off her balance and how much total interest she would be paying back if:

- she stops charging on this card altogether and continues to make only the minimum payment each month, and

- she stops charging on this card altogether and pays $200 per month instead of the minimum payment.

- She uses the Federal Trade Commission's online calculator to figure this out (http://www.ftc.gov/creditcardcalculator). Here's what Dora found out:

- Using the minimum payment approach, it will take Dora seven years to pay off the balance, and she will pay $1,003 in interest charges during those seven years.

- Using the $200 per month payment approach, it will take Dora just 14 months to pay off the balance, and she will pay $290 in interest charges during the 14-month period.

Which is a better approach for Dora? Clearly, she will save money by making monthly payments of $200 instead of the minimum payment approach. She will save $713 in interest charges. And her debt will be wiped out in a little over a year instead of seven years!

Credit Reports and Credit Scores - They Really Do Matter

No history, good history, bad history - it really does matter when it comes to credit. Your credit history is your record of paying loans, credit cards, and other bills. Lenders use your credit history and your credit score in determining whether to give you credit and what interest rate they will charge. Insurance companies, and in some cases an employer, may also review your credit score to determine how financially responsible you are. Utility companies review credit histories when opening new accounts to determine if a deposit is needed.

A good credit history and above average credit scores reflect on-time payments. Completed loans reflect financial responsibility. A history of late payments, loan defaults, and repossessions could result in credit denial, loss of job opportunities, higher credit costs, and a low credit score.

It is not uncommon to have very little credit history when you start your first job. Your growing credit history is compiled into a credit report by credit-reporting agencies, also known as credit bureaus. When you receive a loan or are issued credit, your payment history is reported regularly to the credit- reporting agencies by most creditors. The credit report contains a listing of your debts, how you have paid them (on time or late), any bills that have been turned over to a collection agency, public information such as tax liens and bankruptcies, and a listing of who has requested a copy of your credit report. Negative information can remain in your credit report for seven years, except for bankruptcy, which will remain for 10 years.

The Fair Credit Reporting Act (FCRA) gives you the right to obtain your credit report and to correct any mistakes. FCRA allows you to order one free copy of your Annual Credit Report from each of the three nationwide consumer credit-reporting agencies (Equifax, Experian, and TransUnion) every 12 months. There are three ways to get your free reports:

• On-line at www. Annual creditreport.com. This is the official website authorized to fill orders for your free credit file disclosure, commonly called a credit report. Beware of "imposter" websites that use terms or claims of "free credit reports"; some will charge fees to your credit card for the report, which by law, is available free of charge. To protect yourself, only use the official website listed here.

• Telephone. Call 1-877-322- 8228. Deaf and hard-of-hearing consumers can access TDD service by calling 7-1-1 and referring the Relay Operator to 1-800-821-7232.

• Mail. Download the Annual Credit Report Request Form from www.annualcreditreport.com or from the Federal Trade Commission (http://www.ftc.gov/bcp/edu/resources/forms/requestformfinal.pdf). Mail the completed form to: Annual Credit Report Request Service, P.O. Box 105281, Atlanta, GA 30348-5281.

What you see in your credit report may vary by credit-reporting agency because some creditors do not report information to all three agencies. The credit report does not include your credit score. You have to pay to see your credit score.

In addition to the free annual report from each of the three agencies, you are entitled to a free credit report if you believe you are the victim of identity theft, if you have been denied credit in the past 60 days, if you receive welfare benefits, or if you are unemployed.

Not just anyone is allowed to obtain a copy of your credit report. Only those who can show a legitimate need for the information may have a copy. Generally, your oral or written permission is required, such as your signature on a credit application. Creditors, landlords, employers, and financial institutions are among those who can show a need and may ask permission to obtain a copy of your credit report. The last section of your credit report contains a listing of those who have requested your credit report in the last two years.

If you find inaccurate information in your credit report, you have a right to correct the information as provided by the Fair Credit Reporting Act. You should contact both the credit-reporting agency and the information provider (e.g., the creditor). You will need to let the credit-reporting agency know, in writing, what information you believe to be inaccurate. Provide any relevant data or information you have that supports your claim. The credit-reporting agency will then investigate the items, usually within 30 days. They will notify the creditor of the items in dispute and must provide all the data you provide the credit-reporting agency. The creditor will investigate your claim and report their results back to the credit--reporting agency. If the creditor finds their information to be inaccurate, it must notify all credit-reporting agencies so it can be corrected in your file.

Real Life, Real Money

Carolina learned the hard way how mistakes in her credit report made it look like she was a poor credit risk. After obtaining a copy of her credit report, she noticed that there were more accounts than she knew she had. When she reported the discrepancies back to the credit reporting agency and they investigated, it turned out that the credit history of another person with an identical Hispanic surname had been erroneously recorded as Carolina's credit history!

The result: wrong name, wrong history, and lower credit score! Because she knew what steps to take, her credit report was corrected. She still monitors her credit report to make sure the problem doesn't happen again

When the investigation is complete, the credit-reporting agency must send you the written results and a free copy of your credit report if the dispute resulted in a change. Any item changed or removed cannot be put back in your credit report unless the creditor verified that it was accurate and the credit-reporting agency notifies you in writing with the name, address, and phone number of the creditor. If the creditor maintains the information IS accurate, you are entitled to include a 100-word written explanation in your credit file telling your side of the problem. This statement becomes a part of your credit report and is included whenever a copy of your file is requested.

Getting Your Credit Score

Your credit report score is calculated using the information in your credit report. The credit score is a computer-generated number indicating the likelihood that you will repay credit you receive. The most common credit scores are developed by the Fair Isaac Company and are referred to as FICO scores. Scores range from about 300 to 850. Generally, consumers with higher scores are more likely to repay their debts than those with lower scores. For more information about credit scores, visit **www.myfico.com**

If you wish to access your credit score, contact the credit-reporting agency directly, and be prepared to pay a fee to get your credit score.

Experian
www.experian.com
888-397-3742 (credit report request) 888-397-3742 (fraud alert)

Trans Union
www. transunion.com
800-916-8800 (credit report request) 800-680-7289 (fraud alert)

Equifax
www.equifax.com
800-685-1111 (credit report request) 800-525-6285 (fraud alert)

How to Improve Your Credit Score

Earlier in this chapter, you learned that credit scores are used in many ways. The higher your score, the more money you are likely to be able to borrow and the lower the interest rate. People with a high credit score are considered good credit risks, meaning that they are very likely to pay back their debts in a timely fashion. Many lenders have "risk-based" lending policies, which means that borrowers will qualify for certain interest rates based on their credit score.

This refers to how long your credit accounts have been open and how long since you have had account activity. Having only a few accounts, especially older accounts, is better.

In reality, you have three FICO scores - one for each of the three credit-reporting agencies. Depending on what is reported to each of the agencies, your score can differ among the three. Consumers often wonder what goes into making up your credit score and what can be done to improve the score. **Here's the breakdown:**

• Payment history determines 35 percent of the score. Paying everything on time (bills, fines, and even parking tickets) is very important because if any creditor reports your payment history to the credit bureau, it will impact your score.

• How much you owe your creditors in relation to your available credit makes up 30 percent of the score. If you owe up to your credit limit, your score will be lower than if you were not maxing out your cards.

• Length of your credit history makes up 15 percent of the score.

• The number of recent new accounts and the number of recent credit report inquiries made by lenders where you have applied for credit makes up 10 percent of the score. Credit scores can drop if it looks like you are looking for new sources of credit, especially applying for new credit cards. Avoid opening a new credit card account when clerks tell you that you can "save 15 percent on your entire purchase if you apply for a card with us today." Grabbing that offer can lower your credit score.

• The types of credit you use determine 10 percent of your score. Type of credit refers to the kind of debt you are carrying, such as mortgages, credit cards, vehicle loans, secured loans, personal loans, etc.

Remember that your credit score will change over time, depending on the factors just described. If your score is in the 600 to 700 range, it is worth your effort to improve your score by being careful about taking on new debt, opening additional accounts, not maxing out your credit cards, and paying bills on time.

Evaluate Your Credit Reports

1. Request a copy of your credit report in one of the three ways mentioned in this chapter:

   • Online: www.annualcreditreport.com

   • Telephone: 1-877-322-8228

   • Mail: Complete the Annual Credit Report Request form (http://www.ftc.gov/bcp/edu/resources/forms/requestformfinal.pdf), and mail it to Annual Credit Report Request Service, P.O. Box 105281, Atlanta, GA 30348-5281.

2. When you receive your report, check it over carefully. Is all of the information on your report accurate? If not, what steps will you follow to dispute the inaccurate information?

3. Look closely to see who has requested a copy of your credit report lately.

4. Mark your calendar to show the next time you will request a free credit report. Since you can get one from each of the three credit-reporting agencies once a year, a common strategy is to request a different one every four months

---

How Finance Charges and Fees Are Determined

When you don't pay off your credit card balance each month, you will pay a finance charge. The Annual Percentage Rate (APR) on your card and the method the credit card company uses to calculate the finance charges will impact how much you will pay. The calculation method used will be described in the card member agreement, so make sure you read the fine print.

• The average daily balance method totals the unpaid balance for each day in a billing period and divides it by the number of days in the billing period. The finance charge is figured on this average balance. Cash advances and new purchases are usually included in figuring the daily unpaid balance.

• The two-cycle average daily balance method uses two months of credit transactions. An average daily balance is calculated for the current billing period and the previous billing period, with the total being divided by the total number of days in both billing periods. This method is the least advantageous to consumers and results in a much higher finance charge. To avoid paying any finance charges, you must pay off your balance for at least two months.

• The adjusted balance method takes the balance at the beginning of the current billing period and subtracts any payments and credits received during the current billing period. The resulting total is used to compute any finance charges. This method is less common but is the most advantageous to consumers.

How Are Your Finance Charges and Fees Determined?

Have you read the fine print in your credit card member agreement lately? Do you know which method your credit card companies use to determine finance charges? Take a few minutes to complete the following exercise.

1. Make a list of all your credit card accounts.

2. Locate the card member agreement for each account- it's the one with the small print! Next to each account, indicate which method is used to calculate finance charges. Don't have the agreement? Call the company and ask how finance charges are determined.

3. While you're at it, write down the APR to remind yourself that debt has a price. Check if the APR can change and under what conditions this change will happen.

4. Check the other conditions affecting how much you could be charged in fees. How much is the late payment fee? The over-the-credit limit fee? What other fees apply?

Establishing Credit

If you don't have a credit history because you have never had a credit card or taken out a loan, there are steps you can take to begin to establish credit.

• Make sure you pay all of your bills on time - such as your telephone, utilities, and rent.

• Open a checking or savings account in your name. Pick a bank or credit union that offers a national credit card program. After you have had the account for several months, ask what you need to do to get a credit card. Keep the credit limit small, and pay off the balance at the end of each month.

* Apply for a charge account in your name at a local department store. Only charge what you can pay off each month.

• Take out a small loan. Make the payments on time. Don't pay the loan off early. You want to show that you can make payments on time. Paying the loan early doesn't help you develop that track record.

• Open a secured credit card account. With this type of credit card, you deposit money with the card issuer, which will be used if you don't pay your bill. Your credit limit is usually equal to the amount you have on deposit.

• If one lender turns you down, try another. Different lenders use different criteria in evaluating an application.

• Apply for a loan using a co- signer. A co-signer is someone with an established credit record who agrees to make the payments if you do not. Having the co- signer helps you get the loan, but you will need to make payments on time to establish a credit history.

How to Shop for Credit

Whether you are shopping for a loan or a credit card, it's important to shop around. Look for the following terms and conditions when shopping for a credit card. This information must be disclosed in credit card solicitations.

• Is there an annual fee? This is a fee you pay to have the card whether you use it or not. Not all companies charge an annual fee.

• What is the Annual Percentage Rate (APR)? This is the interest rate you will be charged if you carry a balance on your card. Interest rates vary a great deal, so it is important to compare different offers, especially if you will be carrying a balance. Most companies charge a different APR for purchases, cash advances, and balance transfers. Some companies offer a very low "teaser" rate for a short period of time when you first open the account. Make sure you know what the rate will increase to when the introductory rate expires. Is the APR fixed or variable? A fixed rate will stay the same until the company notifies you in writing that it will change. A variable rate can change from month to month.

• Is there a grace period? This is the time between the billing date and when finance charges will begin to accrue. Grace periods now range from 15-25 days. If there is no grace period, you will be charged a finance charge on your purchase even if you pay off the balance each month.

• What other fees may be charged? These include late payment fees, fees for going over your credit limit, cash advance fees, and balance transfer fees.

• What method is used to compute finance charges?

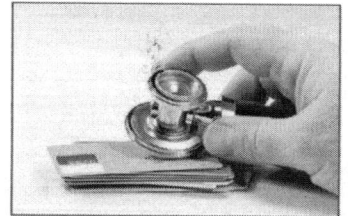

If you are shopping for a loan, consider the following:

• What is the APR? When comparing loans look for the lowest APR. The APR states interest and other finance charges in a standardized form so you are comparing apples to apples.

• What other fees will be charged? Are there application fees or credit check fees? Mortgage loans include a number of fees. Lenders should provide you with a good faith estimate of all of the closing costs.

• Do you understand the contract? What will happen if you make a payment late? Make sure you have all questions answered before you sign.

• What is the length of the loan? When will payments be due? Can you afford the payments?

• What will be the total cost of the loan? This includes the initial cost plus interest and fees.

Resolving Credit Problems

Many people face financial crises at some time in their lives. Whether the crisis is caused by personal or family illness, the loss of a job, or simple overspending, it can seem overwhelming but often can be overcome. The fact of the matter is that your financial situation doesn't have to go from bad to worse.

Do-It-Yourself By Contacting Your Creditors.

The first step toward taking control of your financial situation is to do a realistic assessment of how much money comes in and how much money you spend. Examine your budget for those expenses that are necessary, and prioritize the rest. Examine ways to bring in additional income. The goal is to make sure you can make ends meet on the basics: housing, food, health care, insurance, and education. Contact your creditors immediately if you are having trouble making ends meet. Tell them why it's difficult for you, and try to work out a modified payment plan that reduces your payments to a more manageable level. Don't wait until your accounts have been turned over to a debt collector.

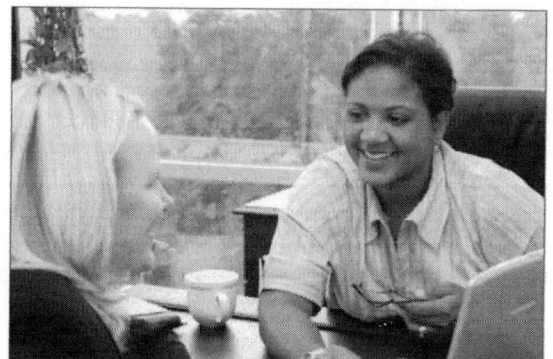

Credit Counseling Services.

If you aren't disciplined enough to create a workable budget and stick to it, can't work out a repayment plan with your creditors, or can't keep track of mounting bills, consider contacting a credit counseling service. Your creditors may be willing to accept reduced payments if you enter a debt repayment plan with a reputable organization. In these plans, you deposit money each month with the credit counseling service. Your deposits are used to pay your creditors according to a payment schedule developed by the counselor. Some credit counseling services charge little or nothing for managing the plan; others charge a monthly fee that could add up to a significant charge over time. Some credit counseling services are funded, in part, by contributions from creditors. Visit www.nfcc.org to find a credit counseling service office near you. For help in evaluating credit counseling services, see the Federal Trade Commission publication, Fiscal Fitness: Choosing a Credit Counselor, at http://www.ftc .gov/bcp/edu/pubs/ consumer Icredit/ cre26 .pdf.

Debt repayment plans usually cover unsecured debt (debt issued and supported only by the borrower's creditworthiness, rather than by some sort of collateral). Your auto and home loan, which are considered secured debt, may not be included. You must continue to make payments to these creditors directly. If you still find it difficult to make your car payments, you may be better off selling the car and paying off the debt. You would avoid the added costs of repossession and a negative entry on your credit report. If you fall behind on your mortgage, contact your lender immediately to avoid foreclosure. Most lenders are willing to work with you if they believe you're acting in good faith and the situation is temporary. Some lenders may reduce or suspend your payments for a short time.

Bankruptcy

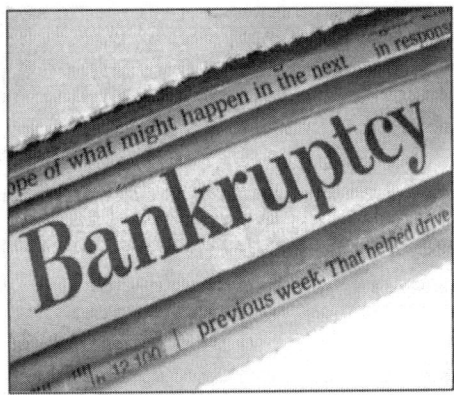

Personal bankruptcy is generally considered the option of last resort because the results are long lasting and far-reaching. A bankruptcy stays on your credit report for 10 years, making it difficult to acquire credit, buy a home, get life insurance, or sometimes get a job. However, it is a legal procedure that offers a fresh start for people who can't satisfy their debts. Individuals who follow the bankruptcy rules receive a discharge - a court order that says they do not have to repay certain debts.

Bankruptcy laws changed in 2005. With limited exceptions, people who plan to file for bankruptcy must get credit counseling from a government-approved organization within 180 days before filing. The law also requires people who file bankruptcy to complete an approved debtor education course before their debts can be discharged.

Bankruptcy cases are filed in a federal bankruptcy court. There are two primary types of personal bankruptcy: Chapter 13 and Chapter 7. A means test that is based on income is used to determine who may file under each category. In Chapter 13 bankruptcy, the court approves a repayment plan that allows you to pay off a default during a three-to-five-year period rather than surrender any property. After you have made all payments under the plan, you receive a discharge of your debts.

Known as straight bankruptcy, Chapter 7 involves liquidation of (getting rid of) all assets (property available for the payment of debts) that are not exempt. Exempt property may include automobiles, work-related tools, and basic household furnishings. Some of your property may be sold by a court-appointed official – a trustee – or turned over to your creditors. You can receive a discharge of your debts through Chapter 7 only once every six years. Under the new bankruptcy law, you may or may not be eligible to file under Chapter 7.

Both types of bankruptcy may get rid of unsecured debts and stop foreclosures, repossessions, garnishments, utility shut-offs, and debt collection activities. Both also provide exemptions that vary by state and allow people to keep certain assets. Note that personal bankruptcy usually does not erase child support, alimony, fines, taxes, and some student loan obligations. And unless you have an acceptable plan to catch up on your debt under Chapter 13, bankruptcy usually does not allow you to keep property when your creditor has an unpaid mortgage or lien on it. Visit the American Bankruptcy Institute for more information about consumer bankruptcy (http://www.abiworld. org).

Protecting Your Financial Identity

Identity theft is one of the fastest- growing types of financial fraud. Identity theft occurs when someone uses your personal information, without your permission, to open fraudulent accounts or commit other crimes (like giving your name when they are arrested). Account theft occurs when thieves use stolen information to steal from your existing accounts.

Thieves obtain your information in a variety of ways, including stealing it from businesses or institutions you do business with, rummaging through trash, falsely obtaining credit reports, stealing account numbers from receipts or records, stealing wallets or purses, stealing your mail, and posing as a business or government official to scam information from you. Once a thief has your information, they can use it to open new accounts; obtain loans for homes, cars, or education; obtain a phone or wireless service; counterfeit checks or debit cards; or change the mailing address on your accounts – all in your name!

If you begin to notice that your bills are not arriving, you have unauthorized withdrawals or charges on your existing accounts, are denied credit, or begin to receive calls from bill collectors for goods or services you didn't purchase, you may be a victim of identity theft. There are several steps you should take immediately.

• Request a copy of your credit report to check for unauthorized accounts.

• Immediately file an Identity Theft Report with local police or the police in the community where the identity theft took place. You will need a case number and copy of your report to provide
to creditors when disputing unauthorized charges.

• Contact the fraud division of the credit bureaus, and request that a Fraud Alert be placed on
your credit file. They will want a copy of the police report or your case number. Include a Victim's Statement in your credit report. You can get a free copy of your credit report from each of the three credit-reporting agencies, as suggested earlier in this chapter.

• Close any accounts opened fraudulently or that have been tampered with. You will need to dispute any unauthorized charges.

• File a complaint on-line with the Federal Trade Commission (FTC) at http://www.ftccomplaintassistant.gov/. The FTC collects complaints and shares the complaint information database with civil and criminal law enforcement authorities worldwide. The FTC does not resolve individual consumer complaints.

Take these steps to protect yourself from becoming a victim of identity theft:

1. Get a copy of your free credit report from each of the three major credit-reporting agencies every year. Check to be sure that everything is accurate, that all of the accounts are yours, and that accounts you have requested to be closed are marked closed. Refer
to the information in this chapter on how to obtain a copy of your credit report.

2. Examine your monthly account statements thoroughly. That's an easy way for you to be sure that all of the activity in your accounts was initiated by you.

3. Tear up or shred all pre-approved credit offers, receipts, and other personal information that link your name to account numbers before throwing them in the trash. And don't leave your ATM or credit card receipt in public trash cans. Thieves are known to go through trash to get account numbers and other items that will
give them just enough information to get credit in your name.

4. Keep track of the renewal dates for your credit cards. If your renewal credit card or bills are more than two weeks late, you should contact the issuer to ask when the item was mailed and to notify the issuer that you have not received the credit card or bill. Additionally, contact the Postal Service to see if someone has forwarded your mail to another address.

5. Mail your payments at the post office. Never use your mailbox with the red flag up. Thieves could steal your mail and obtain your information.

6. Protect your account information. Don't write your personal identification number (PIN) or passwords on your ATM or debit card. Don't write your Social Security number or credit card account number on a check. Don't carry your Social Security card, passport, or birth certificate unless you need it that day. Never provide personal or account information over the phone, unless you initiated the call and know with whom you are dealing. Thieves are known to call with news that you've won a prize, and all they need is your credit card number for verification. Don't fall for it. Remember the old saying, "if it sounds too good to be true, it probably is."

7. Carry only the ID, credit cards, and bank account information you need. And know exactly what you carry in case you lose something or your wallet is stolen.

8. Ask how your employer safeguards your personal information against unauthorized access.

9. You can protect yourself from identity theft by removing your name from credit bureau mailing lists. One call to the Opt In Opt Out Request Line (for Equifax, Trans Union, Experian, and Consumer Credit Associates) is all it takes to permanently remove your name from all marketing lists that credit-reporting agencies supply to direct marketers. You can opt out for a two-year period and renew your request at any time in the future. Call1-888-567- 8688 to opt out.

10. Get off other mailing lists for "junk" mail (i.e., direct mail) for up to three years for $1.00 (2009 cost). Although it can take up to three months before you notice a significant reduction in the amount of direct mail and phone calls you receive, eliminating mail you do not want saves trees and protects your identity. Write a letter to the Direct Marketing Association (www.dmachoice.org) requesting to be taken off national mailing lists. Give your complete name, name variations, and mailing address to: Mail Preference Service (MPS), Direct Marketing Association, P.O. Box 643, Carmel, NY 10512. A sample letter is available from the Privacy Rights Clearinghouse (htti:2iL www.privacyrights.org/Letters/ jm1a .htm). For more information, check out the fact sheet, Junk Mail: How Did They All Get My Address? from the Privacy Rights Clearinghouse at http://www. privacyrights .org/fs/fs4-junk.htm

---

Visit the following websites for more information on identity theft:

- ☐ Federal Trade Commission: http://www.ftc.gov/bcp/edu/microsites/idtheft/
- ☐ Identity Theft Prevention and Survival: http://www.identitytheft.org/
- ☐ Privacy Rights Clearinghouse: http://www.privacyrights.org/
- ☐ Public Interest Research Groups: http://www.uspirg.org/
- ☐ U.S. Department of Justice: http:// www.justice.gov/criminal/fraud/ websites/idtheft.html

Top 10 "Myth-Conceptions" of Credit

Provided by Julie Macc

MYTH #1 You share a credit score with your spouse.

Untrue! Your spouse and your credit report and credit scores are looked at individually. It is based on your social security number, which is unique to you. If you get an authorized user account (also known as "piggybacking") for your spouse, that will also show up on the report. However if none of your accounts are joint, and you don't have any authorized user accounts, there will be nothing that will affect your individual score.

MYTH # 2: Your credit score only counts when you're looking to borrow money.

HUGE Myth! Your credit score, right now, is looked at for almost everything you do. When you are applying for a job, auto insurance, homeowners insurance, life insurance, contractors bond, they look at your credit score, they look at your credit history. That's why it's so important to monitor your credit and clean it up if needed.

MYTH # 3: Always pay your credit card balance in full and that will give you the best credit.

The problem is if you have no balance and you pay it in full every month you will have no payment history. You will want to leave a small balance every month (Ideal amount is 1%) to show that you can pay on time. Don't just pay off a balance and leave it as a zero balance account ongoing, because after six months it is typically looked at as an inactive account, (which can also be closed due to inactivity). If you use the account every few months, and leave a very small balance on it, then it will help you.

MYTH # 4: Too many accounts will hurt, therefore you must close accounts.

This is a HUGE myth! 15% percent of your score is based on the average age of your accounts. Fact, the OLDER the revolving account the BETTER! This does not mean run out and open several new accounts. It is also a good idea to carry a small balance to keep the accounts open.

Myth #5: If a judge in a divorce proceeding orders a spouse to pay a debt, it's no longer affects my credit.

Well the reality is that a judge's orders do not negate the existing contract. Make sure to close all existing joint accounts and make sure that they are paid in full on time even if the other spouse was ordered to pay and you have to pay them to keep your credit intact.

MYTH # 6: Multiple auto or mortgage loan inquires will hurt your score for each inquiry.

The truth is your score was affected with older scoring methods, but now you can have multiple inquiries for an auto loan in a 30-day period and 45 days for mortgage loans, which will only count, for one inquiry.

MYTH # 7: It will take 7 years to improve my score.

Most negative items will remain for 7 years. There are however exceptions. Oftentimes collections are sold and "re-enaged" and can stay on indefinitely. This is a violation of the FCRA and a credit expert can help remove these violations. Your credit report has no history or memory of your score. What is on one month can completely disappear the next.

MYTH # 8: A serious financial crisis will hurt your score for 7 years.

Foreclosures will remain on your credit report for 7 years, bankruptcies 7 - 10 years depending on whether it's a chapter 7 or 13. There are ways to re-establish your credit and raise your score after a financial crisis.

MYTH # 9: Types of credit don't matter.

The credit scoring system gives weight to different types of credit providers better than others. They give more points to American Express, Visa, and MasterCard by predominant national banks than they do to department stores, furniture stores, or gas cards. Subprime and "secured" Visa and Master Cards do not score as well either.

MYTH # 10: Paying off an old collection or charge off will increase your credit score.

This is a huge myth, because what will happen is as soon as you pay off an old collection or charge off, the new date of last activity becomes re-aged, because you have just changed the date of last activity and they get to report the derogatory information for another 7 years! If you concerned about your credit score, then paying off debts prior to obtaining any other type of loan or mortgage will certainly hurt you greatly because it will be re-aged, and it will affect it as if it just happened yesterday. The recent activity of any derogative item has great affect on how it affects your overall credit score.

Julie has 26 Myth-Conceptions of Credit and they are available by contacting Julie directly see her books and website for contact information or you can download all 26 Myths in the Credit folder of your Mentoring Portal's Education Center.

Chapter Five: Record Your Accomplishments!

Possible Action Items for this Chapter:

☐ I determined my debt to income ratio

☐ I have requested my credit reports.

☐ I reviewed my credit reports.

☐ I know my credit score (credit.com or creditkarma.com)

☐ I have laid out a plan to improve or establish my credit.

☐ I researched and understand how credit cards charge fees

☐ I know how much I am being charged for my debt and I know how much I pay each month just on interest.

☐ I have stopped using a credit card

☐ I started tracking my credit card purchases.

☐ I have taken steps to monitor my credit charges and other accounts to protect myself from Identity Theft.

Accomplishment Tracker

Date _____ Year____ My Name_____ My Mentor is_____

Results from last month's action step(s) or Where I'm at right now...

_____

_____

_____

_____

_____

Challenge(s) I overcame to achieve these results

_____

_____

_____

_____

This is what I would like to accomplish in the next 30 days.

_____

_____

_____

Thoughts and Inspirations:

Chapter Notes and Questions

Chapter Six: Making Debt Work For You

Paying Down Your Debt

One of the biggest disadvantages of using credit is that the money you pay in interest and finance charges is money you don't have available to use for reaching other financial goals. If you are looking for ways to pay off your debts- especially credit card debt- the first step is to STOP taking on additional debt! This means stop using your credit cards. You may need to leave them at home so you are not tempted to use them. Some people find they must close all but one or two accounts. Others find placing their cards in a container of water and freezing them to be a good way to curb their credit card spending. By the time the water has thawed, they are over the impulse to buy!

Next, make a list of all your debts, as discussed previously in this chapter.

Include the name of the creditor, the amount you owe, the monthly payment, the interest rate, and how many more payments you have (for installment loans). Examine your total household spending, and look for ways to cut back in other areas so you can increase the payments you are making, particularly on credit cards.

As you look over your list of debts, look at those with the highest interest rate. The higher the interest rate, the more of your payment goes to interest instead of paying off the principal. Try to pay off these highest-interest rate debts first. Doing so will free up money to pay off your other bills. However, if you need a quick psychological boost, look for the debt with the lowest balance, and try to pay it off first. By eliminating one debt as soon as possible, some people become extra-energized to pay off another, and another, and another! Think in terms of making Power Payments. What's a Power Payment? It's paying off one debt and then taking the amount of money you were applying to that debt and adding it to another debt to pay it off even faster. Consider Mary's example in Real Life, Real Money on the following page.

Real Life, Real Money - Mary

Mary has four debts she is currently repaying: $225/month on her car loan, $125/month on her Visa card, $75/month on her MasterCard, and $35/month on her department store charge card. If Mary continues making these payments, she will pay off her department store card in one year and 11 months. When that debt is paid, she can add $35/month to one of her remaining debts; this would be her Power Payment. If Mary doesn't add the $35 to one of her remaining debts, it will take her another four years and six months before she is debt free. During this time, she will have paid a total of $7816.04 in interest charges alone!

If Mary does make Power Payments, she will reduce the time it takes to pay off her debts by one year and nine months and save a total of $975.01 in interest!!

In addition to making Power Payments also known as the Debt Snowball System, you can reduce the time it takes to become debt free by increasing the amount you pay on your debts each month. How can you do that? By finding money in your budget that you can redirect to debt repayment! "Like what?" you ask. Do you regularly purchase a designer coffee on your way to work in the morning? If instead of the $3 cup you purchased the $1.50 cup, you would free up $30 a month to add to your debt payments. If you regularly eat lunch out and average $7.50 a day, you are spending $150 a month on lunch. If you cut back on eating out to only twice a week, you will free up $90 a month. Assuming it will cost you $30 more a month in groceries to bring a lunch the other three days, you will have an additional $60 a month to add to your debt payments. Are you interested in knowing what a difference of as little as $30 would make in paying off your debts? Let's look at Mary's situation again.

If Mary added $30 more a month to her debt payments and continued making Power Payments, she would be debt free in four years and three months (instead of six years and five months), and she would have saved $1,824.06 in interest! Sound worth it? Give it a try! To calculate how much money you could save by making Power Payments, Women's Money now has a Debt Snowball Calculator. Just go into your Mentoring Portal (available to Program One Members) and look in the Education Center File Folder on Debt and click to open the Debt Snowball Calculator.

Debt Snowball / Power Payments Sample

It helps to see debt snowball savings in black and white. In this example, we are comparing the same debt to pay off - $10 a month versus $100 a month added

Debt Pay-Off with only $10 added a month to your total monthly payments.

Debt Reduction Calculator

http://www.vertex42.com/Calculators/debt-reduction-calculator.html

Balance Date: 1/1/2014

Creditor Information Table

Row	Creditor	Balance	Rate	Payment	Custom	Interest-only
1	Card #1	4,400.00	13.00%	50.00	2	47.67
2	Auto Loan #1	3,200.00	9.81%	30.00	1	26.16
3	Auto Loan #2	5,000.00	12.00%	55.00	3	50.00
4	Card #2	9,000.00	13.50%	110.00	5	101.25
5	Student Loan #1	4,900.00	4.00%	25.00	4	16.34
6						
7						
8						-
9						-
10						-
Totals:		**26,500.00**		**270.00**		

Paying this debt off with minimum payment (no snowball): The debt in this sample is paid off almost 25 and a half years and cost $41, 400.61 paid in interest.

Strategy: No Snowball

Creditors in Chosen Order	Original Balance	Total Interest Paid	Months to Pay Off	Month Paid Off
Card #1	4,400.00	9,821.96	285	Oct-37
Auto Loan #1	3,200.00	4,374.68	253	Feb-35
Auto Loan #2	5,000.00	8,254.76	241	Feb-34
Card #2	9,000.00	15,890.4	227	Dec-32
Student Loan #1	4,900.00	3,058.7	319	Aug-40
	-	-	-	
	-	-	-	
	-	-	-	
	-	-	-	
	-	-	-	

Total Interest Paid: 41,400.61 (Lower is Better)

Results are only estimates

Adding only $10 a month to your minimum payment and paying Lowest Balance Debt First. The debt in this sample is paid off almost 20 years and $35,614.94 paid in interest. Only $10 a month saves six years and $6000 in interest payments!

Strategy: Snowball (Lowest Balance First) ▼

Creditors in Chosen Order	Original Balance	Total Interest Paid	Months to Pay Off	Month Paid Off
Auto Loan #1	3,200.00	2,014.32	131	Dec-24
Card #1	4,400.00	7,110.54	186	Jul-29
Student Loan #1	4,900.00	2,534.25	211	Aug-31
Auto Loan #2	5,000.00	8,084.62	220	May-32
Card #2	9,000.00	15,871.21	222	Jul-32
	-	-	-	
	-	-	-	
	-	-	-	
	-	-	-	
	-	-	-	

Total Interest Paid: 35,614.94 (Lower is Better)

Results are only estimates

Adding only $100 a month to your minimum payments. The debt in this sample is paid off almost 10 years and $17,733.59 paid in interest.

Strategy: Snowball (Lowest Balance First) ▼

Creditors in Chosen Order	Original Balance	Total Interest Paid	Months to Pay Off	Month Paid Off
Auto Loan #1	3,200.00	387.67	28	May-16
Card #1	4,400.00	2,017.31	56	Sep-18
Student Loan #1	4,900.00	1,032.04	78	Jul-20
Auto Loan #2	5,000.00	4,140.22	97	Feb-22
Card #2	9,000.00	10,156.35	120	Jan-24
	-	-	-	
	-	-	-	
	-	-	-	
	-	-	-	
	-	-	-	

Total Interest Paid: 17,733.59 (Lower is Better)

Results are only estimates

You can also choose the Avalanche Method, which is paying the Highest Interest Rate Debt First. In some scenarios it may not make a big difference, but in others instances, like this one using the Avalanche payment method on the $100 a month added to minimum payments scenario by an additional $3,287.92 and pays it off 9 months faster.

Strategy: Avalanche (Highest Interest First) ▼

Creditors in Chosen Order	Original Balance	Total Interest Paid	Months to Pay Off	Month Paid Off
Card #2	9,000.00	3,352.88	59	Dec-18
Card #1	4,400.00	3,194.63	77	Jun-20
Auto Loan #2	5,000.00	4,014.33	92	Sep-21
Auto Loan #1	3,200.00	2,334.90	100	May-22
Student Loan #1	4,900.00	1,549.23	111	Apr-23
	–	–	–	
	–	–	–	
	–	–	–	
	–	–	–	
	–	–	–	

Total Interest Paid: 14,445.97 (Lower is Better)

Results are only estimates

Paying Down Debt from College

If you had or have student loans to help finance your college education, then it is likely that repaying college debt is a high priority. When a person graduates, drops out, or is less than a half-time student, there is a "grace period" before repayment has to begin for certain types of loans. It is wise to stay in touch with college financial aid offices to understand and plan for repaying back the loans. A good source of information about Federal Student Aid Programs and Repayment Options, including calculators, is at http://studentaid.ed.gov/PORTALSWebApp/students/english/repaying.jsp. A Public Service Loan Forgiveness Program is available that encourages people to take certain public service jobs. In return, an individual may qualify for forgiveness of the remaining balance on eligible federal student loans after making 120 payments while employed full-time by certain public service employers. More details are available at the Federal Student Aid website listed above.

During the college years, it is not uncommon for students to obtain their first credit card through direct solicitation by credit card companies on college campuses. Some college and university campuses have voluntarily banned certain marketing practices to assure that students do not "get in over their head" by obtaining and using credit cards. It is not worth a free t-shirt to open a credit card account that is not needed or whose terms and conditions are not competitive.

Don't pay for student loan consolidation! Consolidation is a free service offered by the government.

Borrowers should also know whether their loans are through the federal government or a private lender such as Chase or Wells Fargo.

While private loans cannot be consolidated under a federal loan, private lenders may be more than happy to take over your federal loans. That doesn't make it a good idea, says Betsy Mayotte, director of compliance for American Student Assistance, a nonprofit that helps students manage college debt.

"Don't ever consolidate private loans with federal loans," Mayotte says. "Never."

Your Net Worth (a.k.a. Your Financial Snapshot)

Good, solid financial planning is based on facts - money facts. If financial planning is the roadmap, then money facts are its building blocks. You've heard it said, "If you don't know where you're going, any path will do"! You want to build a clear path to your future. That will involve a little detective work and tracking.

This chapter will help you understand how to gather facts about your finances and then analyze these facts. You will be surprised to learn that you are probably better off than you thought you were!

You will learn how to use three important money tools:

       1) Statement of Financial Position (Net Worth Statement),

       2) A Notebook Tool for Tracking Your Spending, and

       3) A Statement of Income and Expense.

Then, you will use the analysis of your money facts as a basis for setting financial goals. Finally, you will learn about tools to use in performing helpful financial calculations.

Your Statement of Financial Position is the first step in planning your financial future is to know where you currently stand. For this, you will take a "snapshot" of your current financial situation. This means knowing exactly what your assets and liabilities are at a particular moment in time. This information will give you a picture of your net worth or, as it is often called, your Statement of Financial Position. A good time to prepare a Statement of Financial Position is when you have all of your financial records for a particular time period, such as at the end of the calendar quarter or year. An especially good time for preparing or updating a Statement of Financial Position is during the month of January, after end-of-year statements arrive.

Real Life, Real Money

I know the facts, all right.

They're spelled d-e-b-t.

I don't feel like I'm getting ahead at all, what with the money I still owe on my college loans, new car, and credit cards. Sure, I'm saving a little, but I feel so depressed. I don't really know where I stand, financially speaking.

To complete this task, you will compile a listing of what you own (assets) and what you owe (liabilities). It really is that simple. If you do not have your money papers organized yet, so back to chapter one.

Preparing a Statement of Financial Position is a fairly easy task because it involves transferring information from money papers you have or will be receiving. These papers include items like monthly, quarterly, or annual statements from your bank, retirement fund, mortgage company, etc. It does not involve an analysis of your income or spending, although it does reflect decisions you have made about spending and saving/investing in the past.

Real Life, Real Money: Lisa Learns Her Net Worth

Lisa is 31 and a single mom of Julie, who is three. Lisa finished her college degree two years ago, found a job as an elementary school teacher, and purchased a home this year using $20,000 of the money she inherited from her grandparents as a down payment. She used the rest of the money for a down payment on a new car and invested $4,000 in the stock market. Since becoming a homeowner, Lisa has developed a serious interest in financial planning. When she obtained her mortgage, she had to prepare a Statement of Financial Position. She has decided she will keep her Statement up-to-date on an annual basis. That way she can see how her net worth changes over time.

Financial Terms to Know

Assets refer to everything that you OWN. They include cash and cash equivalents, invested assets, and use assets. Cash or cash equivalents include checking accounts, savings accounts, money market accounts, and the cash value of life insurance. Invested assets include the money you may have invested in the stock market or in mutual funds, and the money in your retirement portfolios, including individual retirement accounts. Use assets include real estate and personal property, automobiles, and other things you may own. When you add up your assets, you may be surprised to discover how much you "own."

Liabilities refer to everything that you OWE. It includes credit card balances, college loan balances, car note balances, **mortgage** balances, and any other type of personal loan you may have. In Lisa's example, her total liabilities were $163,800.

ASSETS Put Money in Your Pocket
LIABILITIES Take Money Out of Your Pocket

Net worth is determined by subtracting liabilities from assets. In Lisa's case, her net worth is $123,700. This net worth figure is a snapshot of your current financial situation. It is an image that is captured at a moment in time. It is a good idea to determine net worth on an annual basis. That will give you the best idea of how your net worth changes from year to year. When you apply for a loan, the lender will ask you to provide a current Statement of Financial Position before finalizing the loan and may require you to use the form supplied by the lending institution.

Notice on Lisa's Statement of Financial Position (on the right) that the final figure in the right- hand column is called Total Liabilities and Net Worth. This figure is identical to Total Assets and is obtained by adding together net worth and total liabilities.

ASSET	LIABILITY
~~HOME~~ Stocks & Bonds ~~CAR~~ Savings Account ~~BOAT~~ Property Owner renting to others	CREDIT CARDS CAR IOUs HOME COLLEGE LOANS BOAT

Example of Statement of Financial Position

ASSETS (at Fair Market Value)	
Cash/Cash Equivalents	
Checking Accounts	$1,100
Savings Accounts	$3,600
Money Market Account	$1,800
Life Insurance Cash Value	
Total Cash/Cash Equivalents	*$6,500*
Invested Assets	
Stock Portfolio	$5,000
Limited Partnership	
IRAs	$3,000
Pension Plans	$5,000
Total Invested Assets	*$13,000*
Use Assets	
Residence	$165,000
Cars	$28,000
Personal Property	$75,000
Other Real Estate	
Total Use Assests	*$268,000*
TOTAL ASSETS	**$287,500**

LIABILITIES & NET WORTH	
Liabilities	
Credit Card Balances	$2,800
Auto Note Balance	$16,000
Mortgage Note Balance	$145,000
Total Liabilities	*$163,800*
Net Worth	**$123,700**
TOTAL LIABILITIES & NET WORTH	**$287,500**

Step 1. Prepare your own Statement of Financial Position using the *downloadable form found on WomensMoney.org or from your Women's Money Mentor*. Modify the form to account for your various types of assets and liabilities. Put a date on the statement. Remember that a good time to prepare this statement is in January, after end- of-year statements arrive. But you can also prepare the statement at any point in time. Sometimes, the financial statements you use to develop your net worth statement will show different dates. That's all right. Just note the dates next to the asset or liability you have listed on the form. When you estimate your use assets (cars, homes, personal property, etc.), use your best estimate of "fair market value." In other words, what price would you get if you were to sell the asset today? Keep in mind that homes and real estate usually (but not always) appreciate (increase) in value, while automobiles and some personal property (think computers, large screen televisions, refrigerators) depreciate (decrease) in value over time.

Step 2. Analyze your Statement of Financial Position. Is your net worth positive or negative? Are you "worth" more or less than you thought? Are there circumstances beyond your control that have influenced your net worth? Some factors such as a general decline of real estate values in your area or an increase in your debt because you have recently purchased a new car will influence your Statement of Financial Position.

Is there anything you can do to increase your assets and decrease your liabilities, or is your situation the result of larger economic forces? Complete these statements:

• What surprised me most about my Statement of Financial Position is:

• I can increase my assets over the next year by:

• I can decrease my liabilities over the next year by:

Step 3. Make a file folder to archive your Statement of Financial Position. You can add the latest copy each time you update your net worth. Over time, these "snapshots" will help you see the changing nature of your financial position. And someday, your grandchildren may even chuckle at this part of their "family history."

(Optional Step.) If you use some type of computerized accounting system, take the time to enter your asset and liability data into the program. Doing so will allow you to automate the preparation of a Statement of Financial Position through the "reports" function of your accounting package.

Chapter Six: Record Your Accomplishments!

Possible Action Items for this Chapter:

☐ Went to WomensMoney.org to use online calculator to pay off debt fast or logged into PowerPay.org to create a debt pay-off system.

☐ I understand the difference between Assets and Liabilities.

☐ I have reviewed my Assets and Liabilities

☐ I know my TRUE net worth.

☐ I have calculated how much I will save by using the debt pay off acceleration system vs. paying the way I am now. The money I will save is a total of _____.

☐ I have a target date to be debt free!

☐ I have shared this target date and my mission with my Women's Money Group or family to enlist their support to stay on track to become debt free!

☐ What do you intend to do with the money you save by accelerating your debt-pay off? Does it pay for a long-term goal you have? If so, which one?

Accomplishment Tracker

Date _____ Year____ My Name_____ My Mentor is_____

Results from last month's action step(s) or Where I'm at right now...

_____

_____

_____

_____

_____

Challenge(s) I overcame to achieve these results

_____

_____

_____

_____

This is what I would like to accomplish in the next 30 days.

_____

_____

Thoughts and Inspirations:

Chapter Notes and Questions

Chapter Seven: Savings Basics

Saving money isn't always easy, but sometimes getting started is the main roadblock. Many people feel like there just isn't "enough money" to pay bills, let alone think about saving money for the future. Having savings helps to build financial security. Without money set aside for the future, it will be difficult to meet future emergencies; pay large and infrequent bills; or to build resources for important longer-term goals, like a car, a home, a college education, or retirement.

This chapter will help you learn:

1) Why paying yourself first is an important strategy.

2) How to establish an emergency fund and a set-aside account.

3) How to select savings options that make sense for you.

4) Why the time value of money is so powerful.

5) The difference between saving and investing,

As you read about investing, you are certain to come across words and concepts that are unfamiliar to you. Check the Women's Money Glossary for an explanation. A helpful on-line reference is www. Investorwords.com. Write down words you plan to look up.

Real Life, Real Money

"Save money? Are you kidding? It takes 125 percent of what I earn just to make ends meet each month. How can I possibly save any money? I'm barely making it now. "

Why You Should Pay Yourself First

The golden rule of savings is to pay yourself first. By adding to your savings regularly, you will gain control of your financial life. By setting aside money before you can spend it, you may not even miss it! Many people say they will start saving after they have paid all of their bills. They are missing the mark! There will always be ways to spend money! It takes less discipline to pay yourself first than to hunt for ways to save money after the bills are paid.

As soon as you receive your paycheck, make it a habit to pay yourself first. You can even make saving money effortless by automating your savings; have savings automatically drafted from your checking account each month- that way you will not have to think about it. Taking the step to pay yourself first will build a sense of accomplishment and satisfaction when you see your savings account balance grow.

Keep Your Financial Goals in Mind

List your top three financial goals. (If you have completed the goal-setting exercises from previous chapters of this handbook, just copy your top three financial goals here. If this chapter is your starting point, list your three most important financial goals here. Your financial goals provide a roadmap for the future.

1.

2.

3.

First Stop: Emergency Savings

Despite signs that Americans are starting to adopt a new frugality as measured by a rise in the personal savings rate as a share of disposable income, half of U.S. households don't have even modest savings, according to a new study conducted by TNS Group, a market researcher, along with Harvard Business School and Dartmouth College professors. The researchers surveyed households to see how many could come up with $2,000 in 30 days to cope with an emergency like a car breakdown or major home repair. About half said they could not come up with $2,000 for a "rainy day" even if they turned to relatives for help. Researchers pointed to a tougher credit environment that has made it more difficult for consumers to rely on credit for emergencies, thus causing households to live with what one of the researchers calls "financial fragility."

Life is unpredictable. Having an emergency fund is the best way to weather financial storms and uncertainty. Most financial advisers recommend that we have emergency savings equivalent of three to six months' worth of living expenses. However, some experts recommend a fund large enough to cover eight or nine months' living expenses.

How should we go about creating this fund for emergencies? Here are some practical ideas for creating your own emergency fund.

We should note here that unlike any other financial education program, Women's Money advocates for two emergency savings funds. Even though we encourage two funds, please know that you have to do what works best for you and your life. How you get there is not as important as getting and staying there.

Why Create Two Emergency Funds?

Real Life, Real Money: Tanisha Learns a Hard Lesson

Tanisha is 28 and a single mom of Angelina, who is two. Tanisha works as an executive assistant for a casino executive. One day at work, she gets a call that from her daughter's day care that Angelina had a severe head injury on the playground and has been taken to the hospital. Tanisha hangs up, tells her boss of the situation and heads to the hospital. Luckily, Tanisha has good insurance and her emergency savings has three months salary in it, so she can pay for the hospital co-pay, so Tanisha is no worried about the money. She can focus completely on her daughter who was placed in ICU.

Tanisha's daughter is doing well, and will be able to leave ICU shortly. Tanisha's mother holds watch over Angelina, so Tanisha can go back to work the next day. Tanisha didn't even miss a full day of work. She was back to work the next day. Unfortunately, when she returned to work she was fired because she told her boss she was leaving and didn't ask for permission to leave.

When Tanisha sat down to do the numbers, she realized that the hospital co-pay ate up one-third of her emergency savings and now she was left with only two months of living expenses. Her daughter's condition and finding a new job was stressful enough, but now she had once less month to do it in.

Tanisha thought she was prepared, but it turns out she wasn't prepared properly.

First Stop: Create an Emergency Fund

1. Start by looking at your life, family and work. What are some of the possible emergencies that could happen?

    a. Do you have a parent or children across country? You have to be prepared with airfare, hotel and spending money in case you need to fly out for a family emergency.

    b. Do you have a car? Cars break down. If you have an expensive car, your emergency fund may have to be higher than if you had a basic American made car.

    c. Do you have animals? Plan for their potential emergencies.

    d. Do you live in an area where weather-related disasters like a hurricane or flood are likely to occur?

    e. Do you have a home warranty? Research the maximum you would have to pay for the worst covered expense. If you don't have a home warranty, plan to save the price of a washing machine or more. If you don't have a credit card, then estimate the price of a new furnace or water heater.

    f. What else might be an emergency you would have to pay for in your life?

2. Calculate the costs of your possible emergencies.

3. Choose the emergency situation that would cost you the most as the minimum amount you want to have in your emergency fund. Only you can decide what your emergency fund goal should be.

4. Designate a special savings account as your emergency fund. Although current interest rates are low, select an account that will accrue interest or earnings and offers liquidity so you can withdraw funds when an emergency occurs. However, don't make it SO EASY that you will "raid" the fund every time you need a little "extra." That defeats the purpose of having an emergency fund. Look at your emergency fund as your "peace of mind fund." By having funds available to cover future emergencies, you are building a cushion to fall back on should some unforeseen, serious financial emergency occur in your life.

5. Decide how long it will take you to build up your emergency fund. It will take time to build up your emergency fund because you are funding it from your current income. Your current income has many demands on it, including current bills that are due. If you have another source of funds, you can make faster progress in building up your emergency fund. Perhaps you can use a pay raise, a bonus, income from interest or dividends, or a source of income other than your pay to start or increase your emergency fund. If you pay off a debt that you've been paying towards every month, perhaps you can use the money you would have used for the debt to fund or increase your emergency fund. If you receive a tax refund, you could add money from it to your emergency fund.

Second Stop: Create a Pink-Slip Fund™

1. Start by doing the math. What are your "bare bones" living expenses each month? How does this figure compare to what you actually spend right now? A Pink-Slip Fund™ is intended to cover your basic living expenses should you experience losing your source of income. Another way to think about a Pink-Slip Fund™ is to ask yourself the question, "What is the least amount of money I would need to cover the basics and not fall behind with my bills?" In times of emergency, that probably means doing away with spending for non-essentials. We're talking survival here!

2. Once you know the "bare bones" amount for one month's living expenses, multiply that amount by the number of months you want your Pink-Slip Fund™ to ultimately cover. Should it be three, six, eight, or more months? Only you can decide what your emergency fund goal should be.

4. Decide how long it will take you to build up your Pink-Slip Fund™. Remember that Rome was not built in a day, and you cannot fully fund your Pink-Slip Fund™ overnight! Take your time, and be realistic about it. It will take time to build up your emergency fund because you are funding it from your current income. Your current income has many demands on it, including current bills that are due. If you have another source of funds, you can make faster progress in building up your Pink-Slip Fund™. Perhaps you can use a pay raise, a bonus, income from interest or dividends, or a source of income other than your pay to start or increase your Pink-Slip Fund™. If you pay off a debt that you've been paying towards every month, perhaps you can use the money you would have used for the debt to fund or increase your emergency fund. If you receive a tax refund, you could add money from it to your Pink-Slip Fund™.

5. Determine if you already have a fund from your employer that can act as a Pink-Slip Fund™. Do you have employee benefits that you can cash out like accrued sick leave or vacation days you never took? Talk to your employer to see what you may have available to you without penalty of early withdrawal.

6. Designate a special savings account as your Pink-Slip Fund™. Although current interest rates are low, select an account that will accrue interest or earnings and offers liquidity so you can withdraw funds when an emergency occurs. However, don't make it SO EASY that you will "raid" the fund every time you need a little "extra." That defeats the purpose of having an emergency fund. Look at your Pink-Slip Fund™ as your "take a breath fund." By having funds available to cover loss of income, you can take a breath and find the best income replacement and even create a plan to replace that income rather than jumping at the first job offer that comes along.

Real Life, Real Money: Carmen's Emergency Fund Gets Going

When Carmen started her new job, she took a good look at her living expenses and realized that she would need about 75 percent of her current take-home pay of $2800 a month to cover the "essentials." She figured that 25 percent of her take-home pay was being spent on things she could either reduce or eliminate in a real emergency. She decided to set up her emergency fund to cover her "bare bones" living expenses for a five month period in case something happened and she lost her job.

After doing the math, she discovered that her emergency fund goal needed to be $10,500 (75 percent of $2800 H five months). After reviewing her budget, Carmen decided she could start depositing $250 per month into an emergency fund account. At that rate, it will take her 42 months, or just over three years, to fully fund the account. Carmen knows this is a "ballpark" time period. The time it takes her to fund her account will depend on the regularity and actual amount of her savings, as well as the rate of return her savings will earn in her account. She is also aware that if she receives a raise in coming years, she may want or need to make adjustments to her overall emergency fund goal (as opposed to financial goals) or increase her monthly deposit if her "bare bones" needs are increasing. Even if she doesn't need to increase her "bare bones" living expenses, she may choose to devote that raise to her emergency fund as a way of reaching her emergency fund goal sooner.

To make it easier for her to save, Carmen arranged for a monthly payroll deduction to a new emergency fund account that she established with her employer's credit union. Carmen figures that if she doesn't see the money, she won't miss it! By paying herself first, Carmen is taking the first important step to increasing her financial security. Carmen also started to think about ways that she could economize even further so she would have more money left to fund some of her other financial goals. She wished she had started doing this when she started her very first job. She had always heard that an emergency fund was important, but she never got started because she thought she couldn't afford to fund one. Now she's telling her friends and teaching them how to do it.

Here are the steps that Carmen followed in setting up her emergency fund. Complete the "Me" column for yourself, remembering that your situation may be very different from Carmen's.

	Steps for Starting an Emergency Fund	Carmen	Me
A	My current monthly take-home pay	$2800	
B	The percentage of my monthly take-home pay that I need to cover the "essentials" of living	75 percent	
C	How much I need each month to cover the "essentials" *Multiply B H A*	$2100	
D	The number of months' essential living expenses I want to cover through my emergency fund account (from 3-6 months, or more)	five months	
E	The total dollar goal for my emergency fund *Multiply C H D*	$10,500	
F	Amount I will save each month	$250	
G	Number of months it will take me to reach the goal I have set for my emergency fund *Divide E by F*	42 months	
H	Where I'll establish my emergency fund	Employer's Credit Union	

Third Stop: Set-Aside Accounts

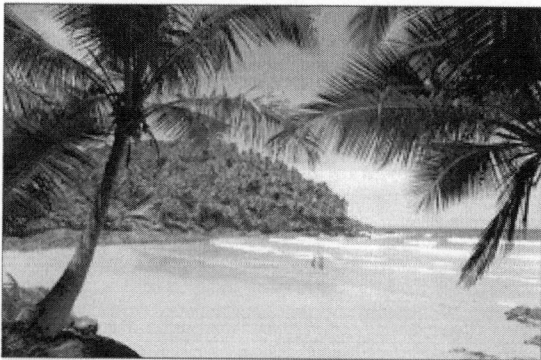

You may be unfamiliar with "set- aside accounts" since not all financial advice books or advisors refer to these special accounts. They aren't quite the same as an emergency fund. Emergency funds are not meant to be tapped regularly, while set-aside accounts are meant to be tapped regularly.

So, what is the point of a set-aside account, you might ask?

It's a place to put money that you know you will need in the future, instead of just keeping it in your primary checking account where using it for other purposes is too easy. Another way of looking at the difference between an emergency fund and a set-aside account is that emergency funds are to be used for sudden, unexpected events; set-aside accounts are for known expenses that occur periodically. A bill for your annual umbrella insurance premium is not an emergency; it is a known occurrence. Of course, if you don't have the money to pay the bill, it is very, very stressful. The following two cases should illustrate two ways in which set-aside accounts can be used, for expenses and for income.

Real Life, Real Money:
Crystal Establishes a Set-Aside Account for Irregular Expenses

Crystal thought she had been doing a good job of budgeting her money, based on her financial goals. But expenses she had forgotten about put things out of whack when the bills arrived. Crystal isn't alone. Many people forget to plan ahead for expenses that don't occur every month. Crystal forgot about her auto insurance (annual premium $988), her holiday gift giving ($450 last year), her annual dream vacation ($1080), and the annual pledge she had made to her favorite charity ($1500 to be paid in two years).

Crystal's usual routine was to put any extra expenses on her credit card. That way she figured she could pay them off as she was able. But of course, the interest charges and other fees make this a very expensive way to finance forgetfulness. She decided that she could get a grip on her situation now that she was making a little more money. She also knew that if she didn't do it now, she could easily fall into the credit trap again. Crystal decided that she needed to set aside the money all year round so it would be there when the bills and obligations arrived. Here's how she did it.

1. She added up all the irregular expenses for this year ($988 + $450 + $1080 + $750 = $3268).

2. She divided the total expense by 12 ($3268 divided by 12 = $272).

3. She started to pay herself first by saving $272 in her set-aside account each month.

4. She uses the money only to pay for the expenses that she elected to fund with her set-aside account.

After using this method for a while, Crystal found there were other irregular bills she had overlooked, so she re-worked the math and set aside a little more money to cover those expenses. She also decided that she would deposit money into this account every month for some of her other financial goals, including a down payment for her own home.

Set Aside Accounts Can Work for Regular Expenses Too

Do you find that you take money from your budget to pay for unexpected extras? For instance, do you overspend on groceries or shopping and then take it from that extra money you were planning to put towards your credit card pay off? This is not uncommon. Being out in the world is pretty tempting, and we don't have an angel on our shoulder reminding us that if we splurge now, we have to take it from somewhere else later. Therefore some people have set-aside "accounts" for regular budgeted expenses too. There are many ways to format these. You have to work this in a way that works for YOU. Try several methods to see what works for you.

Multiple Ways to Create a Regular Expense Set-Aside System

1. **The envelope system.** This is a tried and true system around for many years that has been very successful for many people. How does it work? Get a bunch of envelopes and label them to correspond with each spending category in your budget. Cash your check and put in the budgeted amount in that envelope. Put the envelopes in a safe place. That's what you have to spend in that c category, and because you have cash, you can't go over budget.
2. **The debit card system.** This one is a little tricky, but if you don't feel comfortable with cash and envelopes, this is the same concept but a checking account acts as your "envelope". You open up a free checking account per budget category and have a debit card related to that account. You can only spend what you have in your account. This is also a good way to protect your money from identity theft, as only a small part of your money could be at risk rather than your whole paycheck in your main account.
3. **Flexible vs. Fixed system.** This method is a bit easier to manage than multiple debit cards and checking accounts. Your budget is already divided into fixed and flexible expenses, so you can have two accounts. The fixed expenses account is never touched. Every bill is on auto-pay (rent, car, insurance, etc). The second account is for flexible expenses such as groceries, clothing, gas, etc. You can also split the flexible spending into two accounts one for essentials like groceries and gas and one for fun money like clothing and eating out.
4. **Per Pay-Check system**. Determine which bills you will pay out of each paycheck. Put it in writing. When the paycheck comes in, pay the bills and pay your savings account. Use the remainder for flexible expenses.

Real Life, Real Money:
Jennifer Establishes a Set-Aside Account for Income

Jennifer is a beginning teacher with a nine--month contract. Unlike some schools that issue teachers one check per month, her school district will issue her nine monthly checks during the school year but none during the summer months. She knows it would be tempting to spend all of her money as she receives it, but she has no prospects for summer employment. If she spends it all, she will have nothing for summer. Another teacher told her about creating a set-aside account. Jennifer followed her friend's suggestions and started right away. It took decisive action on her part, but she achieved her goal. Here's how she did it.

1. She multiplied her monthly take-home pay by nine ($2800 x 9 = $25,200).

2. She divided her total annual take-home pay by 12 ($25,200 divided by 12 = $2100).

3. She subtracted this new amount from her monthly take-home pay ($2800- $2100 = $700).

4. She opened a savings account and started depositing $700 from each of her nine paychecks in this set-aside account ($700 x 9 = $6300).

5. She withdrew $2100 each month for three months during the summer ($2100 x 3 = $6300).

Jennifer had enough money to live on throughout the year without feeling deprived during the summer months. In fact, she had an identical amount each month, so it meant she could meet her summer bills easily. If she receives a salary increase for the coming year, she will re-do her math and increase the amount she saves each month. She's thinking about asking her school to allow her to have a payroll deduction that goes directly to her savings (set-aside) account.

Jennifer has applied the principle of pay yourself first to make her money last all yearlong. She has adopted the use of a set- aside account for money she knows she will need during the summer. Jennifer is no longer panicking about a summer money emergency. She has it covered! If she does earn additional money during the summer, she is just that much further ahead.

Create a Set-Aside Account

Using Crystal's method, devise a set-aside account for expenses for yourself so your irregular expenses don't catch you off guard.

	Set-Aside Account for Expenses	Crystal	Me
Step 1	Identify all irregular expenses expected during the year:		
	Auto insurance	$988	
	Holiday giftgiving	$450	
	Dream vacation	$1080	
	Annual pledge to favorite charity ($1500 to be paid in two years)	$750	
Step 2	Total irregular expenses expected	$3268	
Step 3	Divide the total in Step 2 by 12	$3268) 12 =	
Step 4	Deposit $272 each month into set-aside account for expenses	Crystal pays	

Following Jennifer's example, create a set-aside account for yourself if you know that you will be paid irregularly during the coming year. Adjust your needs accordingly.

	Set-Aside Account for Income	Jennifer	Me
A	Current monthly take-home pay.	$2800	
B	Total annual take-home pay. Multiply Step A by 9 (or the total number of months that income is received).	$25,200	
C	Divide Step B (the total annual take-home pay) by 12.	$2100	
D	Amount that needs to be set-aside monthly. Subtract the amount in Step C from the amount in Step A.	$700	
E	Total Amount in Set-Aside Account for Income. Open a savings account and deposit the amount in Step D each month for nine months (or total number of months that income is received).	$6300	
F	Withdraw the amount needed each month that no take-home pay is received.	$2100	

Do You Need Separate Savings Accounts for Your Emergency Fund and Your Set-Aside Accounts?

No? Maybe? Yes?

The answer is "yes" if it is easier for you to maintain separate accounts. The answer is "no" if your long-term strategy is to use a single account as a "holding tank" for money you plan to accumulate in the account and periodically transfer funds to pay for set-asides or for emergencies. It may be less costly to have a single account because it is easier to meet minimum balance requirements. You may also prefer receiving a single statement with all of your transactions. Within a single account, track your sub- account balances. This is easy if you use a computerized financial recordkeeping system.

Comparing Savings Options

Where to Put Your Money Not only must you decide what type of savings option to select, you must be able to compare choices within those options. For example, savings accounts appear to be alike when they advertise an identical Annual Percentage Rate (APR), but research has shown that there can be big differences in earnings because of the numerous ways in which earnings can be calculated. The Truth-in- Savings law requires all financial institutions to disclose the terms and conditions of savings plans. Some general questions to ask before making a decision about any savings plan include:

1. How safe is money in this particular institution and savings plan? Is it insured?

2. Is the financial institution on- line (on the Internet), in my community, or both?

3. Are there minimum balance requirements?

4. Are there penalties and fees for transactions?

5. How convenient is it to make deposits and withdrawals?

6. What is the Annual Percentage Rate?

7. What is the Annual Percentage Yield (APY)?

8. How often is interest compounded?

9. What method is used to compute interest?

10. What special features or services are offered?

11. Are there any tax advantages or disadvantages associated with this savings instrument?

12. Does the account offer Internet- based electronic transfers? How long will it take before amounts that are transferred become available to me?

13. Can the account be accessed and managed on-line?

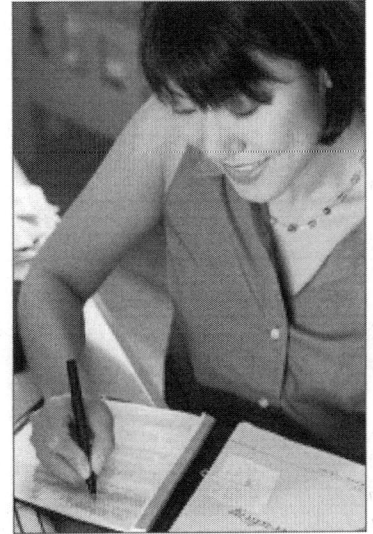

Passbook and Statement Accounts.

Some savers find a passbook account with a bank, savings and loan, or credit union convenient and safe because it is insured. Funds can be withdrawn at any time without penalty. However, the account may not earn enough interest to keep up with inflation. Once you build your savings, keep only a minimal amount in passbook accounts or statement accounts, and move on to savings options that pay a higher rate of return. Most financial institutions no longer issue an actual "passbook" as they did in the past. Instead, periodic statements are provided to the depositor on-line or via mail. On- line-only banks have offered more competitive rates than traditional "bricks and mortar" institutions, but make sure the accounts are insured by either the FDIC (for banks) or NCUA (for credit unions).

Checking Accounts.

Some checking accounts pay interest, but the interest rate is likely to be lower than for a regular savings account or may only apply to amounts over a certain balance. An interest-bearing checking account may be a convenient "holding tank" for short-term set- aside accounts or for emergency funds, but make sure the rate of return is competitive with other savings options and that there are no extra fees or charges associated with the account.

Certificates of Deposit (CDs).

Insured COs at financial institutions are one convenient way for small savers to earn higher interest rates than on regular savings accounts. However, interest rates on COs have declined during the recession that began at the end of 2007, so it pays to comparison shop carefully. Institutions are free to set the interest rate, time period of the CD, and minimum balance required. Early withdrawal penalties are applied to COs, so if you must withdraw your money before the CD matures, you will lose some interest. If you keep the certificate until maturity, you can redeem it for the face amount plus the stated interest. In the CD, you are giving up some liquidity in exchange for a higher rate of return. COs are insured instruments. Federal insurance covers up to $250,000. In today's competitive market environment, use the Internet to help identify the best interest rates. A good place to compare interest rates is www. bankrate.com.

Laddering Your CDs.

People who place their money into COs can benefit from "laddering." Laddering is a different way to build your savings portfolio and offers the potential of earning more interest when interest rates fluctuate. Instead of placing all money into one CD, the money is divided up and placed in different COs, each with a different maturity. For example, in building a five-year ladder with $10,000, you would first divide $10,000 by five. You will build a ladder with $2000 for each "rung" or year of the ladder. The first $2000 would be invested in a five-year CD, the second $2000 in a four-year CD, the third $2000 for 36 months, the fourth $2000 for 24 months, and the last $2000 for one year. When the one-year CD matures, you roll it into a five-year CD, and continue to do this when each CD matures. The idea behind this is that because interest rates tend to be higher over time, you are able to take advantage of some higher rates in the overall savings portfolio while maintaining some liquidity if you need some of your money before all COs mature. You can find more examples of the benefits of laddering at http://www.bankrate .com/finance/ cd!how-do-i-ladder-cd-s.aspx.

Money Market Accounts.

If you feel better with instant access to your funds, have the willpower not to spend every dollar saved, and want interest rates similar to CD rates, then money market accounts may be right for you. However, money market mutual funds are not insured. Companies often require a minimum of $1000 or more to open the account and a $500 or $1000 minimum balance to maintain it. These accounts earn interest at current short-term market rates, and you can write checks in minimum amounts, usually $250 or $500.

Another option is a money market deposit account at a financial institution. Financial institutions are free to set their own terms and conditions about the minimum deposit required to open the account, the interest rates, and minimum balance requirements. Balances that fall below the minimum balance generally earn interest at the passbook account rate. These accounts may permit you to write a limited number of checks per month, often three. These accounts may be called something other than a "money market deposit account."

The following are recommendations to help you choose and maintain your accounts:

- After comparing your options and shopping around for the "best" option(s), select an account or accounts that meet your current needs.
- Be organized about your accounts. You may find it useful to set up a file folder for each account to store account documents, including monthly/ quarterly statements.
- If you move or experience some other life change, notify the financial institution of your new address.
- Monitor the performance of your account. If the account does not yield the return you had expected, continue to compare savings options. Rates change frequently, so you should stay alert to what competing financial institutions may be offering.
- Verify the accuracy and legitimacy of your account periodically, and report discrepancies to the account issuer.

U.S. Treasury Securities and Programs

The U.S. Department of the Treasury has sold U. S. Savings Bonds for more than 50 years. They are affordable, safe, and offer certain tax advantages. They are designed for the long-term investor but still offer flexibility to the investor who needs greater liquidity. Savings bonds are popular savings instruments because of their interest rates, tax advantages, safety, affordability, accessibility, and convenience.

There are many options available to consumers who wish to invest and save by buying securities offered by the U.S. Treasury. You can learn more from the websites, http://www. savingsbonds.gov/ and http://www. treasurydirect.gov. The main types of securities that are available include:

• **Treasury Bills** are short-term government securities with maturities ranging from a few days to 52 weeks. Bills are sold at a discount from their face value.

• **Treasury Notes** are government securities that are issued with maturities of 2, 3, 5, 7, and 10 years and pay interest every six months.

• **Treasury Bonds** pay interest every six months and mature in 30 years.

• **Treasury Inflation-Protected Securities (TIPS)** are marketable securities whose principal is adjusted by changes in the Consumer Price Index (CPI). TIPS pay interest every six months and are issued with maturities of 5, 10, and 20 years.

• **Series I Savings Bonds** are a low- risk savings product that earns interest while protecting the saver from inflation. I Bonds are sold at face value. Compare TIPS and Series I Savings Bonds.

• **Series EE/E Savings Bonds** are safe, low-risk savings products that pay interest based on current market rates for up to 30 years for bonds purchased May 1997 through April 30, 2005. Series EE bonds purchased May 2005 and after earn a fixed rate of return. Electronic EE Savings Bonds are sold at face value when purchased through www. treasurydirect.gov. Paper EE Savings Bonds are sold at ½ face value. You may purchase EE bonds via TreasuryDirect or at almost any financial institution, or through your employer's payroll deduction plan, if available.

The Time Value of Money

Money saved in an interest-bearing account grows by itself. Money in a mattress does not! Of course, it never hurts to keep adding money to an interest-bearing account because it will grow faster. Money that earns interest grows because it compounds over time. Through the magic of compounding, your savings balance will grow. Compounding means that you earn interest on your original deposits AND also on the interest that your deposits have earned.

Time Value Question: How much difference does the annual rate of return make on a $10,000 investment?

The following table shows how $10,000 would grow under various annual rates of return and how much difference the annual rate of return can make on the value of the original savings after 1, 10, and 20 years. In these examples, neither taxation nor the impact of inflation is considered. Note that the differences between the rates of return are more dramatic with the passage of time. After 20 years, the value of the original $10,000 is almost four and one-half times greater at a rate of return of 11 percent ($80,623) than at 3 percent ($18,061). Even after one year, the differences are significant: $200 more is earned at 5 percent than at 3 percent, and $500 more is earned at 8 percent than at 3 percent.

Annual Rate of	Value after 1 year	Value after 10 years	Value after 20 years
3 percent	$10,300	$13,439	$18,061
5 percent	$10,500	$16,289	$26,
8 percent	$10,800	$21,589	$46,610
11 percent	$11,100	$28,394	$80,623

Source of calculations: http://www.leadfusion.com

Time Value Question: Does it matter when I start to save money?

The fast answer to this question is, the EARLIER, the better! Early money always wins, as the Real Life, Real Money example on the following page demonstrates. Unfortunately, most young women do not learn this concept in high school because financial literacy education is not a regular part of the school curriculum. You will be well served to start saving while you are young and to keep up the habit. Because women, on average, live longer than men, they need to recognize that it will take more money to live a longer life. For this reason, saving for the future makes a lot of sense.

Real Life, Real Money: Amber and Connie Save for the Future- The Impact of the Time Value of Money on IRAs at 8 Percent

Amber and Connie were college roommates. When they landed their first jobs after graduation, they made very different decisions about when to start funding their Individual Retirement Accounts (IRAs). Amber started hers right away. She knew that early money would mean that she would have a head start. Connie decided to wait a while before starting to fund her IRA Connie did not realize that by postponing her savings, she would have to save $3,000 a year for 36 years, while Amber only had to save $3,000 a year for just nine years.

Amber will get by with saving just $27,000 of her own money, but Connie will have to save $111,000 of her own money because she is starting to save at a later age. The end result is that Amber will end up with more money ($878,967) in her IRA account than Connie ($828,825). This example uses an annual rate of return of 8 percent, which in today's environment is considered very high, but it does illustrate the point.

Amber's Age	Amount *	Value @ 8 percent	Connie's Age	Amount *	Value @ 8 percent
22	$3,000	$3,240	22	$0	
23	$3,000	$6,739	23	$0	
24	$3,000	$10,518	24	$0	
25	$3,000	$14,600	25	$0	
26	$3,000	$19,008	26	$0	
27	$3,000	$23J68	27	$0	
28	$3,000	$28,910	28	$0	
29	$3,000	$34,463	29	$0	
30	$3,000	$40,460	30	$0	
31		$43,696	31	$3,000	$3,240
32		$47,192	32	$3,000	$6,739
33		$50,968	33	$3,000	$10,518
34		$55,045	34	$3,000	$14,600
35		$59,449	35	$3,000	$19,008
36		$64,204	36	$3,000	$23J68
37		$69,341	37	$3,000	$28,910
38		$74,888	38	$3,000	$34,463
39		$80,879	39	$3,000	$40A60
40		$87)49	40	$3,000	$46,936
			Connie must continue saving $3000 per year from age 41 to 67.		
67		$697,753	67	$3,000	$657,948
68		$753,573	68		$710,584
69		$813,859	69		$767,430
70		$878,967	70		$828,825
Amount Saved	$27,000			$111,000	

What About You?

By signing into your membership account at WomensMoney.org you can use the online calculators to calculate this for yourself using many different options.

The Impact of Inflation

Inflation is always a potential threat to future purchasing power. Inflation occurs when there is an upward price movement of goods and services in the economy, as measured by the Consumer Price Index. This means that over time, as the cost of goods and services increases, the value of what a dollar will purchase declines. Stated simply, it will cost more money to buy the same level of goods and services as they become more expensive. If our incomes and the value of our savings and investments do not keep up with inflation, our purchasing power erodes.

You can use the Inflation Calculator at http://www.bls .gov/ data/inflation calculator.htm to calculate how the buying power of the dollar has changed over the years. The examples below

- $100 in 1998 has the same buying power as $131.62 in 2009.
- $10,000 in 1913 has the same buying power as $216,704.04 in 2009.
- $10,000 in 1980 has the same buying power as $26,036.04 in 2009.
- $1.00 in 2007 has the same buying power as $1.03 in 2009.

Saving vs. Investing Differences From the previous discussion in this chapter, you already know that there are differences between "saving" your money and "investing" it. People often use the terms interchangeably, as if there were no differences. For example, your neighbor may have said, "I decided to invest my money in a CD for this year's Roth IRA." But what your neighbor really did was to save her money rather than invest it. Your mother might say, "All my retirement savings are tied up in company stock," when she really means that her retirement portfolio consists of her investments in company stock. There are differences, however, even though recent changes in how financial products are sold make it possible to save AND invest at the same financial institution or brokerage firm.

So far, this chapter has focused on savings basics - setting funds aside for emergencies and special, short-term financial goals. Savings dollars are usually directed to interest-bearing accounts that are safe (insured up to $100,000) and liquid (can be readily withdrawn). Savings accounts, money market deposit accounts, and time deposits, like CDs, are all savings examples. They earn a lower rate of return in exchange for their safety and liquidity. When you need your money, you can access it quickly. If the financial institution fails, you will still get your money back, thanks to the federal insurance that backs up the deposits in the nation's financial institutions.

Investing your money is quite different. It involves risk, because there are no guarantees that your money will grow as it does in a savings instrument. In fact, you could very easily lose some or all of your original investment. That is the greatest risk in investing your money - the potential loss of principal. Principal refers to the original amount of your investment, in other words, your own money that you have put into the investment.

But investing your money also presents an opportunity for greater reward, that is, greater return from your investment than is possible in a savings account. Investors understand this risk/reward relationship and make investments that they hope will increase their net worth and meet their long-term financial goals. Investments include a complex array of financial products, including stocks, bonds, mutual funds, real estate, and many others.

Because making investments puts you at greater risk for potential financial loss, it is important to make sure you have a solid financial foundation as you enter the world of investing. A good financial foundation includes having appropriate emergency and set- aside accounts established, having adequate insurance coverage, keeping credit under control with a manageable debt-to-income ratio, having a retirement plan to which you are making regular contributions, and building equity in your home.

Chapter Seven: Record Your Accomplishments!

Possible Action Items for this Chapter:

☐ Determined how much money do I need to save each month to reach my goal?

☐ Looked at how much difference will the interest rate will make?

☐ Asked myself: What's it worth to reduce my spending?

☐ I pay myself first by saving regularly, and saving at least 10 percent of my income

☐ Using coupons when I shop and put the money I save in a savings account

☐ Calculating what I need in my Emergency Fund

☐ Establishing an Emergency Fund

☐ Calculating what I need in my Pink-Slip Fund

☐ Establishing an Pink-Slip Fund™ of three to six months living expenses

☐ Saving money to pay cash for big-ticket items instead of charging them to a credit card

☐ Saving for a future high-cost purchase, such as a house or college education

☐ Savings for gifts and holidays

☐ Establishing a set-aside account system (for income and/or for expenses)

☐ Opening a savings account or adding to a current savings account

☐ Identifying ways to reduce expenses so I have more money to save

Accomplishment Tracker

Date _____ Year_____ My Name_____ My Mentor is_____

Results from last month's action step(s) or Where I'm at right now...

_____

_____

_____

_____

_____

Challenge(s) I overcame to achieve these results

_____

_____

_____

_____

This is what I would like to accomplish in the next 30 days.

_____

_____

_____

Chapter Notes and Questions

Chapter Eight: Insurance

Life is full of risks. Some are larger than others. Risk is the uncertainty that a situation or event will turn out the way we expect. You may expect to drive to work every day and not be involved in a crash. There is risk, however, that you might be involved in a crash. Some of the risks we face in life have financial consequences. This chapter will examine the primary way people manage risks with financial consequences.

	High severity	Low severity
Low frequency	Since the loss is potentially large, you could purchase insurance. Because the frequency is low, the premiums should be affordable.	Since the frequency and severity of loss is low, you could consider retaining the risk without insurance coverage.
High frequency	Since the loss is potentially large, you could purchase insurance. But with the frequency also being high, the insurance will likely be expensive.	Retain this risk without insurance coverage since the losses are low, but budget for the frequent losses through an emergency fund.

Risk Management

Engaging in risk management means being able to identify and evaluate situations where you may experience a loss and make a plan for how to deal with the loss. Your goal should be to minimize your risk. There are five steps you should follow when developing a risk management plan:

1. **Gather information about the risks you are exposed to that would result in a loss.** What events and activities do you participate in that expose you to the risk of injury, death, theft, etc.? These are called "perils" by the insurance industry.

2. **Estimate how frequently a loss might occur and the severity of the loss**. A loss from a car crash might not be expected to occur frequently, but it could result in a substantial financial loss from medical expenses, property damage, or liability losses. The following chart illustrates the relationship between frequency and severity of loss.

3. **Decide how you will handle the risk**. By using insurance, you transfer all or part of the financial risk to an insurance company. Other mechanisms include avoiding risk, retaining risk, reducing risk, and controlling loss. If you choose not to own a car, you avoid much of the risk of driving a car. Some risks should be retained by you (not insured against) because the losses aren't large, or they occur infrequently. Using a smoke detector and having locks on your windows and doors are ways of controlling loss. A smoke detector won't prevent a fire, but it can help control the loss that would occur in a fire. In addition to insurance being a way to transfer risk, it is also a way to reduce financial risk. Carrying deductibles on insurance policies reduces your loss to a level you have decided is acceptable or affordable.

4. **Develop and implement a risk management plan**. For most people, this will mean purchasing a variety of insurance plans. This will involve determining the types of coverage needed, the amount of coverage needed, the level of deductibles, etc. Prioritize your insurance needs by: 1) insurance that is necessary if losses could be large and financially devastating to the family, such as life, disability, and liability insurance; 2) insurance that is important because losses could result in your having to take on debt to pay for the losses; and 3) insurance that is optional because losses could be covered with emergency funds or current income.

5. Re-examine your plan and adjust on a regular basis. At least once a year, you will want to review your plan and make sure circumstances and events have not occurred that require you to make changes to your plan. For example, marriage or the birth of a child may result in additional insurance needs.

What Is Insurance, and How Does It Work?

As discussed previously, insurance is a way to reduce or transfer risk. You are transferring risk of a potentially large financial loss from you (the individual) to the insurance company. The insurance company sells coverage to a large group of people. The insurance company pools money (insurance premiums) from this large group of people to cover the losses that group members suffer. The premium is a fee smaller than the loss any one member of the group would suffer and includes funds to pay losses that are likely to occur (calculated by using probabilities), administer the plan, and make a profit for the company. The insurance policy you receive from the company is a contract between you and the insurance company. The policy outlines what is covered, the limits of your coverage, your rights and responsibilities, and procedure s you need to follow to file a claim.

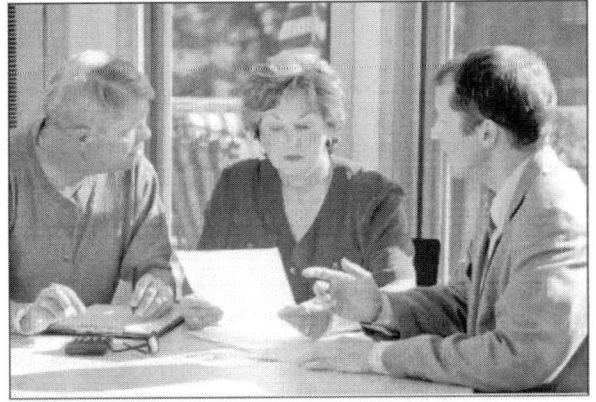

Types of Insurance

Health Insurance. Many people consider health insurance to be one of the most important types of insurance to have. Health insurance offers protection from financial losses that could result from injury, illness, or disability. Without health insurance, you and your family could experience large financial losses. Not all employers provide health insurance to their employees. And many small business owners have been unable to find coverage that is affordable for smaller employee groups.

The March 2009 National Compensation Survey 2 reported that 71 percent of workers in private industry had access to employer-provided medical care benefits, compared with 88 percent among State and local government workers. Only 25 percent of the lowest wage earners in private industry had such access. By contrast, nearly all workers at the highest wage levels had access to medical care benefits. Workers in service occupations had less access to medical care benefits (46 percent) than private industry management, professional, and related workers (86 percent). It is estimated that approximately 74 percent of all civilian workers have access to medical care benefit plans, and 76 percent participate in the plan. However, access and participation vary widely by size of employer. In employment settings with less than 50 workers, only 56 percent have access, although 72 percent of these participate in medical care benefit plans. In employment settings with 500 workers or more, 89 percent have access, and 80 percent of these workers participate in medical care benefit plans.

> ### Real Life, Real Money: Ruth Gambles and Loses
>
> Ruth is 24 and working for an employer who does not offer health insurance. Because she has always been healthy, she decided not to purchase an individual policy. Six months after beginning her job, Ruth went to her family doctor for a checkup. Tests revealed that Ruth had leukemia. Because she has no health insurance, her medical bills left her with large medical debts that will take years to pay off.

There is growing evidence that the high cost of medical bills and bankruptcy are linked. *Himmelstein, et. al.* found that 62.1 percent of all bankruptcies in 2007 had a medical cause. Unaffordable medical bills, income shortfalls, mortgaging homes to pay medical bills, and loss of income due to illness were among the medically related causes participants gave to explain bankruptcies. For 92 percent of the medically bankrupt, high medical bills directly contributed to their bankruptcy. Less than one quarter of debtors were uninsured when they filed for bankruptcy, and medically bankrupt families more often experienced a lapse in coverage during the two years before filing. Families with continuous coverage found themselves under-insured and responsible for out-of-pocket costs, while others lost their private coverage when they became too sick to work. Since 2001, the number of bankruptcies attributed to medical problems has increased by 50 percent.

In March 2010, the Affordable Care Act was signed into law covering comprehensive health insurance reforms that will hold insurance companies more accountable and will lower health care costs, guarantee more health care choices, and enhance the quality of health care for all Americans. Although the Act will not be implemented all at once, portions of the law have already taken effect. Other changes will be implemented through 2014 and beyond.

Among the changes the law will bring about are:

- Sets up a new, competitive private health insurance market through State Exchanges, giving millions of Americans and small businesses access to affordable coverage and the same choices of insurance that members of Congress will have.

- Holds insurance companies accountable by keeping premiums down and preventing many types of insurance industry abuses and denials of care, and ending discrimination against Americans with pre-existing conditions.

Visit www .healthcare.gov for additional information.

Like Ruth (see the Real Life, Real Money sidebar), many young people think they can get by with no health insurance because they have always been healthy. Unfortunately, illness and injury can happen at any time.

Health insurance can be purchased on a group or individual basis. Many people have access to health insurance through their employer as an employee benefit as part of a group plan. Others can purchase individual policies from a health insurance company. Group policies have several advantages over individual policies. Group policies may have lower cost; employers may contribute to the cost, and those with existing health problems may find it easier to obtain coverage.

When selecting health coverage, you may need to decide between a traditional health insurance plan and a managed care plan. Traditional health insurance plans may cover hospital, surgical, dental; and other medical expenses associated with illness and injury. You usually get to decide what doctors to see and where you receive care. Managed care plans exert more control over the conditions under which you obtain care, such as pre-approval of hospital admissions and specifying which doctors and hospitals you can use.

The two most common types of managed care plans are health maintenance organizations (HMOs) and preferred provider organizations (PPOs). An HMO is an organization of health-care professionals that provides health-care services to members on a prepaid basis. There is a monthly fee charged for health care in addition to some deductibles and co-payments. Some HMOs have their own clinic and hospital facilities; other HMOs contract with doctors and hospitals to provide care to members. Members have a primary care physician who coordinates their care. Visits to specialists or for other care require a referral from a primary care physician. A PPO is made up of a group of medical care providers (doctors, hospitals, etc.) who contract with a health insurance company to provide services at an agreed upon discount.

Regardless of whether you receive your health care through a traditional health insurance plan or a managed care plan, as an employee benefit or by buying individual coverage, you need to understand your benefits. Begin by noting the definition of terms in your plan.

• Is a distinction made between treatment of an illness and treatment of an injury?

• Check for the definition of pre- existing health conditions. This information will outline how quickly you will receive coverage for an illness or injury you already had before your coverage begins.

• Make sure you understand what is included as covered expenses. Some plans will cover preventive care while other plans will not.

• Don't assume your coverage begins when you begin employment or when you receive your policy. Sometimes new members must wait a set period of time before coverage begins.
Make sure you know the policy limits, deductibles, co-payment and coinsurance requirements, and coordination of benefits. Policy limits are the maximum amounts that your plan will pay for a covered loss. Sometimes the policy limit is stated as an "item" limit that specifies the maximum amount that will be paid for a particular type of care. Sometimes the policy limit is an "episode" limit that specifies the maximum payment for all covered expenses from a single episode of illness or injury. Many policies limit the maximum payment that will be made within a specified time period, for instance within a year. And some policies state an overall maximum of benefits over the life of the policy.

If you are required to pay a deductible, this is the amount you must pay out of your pocket before the insurance begins to pay. Deductibles can apply to specific types of expense items, such as hospitalization and prescriptions, to each episode of illness or injury, or to all expenses over the course of a year. In family policies, there may be a deductible per person covered by the policy, with a maximum deductible for the whole family.

A co-payment is a specific dollar amount you must pay each time you have a specific covered expense. The most common co-payments include a flat fee for each doctor visit or for each prescription. Co-payments for doctors who are specialists are often higher than for general or family practitioners.

If you are likely to require prescription drugs, understand how the drug plan associated with your health insurance works. Drug plans are often tiered - that is, they offer prescription drugs at different price levels depending upon whether the drug is a generic, on the drug plan's formulary list, or is a brand-name drug.

Co-insurance requires you to pay a certain percentage of any claims. The most common co-insurance clause is 80/20, with the health plan covering 80 percent of the covered expense and you paying the remaining 20 percent. Some policies include a cap on the amount of co-insurance you are required to pay. Once you have reached the cap, the plan pays 100 percent of additional covered expenses.

Other sources of health insurance include COBRA and SCHIP.

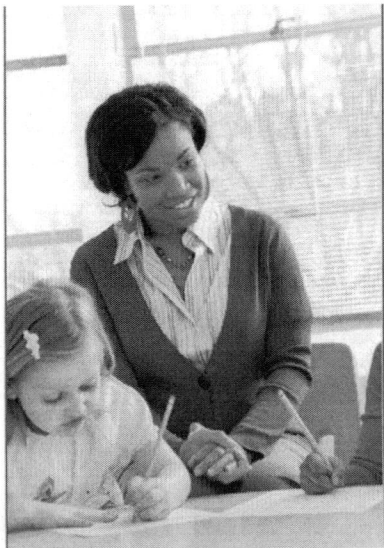

• A law enacted in 1986- the Consolidated Omnibus Budget Reconciliation Act (COBRA) -helps workers and their families keep their group health coverage during times of voluntary or involuntary job loss, reduction in the hours worked, transition between jobs, and in certain other cases. Information about the law can be found on the website of the Employee Benefits Security Administration of the U.S. Department of Labor at www.dol. gov /ebsa/newsroom/fscobra.html.

• The State Children's Health Insurance Program (SCHIP) encourages states to provide health coverage for uninsured children in families whose incomes are too high to qualify for Medicaid but too low to afford private insurance. Since 1997, when SCHIP was enacted, states have had the authority to set their SCHIP income eligibility levels, subject to available funding. In recent years, as the cost of private insurance has increased, states have raised eligibility levels to offer health-care coverage to more families, with families paying a share of the cost based on their income. Information about SCHIP can be found on the website of the U.S. Department of Health and Human Services at www.cms. gov/home/chip .asp.

Life Insurance.

The primary purpose of life insurance is to make sure that anyone who is financially dependent on you will not lose that support if you die. Dependents can include a spouse, children, parents, and siblings.

When you purchase life insurance, you are entering into a contract with the insurance company. In exchange for paying the insurance company a premium, they agree to pay your beneficiaries (people you designate) a certain amount of money (the death benefit) when you die. The amount of insurance you purchase is called the face value of the policy. When you die, the death benefit equals the face value minus any loans you may have taken against the policy (for cash value policies).

When deciding whether or not you need life insurance, ask yourself this question: "Is there anyone dependent on me for his or her financial support?" If you can answer no, then you probably don't need life insurance. People in this category are childless, single adults who provide no financial support to anyone else. If you have children or a parent relies on you for help in making ends meet, or you have a developmentally disabled sibling whom you support, then you probably do need life insurance. Life insurance is the most common and affordable way to provide financial resources for your dependents in the event you were to die. Some singles with no financial responsibility for others may still choose to purchase life insurance to fund specific expenses and financial bequests, such as funeral expenses or money for heirs, special beneficiaries, or charitable organizations upon their death.

Life insurance proceeds can be used by your beneficiaries to replace your income, pay your funeral expenses, pay off any debts you had, and provide for educational needs of your spouse and children. The amount of life insurance you need depends on a number of factors, including how much you have in savings, the value of your assets, and the amount and the type of other benefits your survivors might be eligible for (like Social Security). A number of financial websites include calculators you can use to determine your life insurance needs. These include www.insure.com and www.money-zine.com/Category/ Insurance-Calculators/.

There are two common types of life insurance, term and cash value (also called whole life). Term insurance provides insurance protection for a set period of time. Term policies are written for one, five, 10, or 20 years. If you die before the time period ends, your beneficiaries receive the death benefit. If you do not die in this time period, you will need to purchase a new policy to continue insurance protection. It is recommended that you only purchase guaranteed renewable policies so that you will be able to buy a new policy without having to prove insurability (usually by passing a physical exam). Because term insurance is temporary (in effect only for the stated time period) and is only insurance protection (does not include a savings feature), it provides the most insurance protection for the least annual premium. This makes it ideal if you need a large amount of insurance but have a limited budget, like young families with children. Term life insurance premiums will increase with age because your likelihood of dying increases with age. So each time you renew a term policy, your premium will increase somewhat.

The other kind of insurance is cash value insurance, also called whole life or permanent insurance. While there are different types of cash value insurance, the most common is whole life. Most whole life policies are designed to cover you for your entire life or until you reach age 100. If you live to 100, the insurance would end, and the insurance company would send you a check for the face value of the policy. If you die before 100, the insurance company will pay your beneficiaries the death benefit.

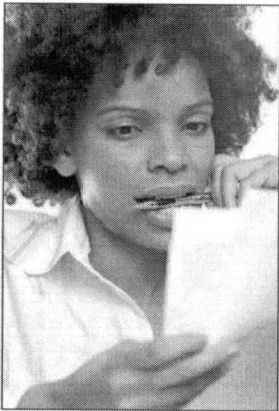

Premiums on whole life policies stay the same throughout the length of the policy. They provide insurance coverage and also build up a cash value. Anytime you decide to end your insurance, you will receive the cash surrender value of the policy. The cash surrender value is different from the face value of the insurance. The face value is the amount you are insured for and the amount that your beneficiaries will receive upon your death, provided your life insurance policy is still in effect.

Keeping premiums level over time may sound appealing to you. At younger ages, however, premiums for whole life policies are much higher than a term policy for the same amount of insurance. Young families often find themselves purchasing a whole life policy for the amount of insurance they need. But the premium may be so high that they often have trouble fitting it into their budgets. They then either drop the insurance, leaving them with no insurance, or they reduce the face value to what they can afford, which leaves them underinsured.

The Living Benefits Rider

The Living Benefits Rider (LBR) can help offer peace of mind at a critical time. It entitles the policy owner to an early (accelerated) payout of policy death benefits, if the insured is diagnosed with a terminal illness. The LBR can help make the insured's remaining time as comfortable and as dignified as possible.

With the escalating costs of medical bills, too many terminally ill patients are faced with financial hardship during the worst possible time. As a person deals with the emotional and physical struggles of terminal illness—as well as the impact on loved ones—the last thing needed is the additional stress of astronomical medical bills. The sad irony is that, while the patient may have substantial collateral in life insurance policies, those funds are technically "off limits." The LBR breaks down the "off limits" fence. By invoking it, the policy owner can access a portion of their eligible policy proceeds, depending on the type of contract. This payment—which is made to the policy owner rather than the beneficiary and reduces the cash value and death benefit paid to the beneficiary.

Policy owners in with a terminal illness may also be able to access funds through a policy loan or a policy surrender; however, the LBR may provide more funds than a policy loan or surrender. This is because policy loans or surrenders are usually based on cash value, while the amount available from the Living Benefits Rider is generally based on the policy's face value, paid-up additions, and (if applicable) an amount payable under a rider that provides a level amount of insurance.

Available at No Cost
At the policy owner's request, this rider can be added to new or existing policies, (if issued after 1985), and in some cases at no additional charge. Find out if your term life insurance policy offers an LBR.

Proceeds may be taxable, and the IRS has not yet clarified how adding this rider to your policy could affect the income tax treatment of the policy. For this reason, it's important to consult with a personal tax advisor prior to making the election to receive benefits.

Automobile Insurance

Automobile insurance is actually a fairly complicated form of protection, requiring decisions in the following areas:

- **Collision Protection**. This covers damage to your automobile from a collision or a roll over, regardless of who is at fault.
- **Comprehensive Coverage**. This is coverage for damage/loss to your vehicle caused by something other than a collision or roll over. It could include fire, theft, vandalism, windshield cracking, or hail damage.
- **Liability Coverage.** All automobile insurance includes liability coverage, so your decision relates to the level of that coverage. Liability insurance pays for someone else's financial loss when you are held responsible. It covers both bodily injury and property damage.

- **Medical Payments Coverage.** This covers all injured occupants of your car, regardless of fault. It also covers members of your family if they are pedestrians struck by a car.

- **Uninsured Motorist Coverage.** This form of coverage pays for treatment of injuries and/or property damage caused by a motorist who does not have insurance coverage or a hit-and- run driver.

- **Underinsured Motorist Coverage**. This coverage allows you to collect from your insurance company for damages caused by someone who does not have adequate insurance. It is not a requirement, but it can protect you from large out-of-pocket expenses.

Most states require that automobile owners carry a minimum level of liability insurance or show proof of financial responsibility. Edmunds provides a summary of required liability limits by state (http://www.edmunds.com/advice/insurance/articles/43773/article.html), but you should consult your own state for the most current information. To determine the level of insurance required in your state, check your state's website for the Office or Department of Insurance. Common minimum liability limits are 20/40/10. Each of these numbers represents coverage in thousands, (i.e., the 20 stands for $20,000). The first number in the series is the maximum amount that will be paid per person for bodily injury in an accident. The second amount is the maximum amount that will be paid for all injuries per accident, regardless of how many people are hurt. The third number represents the maximum amount that will be paid to cover property damage per accident. If you think about it, these minimums are extremely inadequate. Consider the cost of vehicles and the cost of medical care. These days, insurance agents recommend a minimum level of liability coverage of 100/300/50.

Several factors influence the cost of your automobile insurance, including:

Age. Young, inexperienced drivers have more accidents than any other group. This is reflected in the higher premiums this group pays. Once you reach age 25, or 30 for some insurers, your premiums should fall, assuming you haven't been involved in accidents or received any driving citations.

Gender. The number of accidents and losses caused by female drivers 25 years old and younger tend to be lower than for males in the same age group.

Marital status. Statistics indicate that married male drivers practice greater care than those who are unmarried. Cost of repairs. Some cars are more costly to repair than others. Ask your insurance agent what your premium will be on a particular car before you buy it.

Type of car. If you own a car that is susceptible to theft, your premiums will be higher. Value, size, weight, age of your vehicle, and even the cost of replacement parts all impact your premium.

Use of car. Because you are more likely to have an accident the more miles you drive in a year, the more miles you drive, the higher your premium will be.

Location. If you live in a metropolitan area, you are likely to pay higher premiums than someone living in a smaller community.

Other. Some of the other factors that will impact your premium include your driving record, whether or not you smoke, whether your car has anti-theft devices, the number of cars you are insuring, and perhaps your credit score.
Here are some ways you can cut your automobile insurance costs:

- Ask if you qualify for any discounts.

- Notify the insurance company immediately if you sell a car or if an insured driver leaves your household.

- Carry the largest deductibles you can afford. The larger your deductibles, the lower your premiums. If you are carrying a $250 deductible, consider increasing it to $500 or $1000.

- Find out the cost of insurance on a car before you buy.

- Pay premiums in full each year instead of in installments.

Homeowner's/Renter's Insurance. Because your home and personal belongings represent one of the largest expenditures a family will make, it is important for you to protect them against loss from such events as fire and theft. Mortgage lenders will require you to carry adequate homeowner's insurance as a condition of approving your mortgage. If you are a renter, you do not have a mortgage lender requiring you to have insurance, but you should seriously consider purchasing a renter's policy to protect your personal possessions and to provide liability protection. Many renters are under the mistaken impression that their landlord's insurance will cover any loss they experience. This is not the case. If you want your possessions insured, you must purchase a renter's policy.

Homeowner's and renter's insurance are a combination of property and liability insurance. Homeowners' policies cover against loss or damage to the house and other structures on the property, and your personal possessions. Renter's insurance provides protection for your possessions. Both policies provide liability coverage that protects you from having to pay for another person's injury or damaged property when you can be held responsible.

The amount of homeowner's coverage you carry should be equal to or close to the cost of replacing your home if it were totally destroyed. At the very least, you need to have coverage that equals at least 80 percent of the current replacement cost of your home. If your coverage falls below the 80 percent level and you have a partial loss, the insurance company will pay only a percentage of your claim, even though the face value of your policy is more than adequate to cover your total loss.

When you purchase homeowner's or renter's insurance, you may want to look seriously at getting guaranteed replacement cost coverage; in a homeowner's policy, this type of coverage will pay to repair or rebuild your home as it was with like materials, even if the cost exceeds the face value of the policy. In both homeowners' and renters' policies, guaranteed replacement cost coverage will pay to replace lost or damaged possessions, no matter how long you may have owned them or what condition they were in at the time of the loss. There are some possessions that are not included in replacement cost coverage. These include art, antiques, and collectibles. These items, as well as expensive jewelry and specialized equipment, require a special rider to be adequately covered. If you own any of these items, you should discuss it with your insurance agent to make sure you have adequate coverage. If you do not purchase replacement cost coverage, coverage on your possessions will be based on their current cash value.

The amount of coverage your policy provides for your possessions is a set percentage of the value of your home (50-75 percent depending on the company) for those with homeowner's insurance. When you purchase renter's insurance, you purchase the amount of insurance based on the value of your possessions. In both cases, it is important to conduct a personal property inventory to make sure you have adequate coverage. It is also helpful to conduct the inventory to have a record of your possessions in the event of a loss.

Your homeowner or renter's policy will also provide liability coverage to protect you when you, your family members, or even your pets are responsible for injury to people or damage to others' property. Liability coverage also includes medical payments coverage, which pays the medical expenses for anyone who is accidentally injured on your property or injured by you, your family members, or your pet.

Disability Insurance. Disability insurance provides a weekly or monthly income benefit if you are disabled due to a covered injury or sickness. This type of insurance can provide an income to partially replace the wages lost when you are unable to work for an extended time. People never expect to become disabled, but it is wise to consider buying disability insurance. Consider how you would pay your bills if you become disabled.

Many people believe that they will automatically qualify for Social Security disability benefits, but this is not the case. To qualify, you must have worked in jobs covered by Social Security and have a medical condition that meets Social Security's definition of disability. Monthly cash benefits are paid to people unable to work for a year or more because of a disability, but a number of special rules also apply. For more information about Social Security disability benefits, see http://www.ssa .gov/dibplan/dqualify.htm.

Some states such as California, Hawaii, Rhode Island, and New York provide for disability insurance coverage. Check the laws in your state.

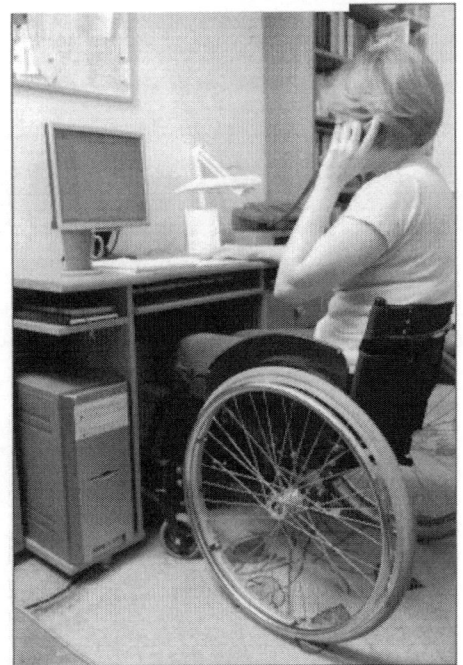

Disability insurance policies have waiting periods before benefits become payable. The waiting period starts after you have become disabled for a covered disability. The longer the waiting period, the lower the premium will be. The periods of time for which benefits are payable can also vary considerably. Benefit periods may depend on whether the disability was caused by an accident or illness.

The amount of monthly benefit provided by a disability income policy may be stated as a percentage of income or as a set dollar amount. The amount of benefit for which you can qualify is usually based on a percentage of your gross earnings, normally around 60 percent.

A disability income policy generally requires that you be totally disabled before benefits are paid. The definitions of total disability vary from policy to policy. There are two different definitions used in disability policies. One definition is that you are unable to perform your own occupation. The other definition is much more comprehensive, requiring that you are unable to perform any occupation (for which you are suited by education or experience). This distinction can be important for jobs that require very specialized physical skills, such as surgeons.

Long-Term Care (LTC) Insurance. The purpose of this insurance is to provide for your "long-term care" if you become unable to take care of yourself because of the loss of functional capacity or cognitive impairment. The word "cognitive" pertains to the mental processes of perception, memory, judgment, and reasoning. 9 Current costs (2009) for such care can exceed $70,000 per year. LTC insurance provides the means to pay for such care in nursing homes and assisted living facilities, through home health care, and adult day care. Policies vary in their coverage and benefit level. The monthly premium increases with age, so buying a policy at a younger age can be a good idea. Because it is difficult to estimate the future costs of LTC, it is very important to understand its features. Among the benefit features to compare when shopping for LTC insurance are the level of daily benefits (the dollar amount that will be paid), the elimination period (the number of days you must wait before benefits are paid), the maximum benefit period (how long benefits will continue to be paid), and inflation protection (how benefit levels will keep up with inflation). Many state insurance department or commission websites provide detailed information about what to look for in considering a long-term care policy. You can find links to your state at the National Association of Insurance Commissioners' website, www .naic .org/state web map.htm .

Some employers offer group policies for LTC insurance, but it can also be purchased as an individual policy from many insurance companies. It is important to be aware of this type of insurance, even if you plan to wait a few years before buying it for yourself. Some employer plans will allow your parents or other family members to obtain coverage. As you or your parents grow older, this may be something important to look into. The most heard complaint about LTC is that is too expensive to purchase. Check LTC policies versus LBR riders to see which best suits your risk tolerance and your price tolerance. For more information about financing long-term care, visit the University of Minnesota website, http ://www. financinglongtermcare.urnn.edu/index.htrnl

Evaluating My Insurance Coverage

Locate your insurance policies, and determine the amount of your current coverage. Evaluate whether or not you have adequate coverage based on your needs. Identify areas where you may need additional coverage. Visit the following websites to assist you in your evaluation: www .insure.com; www.naic.org; http://lifehappens. ill!l).; www .ahip.org; http://www .extension.org/pages/Financial Security: Insurance; and your state insurance department's website.

Insurance as an Employee Benefit

Most employers offer a wide range of insurance as a benefit of employment. Your employer may pay all or part of the premium for this coverage. Even if your employer does not pay any of the premiums, because the coverage will be part of a group policy, the premium is likely less expensive than if you were to buy an individual policy. You should seriously evaluate the range of insurance offered by your employer. The most common forms of insurance offered as an employee benefit include life insurance, health insurance, and disability insurance.

Chapter Eight: Record Your Accomplishments!

Possible Action Items for this Chapter:

- ☐ Identifying the risks in my life.
- ☐ Seek additional information and assistance from the Human Resource Department or your employer's website.
- ☐ I have discovered what employee insurance benefits are available to me
- ☐ Determine what types of insurance your employer offers its employees.
- ☐ Determine which of these options I am participating in. Are there options I am not taking advantage of that may meet my needs?
- ☐ Learning about the types of insurances available
- ☐ Determining what types of insurance I need
- ☐ Check healthcare.gov to see what health insurance options may be available to you.
- ☐ Reviewing my current insurances for competitive pricing.
- ☐ Changing insurances in the cases where is it financially beneficial to me.
- ☐ Addressing the other insurance needs I have

Accomplishment Tracker

Date _____ Year _____ My Name _____ My Mentor is _____

Results from last month's action step(s) or Where I'm at right now...

_____

_____

_____

_____

Challenge(s) I overcame to achieve these results

_____

_____

_____

This is what I would like to accomplish in the next 30 days.

_____

_____

Thoughts and Inspirations:

Chapter Notes and Questions

Chapter Nine: Your Earning Power

The Money in Your Life

The money in your life can come from a variety of sources. Your primary source of income is probably the money you earn from your job, career, or self-employment. For hundreds of different types of jobs, the Occupational Outlook Handbook tells you the training and education needed, earnings, expected job prospects, what workers do on the job, and working conditions. It also gives you job search tips, links to information about the job market in each state, and more. You can access the Handbook at www.bls .gov/oco

In evaluating job or career options, it is important to compare overall compensation, not just the salary offer. There is a tendency to focus on salary or wages exclusively; however, it is more important to focus on the value of overall compensation. Compensation includes your salary or wages and your employer- provided benefits. According to the U.S. Bureau of Labor Statistics (BLS), benefits accounted for nearly 30 percent of employers' total compensation costs in March 2005. Paid leave, such as paid holidays and paid vacation, was the most commonly provided benefit in the private sector in March 2007.

Your employee benefits may include a retirement plan. There are two kinds of employer-based retirement plans: defined-benefit plans and defined-contribution plans (401[k] and 403[b] plans are examples). Defined-contribution plans will not pay a specific dollar benefit at retirement; instead, what you receive will depend on the value of your retirement portfolio. Contributions to defined- benefit plans accumulate and grow (or decline) depending on how long you participate in the plan, how much is invested, and how well the investments do over the years.

During the recession that began at the end of 2007, some employers reduced their contributions to 401(k) plans. An April 2009 survey of U.S. companies by Grant Thornton LLP's Compensation and Benefits practice found that 29 percent had modified or currently intended to modify the matching contribution feature in their 401(k) plans during the 2009 plan year. Of those, two-thirds reported that they would eliminate the match entirely.

Defined-benefit retirement plans will pay a specific dollar benefit at retirement, based generally on a formula that factors in the number of years you have been employed and the salary that you have earned. However, a decreasing number of employers offer defined- benefit plans. In March 2008, 22 percent of private industry workers had access to a defined-benefit plan compared with 62 percent who had access to a defined-contribution plan. Of workers who had access to a defined-benefit plan, 95 percent chose to participate, but only 70 percent of those who had access to a defined-contribution plan participated. About two-thirds of the people who participated in defined-contribution plans were required to contribute to the plans, compared with one out of 25 persons in defined-benefit plans.

Sometimes new employees fail to recognize the importance of starting to build a retirement portfolio as soon as the opportunity is offered to them. Many employees, if given a choice, do NOT contribute to their 401(k) plans, for example. This is unfortunate, especially when employers are willing to provide a full or partial match for the dollars contributed by employees. Failing to contribute is like leaving free money on the table. It is always wise to take advantage of such plans immediately and to be aware of how long it will take to become vested. You do not necessarily have an immediate right to any contributions made by your employer. Federal law provides a maximum number of years a company may require employees to work to earn the vested right to all or some of these benefits.

Other important components of a compensation plan may include various insurance options, such as health insurance, life insurance, disability insurance, and long-term care insurance. Employees should study the costs and benefits of the plans and determine how the plans work with other benefits available through other options, such as a spouse's insurance plans. The chapter on insurance in this Handbook contains more information about types of insurance.

You may have another source of income if you own a business or are an entrepreneur. This income may be very regular or very irregular, depending on how well your business is doing. Some people who have regular jobs also operate a small, home-based business. And many non-employed women with young children at home have found ways to operate a profitable home- based business. Almost half (49 percent) of the nation's businesses are operated from home, according to the U.S. Census Bureau's 2002 Survey of Business Owners (SBO). Fifty-six percent of women-owned firms were home-based in 2002. Many options and resources exist for women wanting to become business owners or entrepreneurs, such as the U.S. Small Business Administration's Online Women's Business Center at http://www.sba.gov.

The other money in your life may be less visible to you, but it is important nonetheless. Money that you are saving or investing, such as your retirement savings, represents important future income for you. The value of spending less money than you earn is that you can invest or save the difference and make your money grow. Think about it this way. When you divert money from current earnings to your savings and investments, you have essentially "instructed" that money to go out and "get a job and earn some money"! Read Carol's story in Real Life, Real Money in the sidebar.

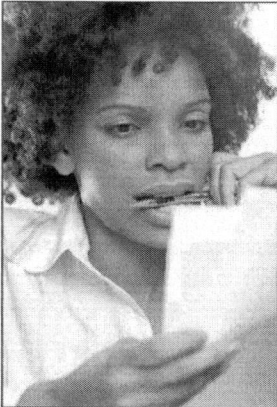

You may have money from other sources. Some dual-earning couples pool their funds or work out a compatible way to support family living expenses, while other dual earners try very hard to live on one income and save the other income, especially if they anticipate "time out" as they start a family. Other sources of income may include alimony or child support payments, unemployment insurance, disability insurance, or Temporary Assistance for Needy Families (TANF). Some people may have income from investments, and some may also continue to receive financial assistance or gifts from parents or other family members. Future money may include inherited money after grandparents or parents die. Other types of income are very important to people experiencing financial difficulties. For example, disability insurance provides partial income replacement for workers who become disabled. Many workers elect to pay for disability insurance through their place of employment when it is offered as an employee benefit. Unemployment insurance is important to workers who lose their jobs. Some workers may qualify, due to financial hardship, for temporary assistance for needy families through the TANF program or other federal, state, or local assistance programs.

Other sources of assistance that help households make ends meet during difficult times include the Food Stamp Program and the Women, Infants and Children (WIC) Program that provides supplemental foods, health care referrals, and nutrition education for low-income pregnant, breastfeeding, and non-breastfeeding postpartum women, and to infants and children up to age five who are at nutritional risk. Working households of moderate means, including many single-parent households, qualify for Earned Income Tax Credit (EITC) and possibly other tax credits, too, which can provide them with additional money to help make ends meet.

Throughout life, money and other resources may come from many different sources. It is important for you to be aware of the sources of your money and to manage your money in such a way that it will last for your lifetime. This means being aware of the risk factors and unplanned events in life that could alter your financial security, as well as those opportunities that can enhance it.

Achieving financial security involves making investments in yourself and planning for the fuh1re, something you have been learning to do throughout your study of the Women's Money Handbook. A regularly updated, comprehensive financial plan will improve your ability to navigate unexpected developments, achieve personal goals, and maximize opportunities. A comprehensive financial plan should reflect your savvy as a consumer, parent, and member of the workforce. A financial plan anchors your aspirations in each of these areas to your personal financial reality. By reflecting on each of these areas, you can begin to imagine the steps necessary to maintain financial security throughout your lifetime.

Investing in Human Capital- You

Today, the name of the game is keeping abreast of change. As a member of the workforce, this means remaining current and making additional investments in your education and training to continue to be competitive in the ever--changing job market.

The percentage of adults participating in adult education courses has continued to rise over the past decade, with work-related courses and personal-interest courses being the most popular forms of adult education in 2005. It means having a "game plan" for your own professional development.

As you draw up your "game plan" for the future, learn about job opportunities that are expected to be "hot." Women's labor force participation will remain strong, with 49 percent of the increase in the labor force between 2006 and 2016 due to women. "Hot jobs" for the 21st century are projected to be in professional and related occupations and in service occupations, according to the Women's Bureau, U.S. Department of Labor.2• 3 Job growth in both of these two categories is expected to grow by about 16.7 percent.

The Fastest Growing Occupations.

The fastest growing occupations are dominated by professional and related occupations associated with health care and the provision of social and mental health services. Examples of these occupations are:

- Health related: personal and home care aides; home health aides; medical assistants; substance abuse and behavior disorder counselors; social and human service assistants; physical therapist assistants; pharmacy technicians; dental hygienists; mental health counselors; mental health and substance abuse social workers; dental assistants; physical therapists; and physician assistants.

- Computer related: network systems and data communications analysts; computer software engineers, applications; computer systems analysts; database administrators; and computer software engineers, systems software.

- Personal Care and Service Related: makeup artists; theatrical and performance; skin care specialists; manicurists and pedicurists.

- Rapid growth in health-related occupations reflects an aging population that requires more health care, a wealthier population that can afford better health care, and advances in medical technology that permit more health problems to be treated more aggressively.

- Women already dominate the fastest growing health-related and personal care occupations. This trend is likely to continue.

- Other fast-growing occupations: veterinary technologists and technicians; personal financial advisors; veterinarians; financial analysts; gaming surveillance officers and gaming investigators; forensic science technicians;

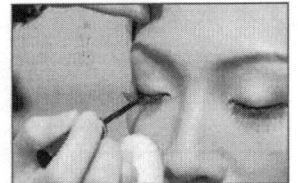

Learn about job opportunities that are expected to be "hot."
Women's labor force participation will remain strong,
with 49 percent of the increase in the labor force
between 2006 and 2016 due to women.

Occupations with the Largest Job Growth.

The 30 occupations with the largest job growth are much less concentrated in professional and related occupations than the 30 fastest growing occupations. Examples of these occupations are:

• Professional and managerial: registered nurses; general and operations managers; computer software engineers, applications; accountants and auditors; management analysts; computer systems analysts; and network systems and data communications analysts.

• Service related: retail salespersons; janitors and cleaners, except maids and housekeeping cleaners; childcare workers; maids and housekeeping cleaners; and security guards.

• Office and Administrative support: office clerks, general; bookkeeping, accounting, and auditing clerks; executive secretaries and administrative assistants; receptionists and information clerks; and customer service representatives.

• Health care support: home health aides; nursing aides, orderlies, and attendants; personal and home care aides; and medical assistants.

• Food preparation and serving related: waiters and waitresses; combined food preparation and serving workers, including fast food; and food preparation workers.

• Teaching: post- secondary teachers; elementary school teachers, except special education; and teacher assistants.

• Transportation and material moving: truck drivers, heavy and tractor- trailer; laborers and freight and stock, and material movers, hand; and truck drivers, light and delivery services.

• Other: landscaping and grounds- keeping workers; carpenters; and maintenance and repair workers, general.

Short-term on-the-job training is the level of post-secondary education or training most workers will need to become fully qualified in the majority of these large growth occupations.

You may want to think about going back to school. Perhaps you want to go back to graduate school, or maybe you were unable to go to college or did not complete your degree. Many young women like you find success by going back to school.

Develop a Professional Game Plan

Think about your current job or career. If you are not presently employed outside of the home, do you expect to be employed in the future? Where are you now, and where would you like to be in the future?

If You Are Presently Employed

How satisfied are you with:
• your current job?
• your current salary/wages?
• your employee benefits?
• your working conditions?
• your opportunities for advancement?
• your work-life balance?

What additional training or education would help you to:
• qualify for a new job with your employer?
• qualify for a different job?
• earn more money?
• enhance your opportunities for advancement?
• improve your work-life balance?

If You Are Not Presently Employed

If you are unemployed and have been unable to find a job:
• Do you know where to get help for additional training and education to qualify for a different job?
• Do you know how to find out if you qualify for benefits/help for the unemployed?
• How will your family be impacted if you find a job? If you don't find a job?
• Are there additional ways for you to economize?

If you decided not to work at this time in your life, have you thought about:
• if, how, and when you might re-enter the workforce?
• what additional training you may need to re- enter the workforce?
• the consequences of never being employed again?
• the work-life consequences of being employed?
• how your financial security is impacted by a job?

Create a professional plan for yourself. Identify jobs that interest you.

Visit the U.S. Department of Labor Women's Bureau website for information and resources on growing job opportunities for women in the United States.

Check out the websites below for further help, if this applies to you. Many options are available for women, including help with financing college costs.

- U.S. Department of Education: http://www.ed.gov
- CIP – College Is Possible: http://www.collegeispossible.org
- American Council on Education: http://www.acenet.edu (click on Adult Learners)
- Career One Stop http://www.careeronestop.org

Both men and women who have earned a bachelor's degree can expect to earn a higher income than those who are high school graduates. The table below shows the latest data (2007) for all full-time workers 25 years of age and over. The median annual income for men with a college degree (bachelor's degree) was $62,090 in 2007, compared to $37,860 for high school graduates. For women college graduates, the median annual income was $45,770 for those with a bachelor's degree, compared to $27,240 for high school graduates. The earnings are higher still for men and women with advanced or professional degrees. The table illustrates a gender gap in earnings, but that is because it includes all workers who are 25 and older, including women who may have left the labor force and then returned to work. Employment interruptions can also mean slower advancement in earnings.

Median Annual Income of Year-Round, Full-Time Workers 25 Years Old and over, by Level of Education Completed and Gender: 2007 (in Current Dollars)[4]		
	Men	Women
All Education Levels	$47,000	$36,090
High School Graduates	$37,860	$27,240
Some College, No Degree	$44,900	$32,840
Associate Degree	$49,040	$36,330
Bachelor's Degree	$62,090	$45,770
Master's Degree	$76,280	$55,430
Professional degree	$100,000	$71,100
Doctoral Degree	$92,090	$68,990

Write down three actions you plan to take in developing a professional development plan:

1.

2.

3.

Seven Simple Ways to Boost Your ROI (Return On Income)

This year your paycheck is probably lower thanks to the expiration of the payroll tax cut. For Americans earning around $50,000, the expiration translates into $80 per month or nearly $1,000 per year.

Here are seven (relatively) easy ways to get that money back:

- Review your W4 with a competent tax professional. The basic rule is that if you're getting more than $500 back on your tax return you're paying too much up front. If you owe more than $500 on your tax return, you're not paying in enough.
- Stop snacking at work. Between coffees, candies, and your basic snacks it totals more than $100 a month!
- Cut your work lunch costs from $200 to $100 per month with a homemade sandwich – fast food is no longer cheap and a typical "lunch run" costs you $10-$15 each time.
- Stop downloading dumb stuff onto your smartphone, which can cost you a boatload ($600+/year). If you're so bored at work that you need to stream Netflix and YouTube, it's time to dig out that resume and get a job you love and pays better.
- Rideshare: A new generation of ride-sharing apps for smartphones is making it easier than ever to find and share rides, thus saving you money on gas and car expenses. If you can't rideshare or take the bus, and you absolutely must drive, then get a hybrid. Hybrid SUVs (you can keep all the luxury and space) save over $1200 a year compared to their gas-guzzling counterparts. They also last longer too – easily lasting 300,000-400,000 miles and beyond.
- Do a fantastic job at work and get noticed. Elaine Starling, author of "Why 5% Succeed: The 5 Principles of Predictable Profit" says that if you focus on providing a rewarding experience for clients and co-workers, you can actually attract people who want to give you more money in the form of sales, a raise, or a better paying job offer.
- Check out your employer's policy on education. You may be able to get your employer to pay for an advanced degree in full or in part. You may also qualify for fellowships that help pay for your living expenses and school. See a scholarship coach or the local university financial aid office to help you out with this after you've spoken to your employer. Once you graduate you're qualified for a better paying promotion or job.

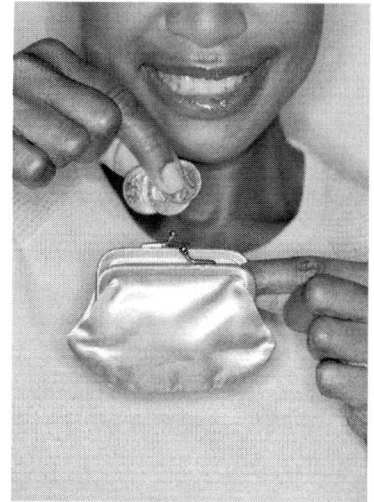

Need Cash Quick?

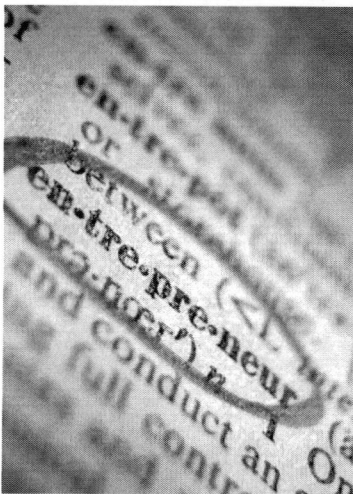

Don't see the Pay Day Lender. See the Avon Lady. One of the many companies that are members of the Direct Selling Association (DSA) were founded on the principles of helping women earn extra money fast or a full time career income fast by selling products and getting immediate cash from your commission on the sales. Today, the direct selling industry has moved beyond what your grandmother may have sold. Now there are full lines of organic health and wellness products, business products, jewelry and more. If you are into it for quick extra cash, don't buy inventory – no matter how much you love the product.

Chapter Nine: Record Your Accomplishments!

Possible Action Items for this Chapter:

☐ Determined if I am earning industry standard for myself

☐ Inquired if I paid equally to my co-workers doing the same job

☐ Investigated if I qualify for any special assistance programs or tax credits

☐ Am I interested in getting a college degree or advanced degree?

☐ Am I interested in being an entrepreneur?

☐ Check my W4 – and adjust deductions if necessary.

☐ Find ways I spend too much money at work and reduce those costs.

☐ Determine how much money I really make with the cost of gas and childcare vs. my net income. Am I earning a personal profit, breaking even, or s my job actually costing me money?

☐ Find out if my employer has education advancement programs or trainings to advance my career.

☐ Take ownership of my attitude at work – how can I be a better employee that people enjoy working with?

☐ Find ways that I enjoy, to earn extra money.

☐ Develop an action plan for my career advancement.

Accomplishment Tracker

Date _____Year____ My Name_____ My Mentor is_____

Results from last month's action step(s) or Where I'm at right now...

_____

_____

_____

_____

_____

Challenge(s) I overcame to achieve these results

_____

_____

_____

_____

This is what I would like to accomplish in the next 30 days.

_____

_____

_____

Thoughts and Inspirations:

Chapter Notes and Questions

Chapter Ten: Investing Basics

Principles Related to Buying and Financing a Home

During the recession that began in 2007, mortgages were front-page news across America. As economic conditions deteriorated in parts of the country, home values began to fall. Some homeowners found they owed more money than their house was worth. These problems for homeowners may have been rooted in the type of mortgage that they had, such as adjustable rate mortgages in which the rate adjusted (upward) over time, with each new "adjustment" requiring a higher monthly mortgage payment. For many households, making a higher payment was not affordable, perhaps because unemployment reduced household income. Housing markets in many areas of the country began to see many foreclosures when homeowners could no longer make their payments. In other cases, people who could not qualify for a conventional mortgage with an affordable interest rate were offered "sub-prime" mortgages, meaning that the interest rate would be much higher than for conventional mortgages, with terms and conditions that could cause hardship and foreclosure for missed payments. And in many cases, the sub-prime mortgage market qualified people eager for homeownership even though they could not afford the mortgage they were being offered.

How can people avoid making the wrong financial decision when buying a home? Because the Women's Money program is not a homebuyer education program, it does not focus in depth on the home buying and financing process; however, a few principles are worth remembering.

- **House payments need to be affordable.** How much house can you really afford? Certainly people may have their "heart set" on a particular house they see, but there is more to housing affordability. One rule of thumb recommended by experts is that a monthly mortgage payment should never be more than about 30 percent of take-home pay. Let's look at Takisha's example in Real Life, Real Money in the sidebar.

- **Mortgage repayment is only part of it. A house payment has four parts to it.** The shorthand for this, PITI, stands for Principal (the part you have borrowed and are now repaying), Interest (the cost you are paying for the privilege of borrowing the money), Taxes (property taxes that you will now owe as a homeowner), and Insurance (homeowner's insurance that protects against financial loss). Other insurance coverage may also be required by the mortgagor (the one who loans you the money.) Many experts give another rule of thumb: 38 percent for PITI plus regular maintenance and possible upgrades. For Takisha, this would be 38 percent of her take-home pay, or $1,140. Other experts may have other rules of thumb.

> ### Real Life, Real Money - Takisha
>
> Takisha wanted a house. With two school--aged children, it had been difficult after her divorce, but she knew that she did not want to continue renting. Rents were increasing, so she figured that if she budgeted carefully, she could probably own a home for just a little more in monthly payments than her current rental. Her take-home pay as a Licensed Practical Nurse amounted to $3,000 a month. With the 30 percent rule of thumb, she could afford a monthly payment of $900.

- **Make the largest down payment you can afford**. It may take several years to save enough money for a down payment, but doing so gives you instant "equity" in your home. Equity means the value that you own outright. For example, suppose you wanted to buy a house selling for $180,000. The lender requires a 20 percent down payment, or $36,000. Where will this money come from? For many people, it comes from the equity they have built up in a previously owned home. But for first-time homebuyers, they have had few options besides saving up the money. In some communities, there are special down-payment assistance programs offered by local authorities. The American Recovery and Reinvestment Act of 2009 provided for a tax credit of up to $8,000 for homebuyers purchasing their first home.

The Worker, Homeownership, and Business Assistance Act of 2009 (signed into law on November 6, 2009) extended the first-time homebuyer credit to April 30, 2010, to buy or enter into a contract to buy a home and June 30, 2010, to close on the home. The new law gives current homeowners a credit of up to $6,500 to buy a replacement principal residence and raises the income limitations for homeowners claiming the credit. See more information about these credits at www.irs .gov/newsroom/article/O,,id=204671,00.htrnl?portlet= 7 and www.hud.gov.

• Learn about types of mortgages and the mortgage process. The Federal Reserve has useful information regarding many aspects of mortgages and the mortgage application process, including your fair lending legal rights. See http://www.federalreserve.gov /consumerinfo/ mortgages.htm for more information. Another source of information is the Department of Housing and Urban Development, whose "Buying a Home" page answers many home-buying questions at http://portal.hud .gov/ portal/page/portal/HUD/ topics/buying a home. Finally, check out www. extension.org where you can find links to housing information provided by
the Cooperative Extension Service of many state universities.

Investing 101 - Some Basic Principles

1. **Risk and reward are inversely related.** The greater risk you are willing to take in investing your money, the greater potential reward you will reap. But there are no guarantees that taking greater risk with your money will result in greater reward. The Pyramid of Investment Risk graphic shows the type of investments that can be made and the degree of risk the investor takes on.

Compound Annual Returns by Investment Category As Measured against the Rate of Inflation, 1926–2008	
Small company stocks	11.7
Large company stocks	9.6 percent
Government bonds	5.7 percent
Treasury bills	3.7 percent
Inflation	3.0 percent

2. **There's a difference between saving and investing your money.** Saving money at a fixed rate of return is safe and certain, even when the rate of return is low. When you save your money, you are not risking loss of your principal. When you invest your money, your entire principal is potentially at risk. You do not know at the onset if you will achieve financial success through your investments. Over the long run, however, the returns on equities or stocks have consistently outperformed instruments you might put your savings in, such as Treasury bills, as shown in these historic returns listed below. Willingness to assume risk has a pay-off.

3. **Know the basic types of investments, especially mutual funds.** The Pyramid of Investment Risk shows low-risk, medium- risk, and high-risk categories of investments. The low-risk category was discussed earlier in this chapter and is discussed in the chapter on insurance. Medium-risk investments include high-quality stocks, bonds, and mutual funds; real estate; and aggressive growth stocks, bonds, and mutual funds. High-risk investments shown are futures contracts and collectibles. Beginning investors should stick to low-risk and medium-risk investments and should never invest their money in something they do not understand.

Stocks. Stocks in a public company may be common stock or preferred stock. If you hold common stock, you have voting rights as a stockholder. If you hold preferred stock, you do not have voting rights but receive fixed dividends on your stock before stockholders of common stock. With common stock, dividend amounts fluctuate with the profitability of the company, making common stock a riskier investment than preferred stock.

When you buy a stock, the price quoted is the price for one share of stock in the company at a given moment. Stocks are traded on the major stock exchanges (New York Stock Exchange, NYSE Amex Equities, formerly known as the American Stock Exchange, and NASDAQ). Investors can buy stock through firms qualified to sell stocks and may also buy stocks through on-line brokerage websites. Not all companies pay out regular dividends or any dividends at all. Companies that do may offer dividend reinvestment plans (DRIPS). Dividends are reinvested to buy more company stock instead of being issued to you as a dividend check. With DRIPS, your stock portfolio will grow as the number of shares you own increases.

For people who need regular dividends paid directly to them, income stocks can be a good choice. Often called blue chip stocks, these stocks are from well-established companies in certain industries or sectors, although depending on economic conditions, the performance by industry or sector can vary. When there is market volatility in the prices of stocks, investors frequently seek dividend- producing investments.

There is both a downside and an upside to investing in stocks. A volatile (fluctuating) market can cause the price of stocks to increase/ decrease erratically. Fundamental problems within an industry or a company can cause volatility, as can widespread fears and realities about the economy or world situation. As we saw with the recession that began in 2007, there is always the potential for losing money in the stock market, just as there is always the potential for gain.

How do you actually "make money" with stock investments? Mainly in two ways: 1) when you receive dividends that are either paid to you directly or reinvested to buy more stock in the same company, thus increasing the value of your investment; and 2) when you sell your stock at a profit. A cardinal rule of investing is to BUY LOW, SELL HIGH. That sounds easy enough, but beginning investors may do just the opposite and wind up losing money instead of making money. You may not have lost money "on paper," but if you don't need that money immediately and don't sell when the market is down, you may be able to recover what you lost. Reference the chart about Compound Annual Returns by Investment Category. Small investors often buy stocks when stock prices are on their way up, and they tend to sell at the first sign of declining prices. The result is no gain, just pain! Small investors need to pay attention during a rising market, too. Instead of holding on, with the hope that the market will continue to rise, a wise strategy may be to sell some of the gains and diversify.

Another way in which investors can potentially "make money" is through stock splits, provided the company remains profitable over time. Companies may decide to split a share of stock into one or more shares from time to time for a variety of reasons. Take the example of McDonald's.

Since going public in 1965, McDonald's has had 12 stock splits. In fact, an investment of $2250 in 100 shares in 1965 grew to 74,360 shares worth almost $4.6 million as of year-end market close on December 31, 2008.

Bonds. In addition to the Treasury bonds already discussed, there are other types of bonds. Companies may issue corporate bonds to raise needed money. Bondholders receive taxable interest on the bonds but also assume risk if the company's credit rating changes or the company goes bankrupt. Public entities (towns, cities, counties, or states) may issue municipal bonds to finance public works projects. Interest from "munis" is exempt from federal income tax as well as state income taxes in some states. Before investing in bonds, be sure to check the bond ratings. Both Moody's and Standard and Poor's (S&P) rate the quality of bonds based on the riskiness of the bond issuer's capacity to pay out interest and pay back the bond principal. Look for the highest rating, not the highest interest rate. You want to make sure you get your money back (your principal) at the end of the bond term, in addition to regular interest payments. The highest bond ratings are AAA (S&P's rating system) and Aaa (Moody's system). A bond rated "C" means "default, recovery unlikely."

Mutual Funds. Mutual funds are a primary investment option for small investors. Almost half of all American households have invested money in mutual funds. Many mutual fund investors remain unclear about this type of investment. Mutual fund companies invest pools of money from individual investors in a variety of investments (stocks, bonds, cash, real estate, government securities, etc.) according to a particular investment philosophy and defined investment objectives for the investment portfolio they create for the fund. There are thousands of different mutual funds available from hundreds of different mutual fund companies. Before you invest, the mutual fund company must provide you with a fund prospectus, which describes the mutual fund, its investment objectives, investment criteria, investment costs, etc.

Mutual funds offer the individual small investor something that is difficult to achieve any other way – portfolio diversification and professional fund management. Although most mutual fund companies have minimum investment requirements to open and add to a mutual fund account, these limits are usually lower for individuals who use mutual funds for their Roth IRA or Traditional IRA. The price of a single share of a mutual fund is called its net asset value (NAV). It is determined daily and published in the financial section of the newspaper and on the World Wide Web, just like individual stocks. The example below is a simplified version of mutual fund quotations in the newspaper. Mutual funds are listed in the financial ages in alphabetical order by fund family. Within the hypothetical fund family below (AAA Fund Family), three individual funds are listed.

In the listing, NAV refers to the net asset value or closing price for the previous day. The Net Change is how much the NAV changed from the previous day. The YTD% Return is how much the NAV has grown "year to date." Under Sales Charge, "NL" stands for No Load (meaning there is no charge to invest), while the 4.50 shows that there is a 4.50 percent sales charge to invest in the Growth and Income Fund.

	NAV	Net Chang	YTD% Return	Sales Charg
AAA Fund Family				
Growth Fund	$14.50	-0.09	+22.3	NL
Growth & Income Fund	$12.54	-0.05	+18.0	4.50
Balanced Fund	$10.65	+0.03	+11.0	NL

On-line sources provide detailed information about mutual fund families and individual funds. From one major financial portal, http://finance.yahoo.com/, select the "Mutual Funds" link. From there you can select "Funds by Family" (http://biz.yahoo.com/p/fam/a-b.html) and obtain detailed information about every fund offered within that family.
How do mutual funds make money for the individual investor? Just as with individual stock investments, mutual funds

make money by the dividends or interest earned on the investments in its portfolio and by selling investments in its portfolio for a profit. These gains are passed on to the mutual fund investor as earnings, which are often reinvested in the mutual fund to buy more shares.

There are four very important things to know about mutual funds before investing:

Investment objective and fund category. Mutual funds are classified in many different ways, but a common way is to categorize them by objectives: aggressive growth, growth, growth and income, and income.

- Aggressive growth funds are from companies expanding rapidly. They carry the highest risk but the greatest potential reward.
- Growth funds offer the potential for long-term growth, with an increase in price being the primary goal.
- Growth and income stocks combine the potential for some appreciation with a promise of dividend payments.
- Income funds seek to provide current income.

Other categories include bond, municipal bond (tax-free), money market, specialty or sector funds, global funds, international funds, small-capitalization or mid-capitalization funds, and index funds. Morningstar (www.morningstar.com) uses a nine-cell style box to classify mutual funds by type (value, blend, growth) and size (small, medium, large). Because mutual fund classifications vary so widely, always be sure you understand the basic underlying investment objective of the fund under consideration. Each of these categories may be further subdivided into categories of funds that meet the general objective. For example, for a growth objective, the fund categories can include growth funds, aggressive growth, small capitalization funds, specialty or sector funds, international funds, global funds, and index funds. Other terms may also be used.

Performance. How has the mutual fund performed? While it is tempting to look at short-term performance, find out: 1) how has this mutual fund performed over time – one year, three years, five years, 10 years, since its inception? and 2) how does the performance of this mutual fund compare to the performance of others in its fund category? What performance rating has it received? Performance ratings by Morningstar are commonly used. Morningstar gives five stars to the highest-rated funds. You can learn more about the Morningstar rating system at the website, www.morningstar.com. To learn how a particular mutual fund is rated and to obtain additional information about any mutual fund, type the mutual fund's ticker symbol in the small box that says, "enter a ticker, name, or topic" and select "quote." If you do not know the ticker symbol, type in the name of the fund.

Fees and expenses. Recent criticism of the mutual fund industry has focused on investment costs and the disclosure of fees and expenses. There may be fees you must pay for specified transactions, such as when you buy, sell, or exchange your shares; and those you pay on an ongoing basis. Higher expenses do not assure better performance. Costs associated with investing impact portfolio growth. There are two basic types of mutual funds: no-load mutual funds and load mutual funds. A $100 investment in a no-load fund means all dollars are fully invested. A mutual fund with a front-end load fee of 5 percent will keep $5 and invest $95 for you. Some load fees apply at the beginning, as in this example, but some mutual funds charge a load fee at the end, after the portfolio has grown. Even with no-load fees, there will be certain other fees and expenses. One such fee is known as a 12(b) fee that is charged each year to cover marketing expenses. Read the prospectus to find out what fees and expenses apply. How do the expenses of investing in a particular mutual fund compare to other mutual funds? Use the on-line calculator at http://www.sec.gov/investor/tools/mfcc/mfcc-int.htm to compare the cost of owning a mutual fund.

Tenure of the fund manager. How long has the current fund manager been at the helm of the mutual fund? Frequent changes in fund managers should alert you to carefully evaluate the fund under consideration, as fund manager turnover may be a result of poor investment performance. Information about tenure may be found in the prospectus or on-line.

Index mutual funds are a viable alternative for mutual fund investors who would prefer to make an investment and forget about it because they plan to remain invested for the long run. Index mutual funds hold stocks in one of the broadly based market indexes, such as the S&P 500, which represents the 500 largest companies; the Russell 2000, which represents 2000 small companies; or EAFE (an international index that represents European, Australian, and Far Eastern companies). Other indexes also exist. Almost every mutual fund company offers one or more index funds. They are characterized by very low expenses. Their performance will mirror the performance of the broadly based market indexes upon which they were patterned. Index mutual funds are considered a good investment for long-term investing. One strategy is to use index mutual funds to fund IRAs.

4. **Pay attention to asset allocation and diversification.** These principles mean that you should not put all of your money into one single type of investment. Don't put all your eggs in one basket! For example, it would not make good sense to put all of your money into one stock alone – say the stock of the company you work for. If something were to happen to your company or the value of its stock, you would be exposed to greater risk because literally all of your investment holdings would be in one basket. This is why sound investment advice suggests diversifying the holdings in your investment portfolio to lessen risk. Asset allocation involves dividing the portfolio among different asset categories, depending on your time horizon and risk tolerance. If you have a variety of different types of investments, such as stocks, bonds, and real estate in your investment portfolio, they are not all likely to move in the same direction, that is, all fall at the same time or all increase at the same time.

5. **Don't panic when the market falters**. Many people panic as soon as the stock market becomes erratic or volatile. Sometimes values fall because something has happened to a particular company's stock. But in other cases, falling values result when people react adversely to other issues ongoing in the economy or because they fear that something bad is going to occur. Over history, the market has faltered and recovered. Wise investors learn how to benefit from both rising and falling markets.

6. **Apply dollar-cost-averaging in investing your money – the secret of successful investors.** Many people new to the investing world assume that there are special secrets to becoming a successful investor. They often think that there has to be a best time to invest, but being unsure of when that might be, they tend to procrastinate. By delaying the decision to invest, the potential investor is sacrificing one of the most important investment principles: regular investments made over a long period of time, regardless of market conditions, will enable the investor to take advantage of the principle of dollar-cost averaging. Dollar-cost-averaging is a strategy where a fixed dollar amount is invested at regular intervals, resulting in more shares purchased when the price per share is low and fewer shares when the price is high. Instead of waiting for an opportune time to enter or exit the investment world, prudent investors keep plugging along, making their contributions regardless of the current economic conditions.

Consulting with Financial Professionals

Sometimes consulting with a financial professional can be very beneficial. Women's Money is helping you to establish the basics, but later you may need help in developing a comprehensive, long-term financial plan. Or you may need help on specific matters, such as insurance, retirement planning, and estate planning.

Interview and evaluate several financial planners to find one that is right for you. The Certified Financial Planner Board of Standards, Inc., suggests you ask the following 10 questions of each person you interview. A useful checklist for choosing a financial planner and other information about the financial planning process is available from the Board's website, http://www.cf:p. net/learn/.

1. What experience do you have?
2. What are your qualifications?
3. What services do you offer?
4. What is your approach to financial planning?
5. Will you be the only person working with me?
6. How will I pay for your services?
7. How much do you typically charge?
8. Could anyone besides me benefit from your recommendations?
9. Have you ever been publicly disciplined for any unlawful or unethical actions in your professional career?
10. Can I have it (the agreement detailing services to be provided) in writing?

It is also important to understand the professional designation(s) used by individuals engaged within the financial services industry. A good starting point for that information is to consult the database maintained by FINRA (Financial Industry Regulatory Authority, Inc.) at http://apps.finra.org/DataDirectory/1/ prodesignations.aspx . You will be able to look up the acronym or title of the professional designations included in the database.

Real Life Real Money:
Miranda Learns the Impact of Dollar-cost- averaging

Miranda had heard about dollar cost averaging but wasn't completely sure how she could benefit. Her financial advisor, Elizabeth, helped her to understand. Elizabeth told her that she should continue to invest a fixed dollar amount each month, regardless of market conditions. That way, she would never have to guess the best time to make an investment. Elizabeth drew up a chart to help Miranda see the meaning of this principle.

After considering several mutual funds, Miranda decided to invest in XYZ mutual fund. Miranda invested $100 the first of every month from February to October. She invested an additional $300 on September 15th after she received a bonus at work. On February 1, the cost was $10 per share, and she purchased 10 shares for $100. On March 1, her $100 investment only bought five shares because the cost per share had risen to $20. The total number of shares she now owned was 15, but each one was worth $20 so her total investment was worth $300 even though she had only invested $200 of her own money, to date. Dividing her $200 investment by the number of shares she owned in February gave her an average cost per share of $13.33.

On April 1, her $100 purchased 20 shares when the net asset value of her mutual fund declined to $5 per share. Elizabeth told Miranda not to worry too much about the lower value of her investment but to recognize that she was able to buy more shares because of the lower price. Her average investment cost also fell to $8.57 per share. Elizabeth explained that through this dollar cost averaging approach, the average cost of her shares was lower than any amount she had actually paid. Elizabeth also told her to get accustomed to fluctuations in the net asset value of her investment. Elizabeth explained that this mutual fund had a good track record and that Miranda should stay invested for the long run. If Miranda had become nervous about her investment, she might have pulled out at just the wrong time.

Investment Date	Amount Invested	NAV	#of Shares Purchased	Total Shares Owned	Total Value of Shares	Average NAV
February 1	$100	$10	10 shares	10 shares	$100	$10.00
March 1	$100	$20	5 shares	15 shares	$300	$13.33
April 1	$100	$5	20 shares	35 shares	$175	$8.57
May 1	$100	$10	10 shares	45 shares	$450	$8.80
June 1	$100	$15	6.67 shares	51.67 shares	$775.05	$9.68
July 1	$100	$10	10 shares	61.67 shares	$616.70	$9.73
August 1	$100	$20	5 shares	66.67 shares	$1333.40	$10.50
September 1	$100	$5	20 shares	86.67 shares	$433.35	$9.23
September 15	$300	$8	37.5 shares	124.17 shares	$993.36	$8.86
October 1	$100	$25	4 shares	128.17 shares	$3204.25	$9.36

Miranda continued to invest on a regular basis. Elizabeth's chart showed the fluctuating number of shares that Miranda purchased each month as well as the fluctuating value of her portfolio. The last column in the chart showed the average cost that Miranda paid for her mutual fund. Miranda's persistence paid off, and so did her growing knowledge about investments. When she received a $300 bonus in September, she thought about buying a new digital camera, but she thought it might be wiser to invest her money in the mutual fund she had been buying all year. With her $300 she was able to buy 37.5 shares! This brought her total shares to 124.17, and even though the overall value of her mutual fund was down on September 15, Miranda knew that it was better to have more shares than to worry about the overall value on any given day. By October 1, the NAV increased to $25 per share! Although her $100 investment only bought her four shares, her overall portfolio was worth over $3200 that day! From February to October, Miranda had invested $1200 in her mutual fund. Her investment was growing, not only in dollar value, but also in the number of shares she held. The average cost of her shares was just $9.36 per share, even though she had paid as much as $25 per share and as little as $5 per share. (This example is used for illustration purposes only. The net asset values of mutual funds are not likely to vary this widely during a short time period.)

Chapter Notes and Questions

Chapter Ten: Record Your Accomplishments!

Possible Action Items for this Chapter:

☐ Determining if owning a home or renting is the best path for my family and me.

☐ Evaluating if my current mortgage is the best financial situation for me.

☐ Cut costs associated with owning my home such as energy, water, etc.

☐ Identifying ways to reduce expenses so I have more money to save

☐ Increasing my knowledge about investing

☐ Saving more than I am currently saving towards my retirement starting

☐ Estimating how much I should be saving for retirement

☐ Taking the steps to purchasing a home or selling current home.

☐ Refinancing my mortgage.

☐ Taking the Participating in a retirement plan at work

☐ Increasing my retirement contributions at work

☐ Interviewing several financial advisers

☐ Developing an action plan

☐ Opening or adding to a Roth or Traditional IRA

☐ Investing in stocks for the first time

☐ Investing in bonds for the first time

☐ Investing in mutual funds for the first time

☐ Changing my investment mix as a result of what I have learned

☐ Calculating the cost of owning mutual funds at the SEC website

☐ Enrolling in an investment course

☐ Setting a financial website for my browser's opening page

☐ Preparing to go into Women's Money® Program Two – Wealth Building

Accomplishment Tracker

Date _____ Year _____ My Name _____ My Mentor is _____

Results from last month's action step(s) or Where I'm at right now...

_____

_____

_____

_____

_____

Challenge(s) I overcame to achieve these results

_____

_____

_____

_____

This is what I would like to accomplish in the next 30 days.

_____

_____

_____

Thoughts and Inspirations:

Chapter Eleven: College Savings

Investing in Human Capital – Your Children

One of the most important investments parents can make is in the post-secondary education of their children. You want your children to achieve the personal happiness and financial security that result from a wise career choice. The future world of work will demand young people who are educated beyond the basics because a global economy demands well-educated and highly skilled workers. Achieving financial security is easier when one's income-earning capacity holds promise through a wise career choice and preparation.

More education translates to higher career earnings. Lifetime earnings projections by the Bureau of the Census tell us that over an adult's working life, high school graduates can expect, on average, to earn $1.2 million; those with a bachelor's degree, $2.1 million; and people with a master's degree, $2.5 million. People with a doctoral degree can expect to earn an average of $3.4 million; and those with a professional degree, $4.4 million, over their working lifetime.

Parents know that college costs continue to rise, and they worry about future affordability. Parents wonder how they will be able to finance college costs. There are four primary strategies: 1) Pay as you go out of current income, extra jobs, or part- time student employment; 2) Paying later through borrowing money and paying loans back after graduation; 3) Getting help through scholarships, grants and financial aid, including help from other relatives and Federal tax incentives; and 4) Saving money before a child is ready to enter college, which involves becoming knowledgeable about alternative saving and investing opportunities. Parents, perhaps with the help of grandparents and/or other relatives, may be able to set aside college money for the future. Many young people have also been able to go to college following completion of military service. Parents who are interested and able to save money towards their children's college expenses have many options open to them. The following four ways are common.

• Prepaid Tuition Programs. With these programs, making a one-time, lump-sum payment or a series of periodic installment payments may lock in today's tuition rates. The program invests the money and pays for tuition when the time comes for the student to enter college. In most cases, the funds may be used to attend college in other states at eligible institutions. Some states offer prepaid tuition programs, but participating in the program does not insure acceptance of your child at an institution of higher education. Some states have discontinued their prepaid tuition programs. Check http:// www.collegesavings.org/ to see if your state offers this option.

• **Savings Plans (529 Plan).** Every state now has at least one 529 investment plan to help families save for future college costs. Investments grow tax-free as long as they stay in the plan. When used to pay for college costs, no federal income tax has to be paid on the distribution. The total amount that can be contributed is very large (over $200,000 in some states). Parents have the option of investing in a 529 plan outside of their own state, if permitted by the plan. A comparison of all plans may be found at http://www. savingforcollege.com.

Considering Saving for College?

We all want the absolute best for our children. Providing for a child's higher education needs is one of the greatest gifts we can pass along. A college education is a gift that will last a lifetime, and will most certainly pave the way to a more successful future. So, how do we begin to save for college?

1. Recognize the necessity and value of a college education for our children.
2. Make saving for college a priority.
3. Identify and execute a plan!

Why College?

Overall, Americans are nearly unequivocal in the value they place on a college education. Those surveyed are in nearly unanimous agreement (average agreement of 97% from 2009- 2014) that college is an investment in the future. More than 8 in 10 agree that a college degree is more important now and that a degree is needed for the student's desired occupation. Additionally, Americans still view a college education as part of the American Dream (average 80% agreement from 2009-2014). *–How America pays for College 2014 - Ipsos Public Affairs and SallieMae*

83% of college students and parents strongly agreed that higher education is an investment in the future; college is needed now more than ever (70%), and is the path to earning more money (69%). *-- 2012 survey - Ipsos Public Affairs and SallieMae*

According to the U.S. Bureau of Labor Statistics (BLS), in 2011 those with a bachelor's degree earned $1,053 a week, on average, while those with only a high school diploma earned $638. Thus, a college graduate earns an extra $21,580 a year. If we assume a 40-year period of working full time, this adds up to an extra $863,200 over the worker's lifetime.

The Rich Times, June 4, 2012.

Make Saving for College a Priority, and Plan Accordingly!

• Families with a plan to pay for college are less likely to borrow. Even among borrowing families, those who have a plan to pay the full cost of college prior to enrollment borrow significantly less than families who do not plan at all for paying for college —on average $2,892 compared with $5,551, a 48 percent difference!

2012 survey conducted by Ipsos Public Affairs and SallieMae

• While 74 percent of students have decided that they want to save for post-secondary education, only 45 percent have actually begun to save. Even among the savers, fewer are giving up electronics or cars than have in the past, and fewer still know how much they should be saving in the first place.

College Savings Foundation, 2012 Survey of Youth

• The best way to save for college is through Nevada's College Savings Plans and Prepaid Tuition Programs. With the college savings plans, such as the SSgA Upromise 529 Plan, earnings grow tax deferred and qualified withdrawals are exempt from federal income taxes.

• With the SSgA Upromise 529 Plan, for example, you can start with as little as $15 per paycheck through payroll direct deposit.

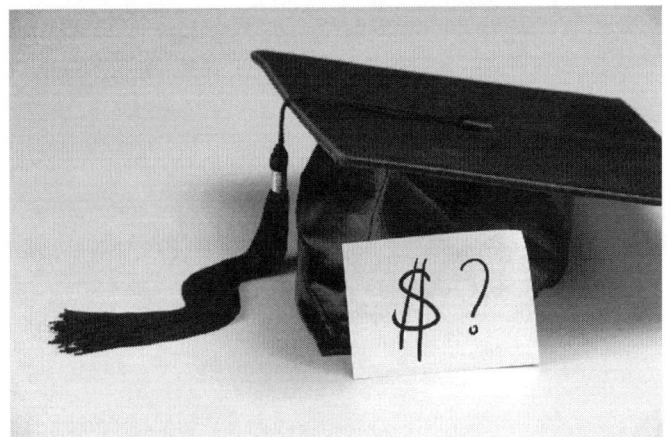

How Do I find Money for College?

If you're not already saving for college, start by evaluating your monthly expenses so you can FIND money to save:

Tip*	Monthly Saving	Yearly Savings
Save $.50 a day in loose change	$15	$180
Cut soda/pop consumption by 1 liter a week	$6	$72
At work, substitute 1 coffee for 1 cappuccino	$40	$480
Bring lunch to work (saving estimated $3/day)	$60	$720
Eat out 2 fewer times a month	$30	$360
Borrow, rather than buying, one book a month	$15	$180
Comparison shop for gas (save est. $.25/gallon)	$4	$48
Maintain checking account minimum to avoid fees	$7	$84
Bounce one less check a month	$20	$240
Pay credit card bill on time to avoid late fee	$25	$300
Pay off $1,000 of credit card debt, reducing interest	$15	$180

*Source – AmericaSaves.org

Evaluate your monthly expenses so you can FIND money to save: Identify your plan now!

My Opportunity	Monthly Savings Potential	Yearly Savings Potential

Does Saving a Little Really Make a Difference? College is So Expensive!

See an example below: Even saving $15/$50/$100 per month really adds up!

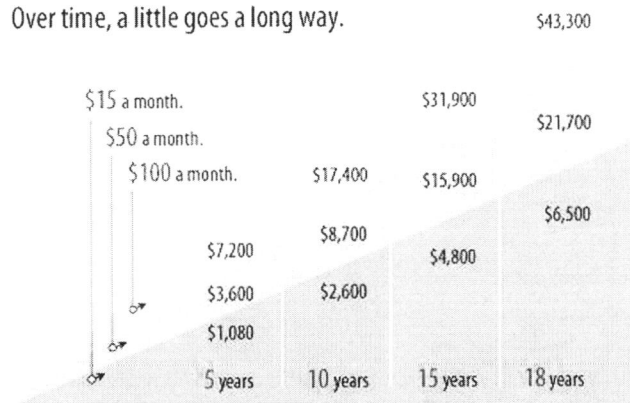

Over time, a little goes a long way. $43,300

$15 a month. $31,900
                                                                              $21,700
  $50 a month.

    $100 a month. $17,400 $15,900

                                                                                $6,500
                           $8,700
              $7,200 $4,800

                 $3,600 $2,600

                    $1,080

              5 years   10 years   15 years   18 years

This chart is a hypothetical example and should not be considered an indication of performance of a 529 plan. These estimates assume that contributions of $15, $50, and $100 per month are made at the beginning of the month with a 7% annual return. Assumes that the money is invested in a tax-free investment vehicle, such as a 529 plan.

*Source: collegesavings.org

What You Should Know About Student Loans

- Student loan indebtedness, the largest component of household debt other than mortgages, rose 3.4% in the quarter, to $904 billion. FEDERAL RESERVE BANK OF NEW YORK, 2012 Q1 Report on Household Debt and Credit
- "Student loan debt continues to grow even as consumers reduce mortgage debt and credit card balances it remains the only form of consumer debt to substantially increase since the peak of household debt in late 2008." Donghoon Lee, senior economist at the New York Fed
- Outstanding educational debt stood at $904 billion as of March 31, 2012. FEDERAL RESERVE BANK OF NEW YORK, 2012 Q1 Report on Household Debt and Credit
- Over the one-year period ending March 31, 2012, student loan balances increased $64 billion. Over the same period, all other forms of household debt (mortgages, HELOCs, auto loans and credit card balances) fell a combined $383 billion. FEDERAL RESERVE BANK OF NEW YORK, 2012 Q1 Report on Household Debt and Credit
- Since the peak in household debt in 2008Q3, student loan debt has increased by $293 billion, while other forms of debt fell a combined $1.53 trillion FEDERAL RESERVE BANK OF NEW YORK, 2012 Q1 Report on Household Debt and Credit
- Student Loan debt summary & why you should act now!
- Students are borrowing record amounts in order to attend college. At the same time, colleges are raising tuition prices at record rates.
- Student loan debt is not only expensive, but there is NO WAY to escape it.
- Utilizing some form of college savings will help minimize your child's student loan debt when he/she graduates college.
- Minimizing student loan debt is crucial because the amount of interest you end up paying with student loans can delay important life events such as buying a house, saving for retirement, and in some cases having kids.

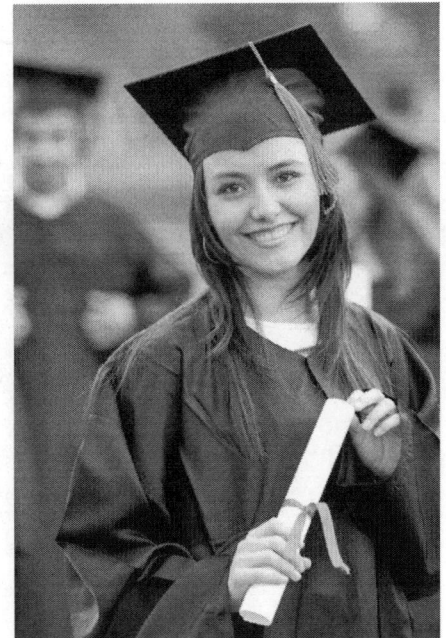

College Savings Programs offered in Nevada

What is a 529 plan?
Named for the Internal Revenue Code section that regulates them, 529 plans offer families a tax advantaged way to save for future college costs. Any earnings on your savings grow tax deferred and are tax exempt if used for qualified expenses at an eligible school. Savings can be used at thousands of schools across the country. With the many attractive features and benefits they offer, 529 plans have become one of the most popular ways to save for college. Millions of families currently save with 529 plans and enjoy the peace of mind that comes from preparing for a child's future.

The Benefits of a 529 Plan
- Professional Investment Management
- Control over how assets are used – as account owner a parent remains in control of the account
- Savings can be used a virtually any technical or vocational, college or university in the country
- Tax-deferred earnings: The money that you invest in a 529 plan account grows tax-deferred, which means that your money can work harder than in a taxable account.
- Tax-free qualified withdrawals: You don't pay federal taxes on withdrawn money when it's used for a qualified, college-related expense.
- No income or age restrictions – accounts can be established for anyone

Nevada Prepaid Tuition Program

Nevada Prepaid Tuition Program allows families to lock in today's college tuition value for use in the future. The Nevada Prepaid Tuition Program, which began in 1998, offers a smart and easy savings option to Nevada residents or graduates of the Nevada System of Higher Education looking to lock-in today's college tuition value for use in the future for their newborn to ninth grade child. The Program allows parents, grandparents, extended family and friends to purchase a contract for a fixed amount of undergraduate credit hours for a child to use credit-for-credit in the future at any eligible Nevada school or take the equivalent value to attend an eligible school anywhere in the country. To date, over 16,000 children have enrolled in the program.

Benefits of the Prepaid Tuition Program

- Affordable - A variety of plan and payment options are available to fit your needs. Grandparents, relatives, and friends can even help by making contributions at any time.
- Easy - Choose to make payments by coupon, or set up automatic withdrawals from your bank account or payroll deduction.
- Flexible - The plan option, payment option, or the beneficiary can be changed at any time (subject to applicable program and federal tax rules). You can hold the contract for up to six years after the projected college entrance date of the beneficiary to complete usage of the benefits. The beneficiary can be transferred to another family member, including a first cousin.
- Portable – The program is fully transferable to private or public out-of-state colleges and universities. The contract can be used to pay tuition costs at any eligible college or university nationwide.
- Voluntary - Nevada Prepaid Tuition accounts may be cancelled at any time and a refund issued, minus a $100 administrative fee.
- Tax-free Savings - Program earnings are free from federal taxes if the benefits are used to pay for the cost of future college tuition.

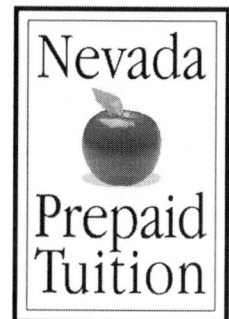

Nevada Prepaid Tuition

Nevada Prepaid Tuition Plans

Plan Options:

- 4 Year University
- 2 Year University
- 1 Year University
- 2 Year Community College
- 2 Year Community College/
  2-Year University Combination

Payment Options:

- One Time Payment
- 5 Year Monthly Payment Option
- Long-term Monthly Payments

The annual enrollment period for the Nevada Prepaid Tuition Program occurs each year from December 1st through February 28th, with enrollment for newborns extending through June 30th. For more information on the Nevada Prepaid Tuition Program, please call 1.888.477.2667 or visit NVPrepaid.gov.

Take Action NOW!

Consider Nevada's Prepaid Tuition program or one of the other 529 programs highlighted above.

- Visit www.NevadaTreasurer.gov
- Formulate a Plan, and Start Saving Now
- Take Advantage of The Silver State Matching Grant for FREE Money
- Save for College One Step at a Time

The following resources may be helpful, whether your child is a newborn or getting ready to go to college soon:

- College Savings Plans Network: http://www.collegesavings.org/

- College Is Possible: http://www. collegeispossible.org

- Saving for College: http://www. savingforcollege.com

- Paying for Education: http:// www.mymoney.gov/education. shtml

- Students.gov: http://www. students.gov/STUGOVWebApp/ Public

- U.S. Dept. of Education: http:// www2.ed.gov/students/landing. jhtml (for students)

- U.S. Dept. of Education: http:// www2.ed.gov/parents/landing. jhtml (for parents)

- Free Application for Federal Student Aid (FAFSA): http:// www.fafsa.ed.gov/

- College Board: http://www. collegeboard.com/

- College Parents of America: http://www.collegeparents.org

- Student Guide to Financial Aid: http://studentaid.ed.gov/students/ publications/student_guide/ index.html

- The Sallie Mae Fund: www.thesalliemaefund.org

Parenting for Financial Literacy

Parents today want to know how to raise financially literate children. The Jump$tart Coalition for Financial Literacy (www.jumpstart.org), a group that promotes financial education for children and youth, has identified 12 principles that every yatmg person should know. These principles (htt:p://www.jumpstart. org/principles.cfm) are important to keep in mind as you raise your own children. Notice how consistent these principles are with what you have learned from the Women's Money Handbook!

1. **Map your financial future.** Take time to list your financial goals, along with a realistic plan for achieving them. You can go places you want to go without a roadmap- but seldom on the first try.

2. **Don't expect something for nothing.** Be leery of advertisements, sales people, or other sources of financial offers promising anything free. Like non-financial opportunities, if it sounds too good to be true, it probably is.

3. **High returns equal high risks.** Recognize that no one will pay you high interest rates on a sure thing. In most cases, the higher the interest rate offered to you, the investor, the higher the risk of losing some- or all - of the money you invests. Diversification of assets is the best protection against risk.

4. **Know your take-home pay**. Before committing to significant expenditures, estimate how much income is likely to be available for you. Net income, after all mandatory deductions, is more important to estimate than gross income before deductions.

5. **Compare interest rates**. Obtain rate information from multiple financial services firms to get the best value for your money.

6. **Pay yourself first**. Before paying bills and other financial obligations, set aside an affordable amount each month in accounts designated for long-range goals and unexpected emergencies.

7. **Money doubles by the "Rule of 72."** To determine how long it will take your money to double, divide the interest rate into 72. For example, an account earning 6 percent interest will double in 12 years (72÷6 = 12).

8. **Your credit past is your credit future**. Be aware that credit bureaus maintain credit reports, which record borrowers' histories of repaying loans. Negative information in credit reports can affect your ability to borrow at a later point.

9. **Start saving young**. Recognize that your total savings are determined both by the interest you earn on those savings and the time period over which you save. The sooner you start saving, the more funds you'll be able to amass over time.

10. **Stay insured**. Purchase insurance to avoid being wiped out by a financial loss, such as an illness or accident. An insurance plan should be part of every personal financial plan.

11. **Budget your money**. Create an annual budget to identify expected income and expenses, including savings. This will serve as a guide to help you live within your income.

12. **Don't borrow what you can't repay**. Be a responsible borrower who repays as promised, showing you are worthy of getting credit in the future. Before you borrow, compare your total payment obligations with income that you will have available to make these payments.

- Use allowances as a lesson in money management.
- Encourage interests that lead to a career.
- Discuss the importance of financial independence.
- Encourage girls in math.
- Play investment games together.

Another source of parenting advice specifically for parents who want to raise financially savvy girls is from Girls Inc. (http://www.girlsinc.org/ resources/ tips/p3-3-1 .h tml): Girls Inc. also has a new initiative related to girls and economic literacy (http://www.girlsinc.org/about/ programs/ economic-literacy.html).

Real Life, Real Money

Karen married when she was a junior in college. She lacked only a semester to complete her degree before dropping out when her first child was born. She held a series of jobs to help put her husband through graduate school while raising two children and putting her own dreams on hold. The divorce came later. She never thought she'd be raising two kids on her own. And every "good" job she applied for slipped by her. "I've just got to go back to school," she thought, but wondered how she could possibly do it and still be a good mom.

Chapter Eleven: Record Your Accomplishments!

Possible Action Steps for this Chapter:

- ☐ Determining what I need to pay for more education for my child, myself, and/or spouse.
- ☐ Investigated the options best suited for saving for college
- ☐ Evaluated 529 plans
- ☐ Evaluated Prepaid Tuition programs
- ☐ Started an account/program to save for college
- ☐ Discussed financial literacy with my children
- ☐ Saving more than I am currently saving towards my college savings
- ☐ Estimating how much I should be saving for college
- ☐ Discussed my options with college funding experts.
- ☐ Creating a College Action Plan for my children
- ☐ Looking into scholarships and create a scholarship plan
- ☐ Discussed plans for college with my family and my child's teacher(s) to enlist their communication and support.
- ☐ Determined if getting an advanced or different degree would increase my income and job satisfaction.

Accomplishment Tracker

Date _____ Year ____ My Name _____ My Mentor is _____

Results from last month's action step(s) or Where I'm at right now...

_____

_____

_____

_____

_____

Challenge(s) I overcame to achieve these results

_____

_____

_____

_____

This is what I would like to accomplish in the next 30 days.

_____

_____

_____

Thoughts and Inspirations:

_____

Chapter Notes and Questions

Chapter Twelve: Retirement Planning Basics

Retirement planning is important for everyone, but especially for women. Even if retirement is many years away, the planning and action steps you take now affect your future retirement security. Learning how to plan and invest for retirement should be high on your financial priority list. Lack of understanding about retirement plans and confusion about investment choices can lead to fear and inaction about investing for retirement. This chapter aims to clear up some of the uncertainty.

This chapter builds on the saving and investing material covered in Chapter 5 of Women's Money. It focuses on why retirement planning is important to women, the importance of investing early for retirement, how to estimate retirement income and savings needs, taking advantage of employer-provided plans, investing in IRAs, and what women should know about Social Security. Avoiding investment fraud is also covered.

Why Retirement Planning Matters to Women

There are important reasons why retirement planning and saving are especially important for women, according to the Employee Benefits Security Administration of the U.S. Department of Labor.

- Women are more likely to work in part-time jobs that don't qualify for a retirement plan.

- Working women are more likely than men to interrupt their careers to take care of family members. Therefore, they work fewer years and contribute less toward their retirement, resulting in lower lifetime savings.

- Of the 62 million wage and salaried women (age 21 to 64) working in the United States, just 45 percent participate in a retirement plan.

- On average, a female retiring at age 65 can expect to live another 19 years - 3 years longer than a man retiring at the same age.

- By and large, women invest more conservatively than men.

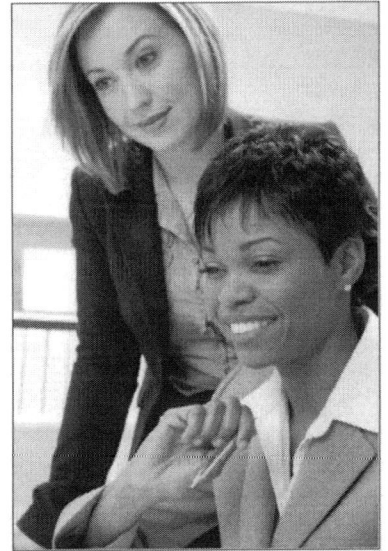

> ## Real Life, Real Money
>
> When I took my first job, I was overwhelmed by the many important decisions I had to make about my employee benefits. There was so little time to decide what to do! I was supposed to decide how to invest the money my employer and I would be contributing to my 401(k) plan, but I didn't know the first thing about mutual funds. I'd never invested before, so I decided not to contribute to my 401 (k) right away – a big mistake, I found out later!

Given these facts, there are important steps women should take. If you work and if you qualify, join a retirement plan now or as soon as you are eligible. Remember that small amounts saved or invested can grow and add up over time. The earlier you begin to save and invest money, the more opportunity your retirement nest eggs (yes, you should have more than one egg!) have to grow. Consistent retirement savings will increase a woman's chances of having enough money to last during retirement. However, you will have to choose carefully where you put your money and learn how to make your investments grow.

Retirement Confidence in America

For 20 years, the Retirement Confidence Survey (RCS) has been conducted by the Employee Benefits Research Institute to gauge the views and attitudes of workers 25 and older and retired Americans regarding retirement, their preparations for retirement, and their retirement confidence. The 2010 Survey showed both gaps and similarities between women and men.

- Retirement confidence stabilizing. The percentage of workers very confident about having enough money for a comfortable retirement remained steady at 16 percent, which is similar to 2009. However, only 12 percent of women are very confident, compared to 19 percent of men. Men are more confident than women in their ability to prepare financially for retirement. Four percent of women and 15 percent of men believe they will have enough money to pay for long-term care during retirement. A quarter of the women and one- third of the men believe they will have enough money to take care of basic expenses during retirement.

- Saving for retirement. Men and women are equally likely to say they (and/or their spouse) have saved for retirement and to say they are currently saving for retirement. Women (42 percent) are as statistically likely as men (38 percent) to say they are currently contributing to a retirement plan at work. Likewise, men (47 percent) and women (46 percent) are similar statistically when it comes to saying that they have an individual retirement account (IRA or rollover IRA). Calculating retirement accumulation needs. Forty-five percent of women and 47 percent of men have calculated how much they need to have in retirement savings by the time they retire to live comfortably. Men, however, are more likely than women to think they need $1 million or more, while women more often say they do not know.

Because of a longer work life projection for many, other findings from the 2010 Survey cast doubt about the ability of those surveyed to achieve financial security in retirement.

• Just 60 percent reported they are currently saving for retirement.

• Among workers reporting they have virtually no savings or investments, 27 percent say they have less than $1,000 in savings. Overall, 54 percent report the total value of household savings and investments (excluding the value of their home and defined benefit plans) to be less than $25,000.

• A quarter (24 percent) have decided to postpone their planned retirement age, but the percentage of workers expecting to retire after age 65 has increased significantly - from 11 percent in 1991 to 19 percent in 2000, and 33 percent in 2010.

Projecting Down the Road - How Much Will You Need?

Depending on your current age, you may be giving serious thought to the future and what your income needs will be during retirement. They may be different from your income needs right now. Perhaps you have consulted with a financial planner to start the process. One rule of thumb frequently used in projecting retirement income needs is an easy one to remember: plan to replace about 70 to 90 percent of your pre-retirement income to maintain your same pre- retirement level of living. Some experts suggest a replacement level close to 100 percent, while others may suggest different levels. No single recommendation fits everyone! Some expenses will disappear in retirement, such as work-related expenses, but others, such as medical bills, may increase. Your mortgage balance and other debt at the time of retirement will influence how much money you will need. Many financial experts recommend paying down debt and paying off the mortgage balance before retirement. One thing is certain, however; if you can build up your nest egg(s) starting now, retirement will be a lot easier.

Choose to Save, one of the programs of the Employee Benefit Research Institute's Education and Research Fund, provides a useful tool to help people estimate how much money they need to save for retirement. For years now, they have promoted the use of the Ballpark E$timate® to help consumers become motivated to start their retirement planning. The Real Life, Real Money story below provides our example.

The Ballpark E$timate® is available as an interactive worksheet on-line at http ://www.choosetosave.org/ballpark/index .cfm. There is also a non-interactive (printable) version. Employees who are covered by the Civil Service Retirement System (CSRS), CSRS-Offset, or the Federal Employees Retirement System (FERS) who plan to retire under the voluntary age and service rules can use a specialized version developed by EBRI, the Federal Government Employees Ballpark Estimator, available at the same website.

You can access a printable estimator through your Women's Money Mentoring Portal's Education Center.

For Example: Juliana's Summary: she is 38, earns $40,000 per year, plans to retire at her full retirement age of 67, wants to replace 90 percent of her income at retirement, expects to live to age 92, thinks inflation and her raises will both average 2 percent a year, thinks her investments will grow 5 percent a year before and after retirement, has $15,000 currently saved for retirement, and calculated (at the Social Security website) that she will receive $4085 per month in Social Security at age 67.

Juliana's Ballpark E$timate® results from the on-line interactive version were very encouraging: "Based on the assumptions you entered, you have now saved enough to allow you to replace 74 percent of your final wages (this includes income from Social Security). The percentage of total salary you will need to save from now until retirement age to achieve your desired income replacement rate is 7 percent. (She wants to replace 90 percent.) The dollar amount you will need to save this year is $2,608" (about $217 per month).

> ## Real Life, Real Money -Juliana Starts Her Action Plan with the Ballpark EStimate®
>
> Juliana learned about the Ballpark E$timate® when she took the Women's Money class on Retirement Basics offered by her employer. Retirement seemed a long way off to her, but at age 38 she knew she needed to "get going." Before taking the class, Juliana had been frightened by all the predictions she heard on television that any woman without one or two million dollars in the bank would wind up as a bag lady in retirement. The Ballpark E$timate® took a different approach because all it required was for her to input a few basic facts into the interactive version. The results it produced encouraged her to take action now.

What Should Juliana Do? She could make adjustments in the inputs to the Ballpark E$timate®, such as changing the replacement rate up or down, anticipating part-time income during retirement, or other factors. She should remember that the recommendation to save 7 percent of her total salary needs to be adjusted annually. This year she should save $2,608 (about $217 per month), but if she gets a 2 percent raise next year, 7 percent of her new salary of $40,800 will be $2,856. She can't allow herself to get "stuck" by saving only the dollar amount shown in the results. She has to adjust it upwards every year.   Decision Time for Juliana: Juliana had never had a Roth IRA, so she decided she would start one and have the money transferred automatically each month from her checking account to her new Roth IRA.

Your Turn

1. If you have on-line access, go to http://www.choosetosave.org to select the interactive version of the Ballpark E$timate® and enter your data. Note that you do not have to provide any identifying information, and your data are not used by EBRI in any way. The exercise will take you to another calculator on the Social Security website to calculate your future benefits. [If you are a Federal government employee, use the special version for federal employees.] You can also access a printable estimator in your Mentoring Portal's Education Center.

2. Note that you can revise your estimates in the interactive version. When you are satisfied with what you have entered, click the "submit" button to see your results.

3. My Results: Based on my assumptions, I have now saved enough to allow me to replace percent of my final wages, including Social Security. The percentage of total salary I will need to save from now until retirement age to achieve my desired income is _____percent. The dollar amount I will need to save this year is $ _____.

4. How did this exercise make you feel? Surprised? Frustrated? Depressed? Motivated?

5. Do you have Action Steps for saving the money?

Building Your Retirement Nest Egg(s)

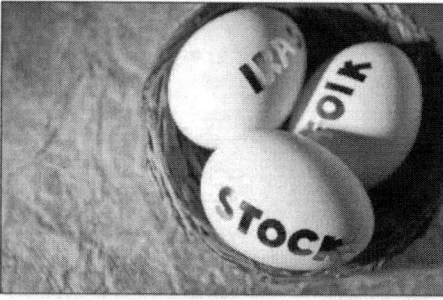

Financial planners and educators often use metaphors when discussing retirement planning. The metaphor, "nest egg" suggests an asset-building process that results in golden eggs to be tapped in the future. Another metaphor views sources of retirement income as a "three or four or five-legged stool." How many legs will your retirement income stool have? One source alone will not be sufficient in the future, yet many people, particularly elderly women, rely on a single stream of income, Social Security. Without it, they would be destitute. Perhaps they never worked in a job that provided retirement benefits, did not work for pay, or were unable to save for retirement on their own.

Where will your future retirement income come from? Envision the legs on your future retirement income stool. Will there be many or few? Use the checklist on the following page to consider your possibilities. For some people, the stool might look more like an octopus than a stool!

Use the checklist below to determine your future sources of retirement income.

My Future Retirement Income...will come from	Yes	No
Social Security		
CSRS, CSRS-Offset, or FERS		
Government Thrift Plan (for Federal employees)		
Pension from a Defined Benefit Plan		
401(k) or 403(b) or similar Defined Contribution Plan (with employer contribution or match)		
Tax-deferred plan at work (voluntary, not matched)		
IRAs, Roth IRAs, or other plans for self-employed		
Other non-retirement savings		
An inheritance		
Income during retirement from work, hobbies, consulting,		
Proceeds from sale of my home		
Other:		
Other:		
Other:		

Does this list suggest retirement planning options you should check into?

Take Advantage of Employer- Provided Retirement Plans

Not everyone has an employer- provided retirement plan, but those who do are fortunate. One of the most compelling reasons for becoming a knowledgeable investor is to take advantage of employer- provided retirement benefits, even if retirement is decades away. Today, many workers, including many women workers, are literally leaving money on the table by not taking advantage of a good deal at work.

Some workers fail to understand how important it is to prepare for retirement early in their lives. Others overlook the opportunities for retirement investing at work. Still other workers would like to participate as investors, but they do not know where to begin.

Workers who change jobs need to understand how their current retirement plan will be affected. Many workers "cash out" their current retirement accounts when they switch jobs. This has two serious implications. First, additional income tax will be due when tax-deferred money is withdrawn early. But more importantly, spending the retirement funds for other purposes depletes an important "nest egg," even if the amount in the account is small. Instead, workers should examine their options to determine whether their funds can be "rolled over" into a new job's retirement plan.

Get to Know Your Retirement Plan at Work Employer-provided retirement plans are not all the same. Some employers offer a defined benefit plan, while others offer a defined contribution plan. Fewer employers offer defined benefit plans than in the past.

A defined benefit plan promises you a specified monthly benefit at retirement. The plan may state this promised benefit as an exact dollar amount, such as $100 per month at retirement. Or, more commonly, it may calculate a benefit through a plan formula that considers such factors as salary and service, for example, 1 percent of your average salary for the last 5 years of employment for every year of service with your employer.

Other plan formulas consider number of years of service, age, and an average "high" salary in determining the amount of the benefit.

A defined contribution plan, on the other hand, does not promise you a specific amount of benefits at retirement. In these plans, you or your employer (or both) contribute to your individual account under the plan, sometimes at a set rate, such as 5 percent of your earnings annually. These contributions generally are invested on your behalf. You will ultimately receive the balance in your account, which is based on contributions plus or minus investment gains or losses. The value of your account will fluctuate due to changes in the value of your investments. Examples of defined contribution plans include 401(k) plans, 403(b) plans, employee stock ownership plans, and profit-sharing plans. To determine what type of plan your employer provides, check with your plan administrator or read your summary plan description. To learn more about what you should know about your retirement plan, see the Department of Labor's information at http://www.dol.gov/ebsa/ publications/wyskapr.html.

If you have a defined contribution plan, the amount of your future retirement income will depend on the future value of your retirement portfolio. Wise investing and good portfolio management can help your portfolio value grow, but fluctuations in market value will play a large part in how much money your portfolio accumulates over time, when you retire, and how much you draw down each month during retirement. Often the responsibility for selecting investments from an array of options selected by the employer falls to the individual employee. I£ you have a 401(k) plan, a 403(b) plan (for qualifying public- sector employees), or a thrift savings plans (TSP for federal workers), becoming knowledgeable about your investment options is very important.

The value of most defined contribution plans changes with market conditions. When the value of their portfolio is rising, investors are happy, but when the value is going down, they get nervous. Investors should exercise caution in buying and selling their investments when the market is experiencing a lot of ups and downs. It is important to remember that selling "low" -that is, selling at a time when the value of investments is going down - locks in a real loss that may not be recovered. Knowing one's tolerance for investment risk is important and helps investors to avoid engaging in panic selling when the stock market is going down.

Take Advantage of Tax Breaks When You Invest

Reducing income taxes through employer-sponsored programs or other tax-advantaged programs is often a powerful incentive to save for retirement. During the accumulation phase, when you are building up your investment portfolio, your savings and investments grow much faster when they can grow tax-deferred.

To take the best advantage of this tax-deferred accumulation period, start as early as possible, and be a consistent, regular saver/investor. Many women postpone the decision to start saving or investing until it is late in their working career. Clearly, having enough money to save or invest is always a concern, but as you have learned by working through this Handbook, there are ways to free up money when you have a major financial goal in mind.

The effect of tax-deferred investment growth. As shown in the table above, an investment of $100 per month that yields an annual investment return of 6 percent has different end results when the impact of taxation is considered. The three women in the example have two options: 1) make a tax- deferred investment (this means their funds will grow without being taxed until they start to withdraw them), or 2) make a non-tax-deferred investment (this means that there is no tax benefit to their investment). In this example, the earnings are compounded annually, which means that all interest/dividends are added back into the principal amount invested. Each year, the new amounts of principal plus interest continue to grow.

Value of Investing $100 per Month, Tax-deferred vs. Non-tax-deferred Investments		Tax-deferred	Non-tax -deferred
Sally	5-year investor	$6,982	$6,703
Melanie	15-year investor	$28,831	$25,301
Gabriela	30-year investor	$97,926	$73,428

Sally, who invests $100 per month for five years, will have savings worth $6,982 if she invests her money on a tax- deferred basis and $6,703 if invested on a non-tax-deferred basis. Melanie is a 15-year investor and will accumulate $28,831 tax-deferred but only $25,301 non-tax-deferred. Gabriela, who has invested $100 per month for 30 years, will wind up with $97,926 if she invests on a tax--deferred basis but only $73,428 if she invests on a non-tax-deferred basis.

Why is there such a difference between the two approaches? Assume that these women are in the 27 percent tax bracket. This means that each $100 invested on a non-tax- deferred basis is really equivalent to $73 (27 percent means $27 will go for taxes, leaving just $73 to invest and to grow). Additional taxes also may be owed on the non-tax-deferred investment every year that the investment grows.

Take Advantage of Other Retirement Planning Incentives – IRAs

Individual Retirement Accounts (IRAs) provide an avenue with significant tax advantages, whether you have a retirement plan at work or not. Roth IRAs and/or Traditional IRAs can become an important "leg" of your future retirement stool. Consult IRS Publication 590 for more detailed information about IRAs.

Real Life, Real Money
Sirena Gets Her IRA Question Answered

Sirena had been wondering about IRAs for a long time, but she was afraid she didn't know enough to move ahead with one. She knew that there were clear tax advantages and that an investment would grow faster in an IRA. But one question continued to plague her: "What, exactly, was an IRA...just what kind of an investment was it?" And where could she find one to meet her needs? One day at lunch, her friend, Elaine, said she had just opened a Roth IRA, so Sirena asked her the question that had been plaguing her. What Elaine told her was this: "Sirena, look at it this way. The IRA is just the envelope...you can put almost any type   of savings option or investment inside that envelope....Certificates of Deposit, stocks, bonds, mutual funds, to name just a few. It's the stuff inside that creates your IRA investment portfolio."

The significant advantages of a Roth IRA are that withdrawals are tax-free (see exceptions in the table below) and are not required to be taken after reaching age 70-½. Withdrawals from Traditional IRAs must be taken after reaching age 70-½ and are subject to taxation.

	Roth IRA	Traditional IRA
You can contribute if:	• you have earned income (or file taxes jointly with an earner), with Modified Adjusted Gross Income of up to:	• you are under the age of 70-½ and have income from compensation (or file taxes jointly with an earner)
Each year, you can contribute up to:	$ $5,000 from 2008-2010 • $5,000 plus inflation starting in 2011 • Persons over age 50 can contribute an additional $1,000; in 2011, this amount will be adjusted by an inflation factor. • The total amount of all IRA contributions (Roth and Traditional) cannot exceed the annual amounts shown above.	
Tax-deductibility of your contribution	• not tax-deductible	• fully tax-deductible if you do not have an employer-provided retirement plan • deductibility for those with an employer-provided retirement plan depends on amount of Modified Adjusted Gross Income and filing status

Tax advantages	• account value grows tax-free
	• contributions can be withdrawn at any time, tax-free and penalty-free
	• after account has been open for five years, earnings can be withdrawn totally tax-free and penalty-free for the following:
	  o reaching age 59-½
	  o disability
	  o death
	  o first-time home purchase
	• unlike Traditional IRA, do not have to start withdrawing money at age 70-½
		• earnings grow tax-deferred
		• contributions may be tax-deductible (see above)
		• funds may be withdrawn penalty-free for:
		  o reaching age 59-½
		  o qualified higher education expenses
		  o first-time home purchase
		  o disability
		  o qualifying medical expenses exceeding 7.5 percent of adjusted gross income
		  o payment of health insurance premiums while unemployed for 12 weeks or longer
		  o payment to beneficiaries upon death
		• subject to Required Minimum Distributions after reaching age 70-½

Investment alternative s available	Almost any type of an investment can be made and designated as either a Roth IRA or Traditional IRA.	

Take Advantage of Other Retirement Planning Incentives – IRA-based Retirement Plans for Small Businesses The chart below illustrates four IRA-based plans that are designed for small businesses. If you own or work for a small company, you may wish to learn more about these plans. Note that contribution maximums differ among the plans.

IRA-based Retirement Plans				
	Payroll Deduction IRA	**SEP**	**SIMPLE IRA Plan**	**Safe Harbor 401(k)**
Key Advantage	Easy to set up and maintain	Easy to set up and maintain	Salary reduction plan with little administrative paperwork	Permits high level of salary deferrals by employees without annual discrimination testing
Employer Eligibility	Any employer with one or more employees	Any employer with one or more employees	Any employer with 100 or fewer employees that does not currently maintain another retirement plan	Any employer with one or more employees
Contributors to the Plan	Employee contributions remitted through payroll deduction	Employer contributions only	Employee salary reduction contributions and employer contributions	Employee salary reduction contributions and employer contributions
Employee Contributions (annual maximum)	Up to $5,000	0	Up to $11,500	Up to $16,500
Employer contributions (annual maximum)	0	Optional	Required	Required
Age 50+ catch-up contributions	Up to $1,000	0	Up to $2,500	Up to $5,500
Loans allowed	No	No	No	Yes
Hardship withdrawals allowed	Yes	Yes	Yes	Yes

Resources for learning more about these plans include:

- IRS Retirement Plans Navigator (http://www.retirementplans.irs. gov/plan-comparison-table/).

- Choosing a Retirement Solution for Your Small Business (httpJL www.irs.gov/pub/irs-pdf/p3998. pdf).

Social Security and Women - A Few Basics

Retirement income from Social Security is important for women. Women represent 57 percent of all Social Security beneficiaries age 62 and older and about 69 percent of beneficiaries age 85 and older. Moreover, 47 percent of all elderly unmarried females receiving Social Security benefits in 2007 relied on Social Security for 90 percent or more of their income.4 And because more women are in the workforce, more women are earning retirement income credit than ever before. Women who do not work but who are married often receive benefits through their husbands' work history. The level of Social Security protection for women has been strengthened over the years. The benefits amount for surviving spouses has been raised, and benefits for disabled spouses have also increased. For divorced women, an important economic protection was gained when the requirement that the divorced wife be dependent on her husband was removed. Divorced women who were previously married for 10 years can qualify for Social Security benefits based on their ex-spouse's earnings.

The Social Security Administration wants women to be aware of several key points. Note that the Social Security Administration issues the publications and forms referenced below unless otherwise noted.

• Make sure that your name and your tax and reporting obligations by reviewing Publication No. 05- 10021, Household Workers.

• If you have served in the military, you may be eligible for both Social Security benefits and military

• If you are a worker age 25 or older, you should be receiving an annual Social Security Statement that gives you a record of your earnings and estimates what your future Social Security benefits will be at different retirement ages. Report any discrepancies between the Statement and your W-2 statements so that corrections can be made.

• If you change your name, report the change to Social Security. Otherwise, your earnings may be recorded incorrectly. You must provide acceptable evidence of your legal name change along with Form SS-5, Application for a Social Security Card.

• Victims of domestic violence may apply for a new SSN when their benefits, with no reduction in Social Security benefits. Ask for Publication No. 05-10093, New Numbers for Domestic Violence Victims.

• Apply for a SSN for your baby when you apply for his/her birth certificate. Children's SSNs must be reported on income tax returns.

• Apply for a SSN for your baby when you apply for his/her birth certificate. Children's SSNs must be reported on income tax returns.

• Apply for Medicare in the months before reaching age 65.

• The money you and your employer pay into Social Security provide retirement benefits to retired workers as early as age 62, disability benefits at any age to those who qualify, family benefits to the spouse and children of retired or disabled workers, and survivors benefits to the widow/widower and children.

• If you are self-employed and your net earnings are $400 or more in a year, you must report your earnings on IRS Schedule SE when you file your federal income tax return and pay your Social Security taxes directly to the IRS.

• If you employ household workers, be sure to understand your tax and reporting obligations by reviewing Publication No. 05- 10021, Household Workers.

• If you have served in the military, you may be eligible for both Social Security benefits and military benefits, with no reduction in Social Security benefits.

• You need 10 years of work (40 credits) to qualify for retirement benefits.

• The age when you begin to collect Social Security benefits impacts substantially how much you will receive. Security Retirement Estimator at http://www.ssa.gov/estimator/ to estimate your benefits at retirement. If you are eligible for benefits on more than one work record (i.e., yours and your spouse's/ex-spouse's), you will receive the highest benefit for which you are eligible.

- If you become disabled, you may qualify for disability benefits. Consult http://www. socialsecurity.gov/disability for further information.

- Family benefits may be available under certain conditions when Social Security or disability benefits are initiated, particularly if the principal or a spouse dies.

- People - often government workers -who worked at a job that did not include Social Security coverage can be impacted at retirement by two laws: Windfall Elimination Provision (WEP) and Government Pension Offset (GPO). For more information, go to http://www.socialsecurity.gov/gpo-wep. Benefit calculators are also available that take WEP and GPO into consideration.

- Widow/Widower benefits can begin as early as age 60 or age 50 if you are disabled and your spouse dies. But remarriage before 60 (or age 50 if disabled) will effectively stop those benefits as long as the new marriage is in effect. Remarriage after those ages will not stop the benefits, but it is a good idea to see if your new spouse's earnings record will result in a higher spousal benefit for you.

- Divorced women can receive benefits based on their ex- spouse's work record if the marriage lasted 10 years or longer, you are unmarried, and you are age 62 or older. Other provisions also may apply. Many women receive a higher benefit based on their ex-spouse's work record rather than based on their own earnings. Benefits can begin at 60 if the ex-spouse is deceased.

- You may qualify for the Supplemental Security Income (SSI) program if you are age 65 or older, or blind or disabled, and your income and value of your resources is limited.

- If you are responsible for the care of an elderly or disabled relative who needs help managing monthly Social Security or SSI benefits, you can apply to become a representative payee, whereby you will be paid the benefits to use in caring for the individual. Consult http://www. Socialsecurity.gov/payee for additional information.

- You will find more information specifically geared to women at http://www.socialsecurity.gov/ women.

Avoid Investment Fraud

If an investment offer sound too good to be true, it probably is. Caveat emptor means, "let the buyer beware." Never invest in anything that makes absolute out- of-the-realm-of-reality promises. Investment fraud is becoming more sophisticated, so greater vigilance is required. Never invest in something you do not understand. Just as you would not buy a car you couldn't drive, you shouldn't invest in something you don't understand. The U.S. Securities and Exchange Commission (SEC) and the Financial Industry Regulatory Authority (FINRA) suggest that you protect your money by researching brokers and advisers. Federal or state securities laws require brokers, advisers, and their firms to be licensed or registered and to make important information public. But it is your responsibility to find out if the person you are dealing with is indeed reputable.

• Use the SEC's Central Registration Depository website (http://www. sec.gov/investor/brokers.htm) to obtain information about most brokers, their representatives, and the firms they work for.

• Use the FINRA BrokerCheck website (http://www.finra.org/Investors/ToolsCalculators/ BrokerCheck/index.htm) to check the background of your investment professional.

• Investment and financial professionals may have one or more professional designations, which often appear as a set of initials following a person's name. The number of designations has expanded greatly. You can look up the meaning of these designations at FINRA's Understanding Professional Designations Database (http://apps.finra

.org/DataDirectory/1/prodesignations.aspx). The information will help you understand what education and experience requirements are necessary for a designation and whether the granting organization mandates continuing education, offers a public disciplinary process, provides a means to check a professional's status, and otherwise ensures that a professional designation is more than just a string of letters.

• Connect to your state securities regulating body through the North American Securities Administrators Association, Inc. website for state-specific information, including investment fraud alerts (http://www.nasaa .org/OuickLinks/ ContactYourRegulator.cfm).

• Check the Investor Information component of the U.S. Securities and Exchange Commission website periodically for updates (http://www.sec.gov).

• Take a look at http://investor.gov to learn how to invest wisely and how to avoid fraud. This website is from the U.S. Securities and Exchange Commission.

Women- What's in Your Future?

1. Even if retirement is many years away, it's never too early to trunk about the future and the money you are investing for retirement. Can you answer the eight questions listed below? You can find a complete discussion of the answers in the Women and Retirement Savings6 publication at http://www.dol.gov/ebsa/publications/women. html.

- Do you work for an employer that offers a retirement plan?

- Have you worked at the job long enough to earn retirement benefits?

- Do you keep copies of the documents that define the provisions of your retirement plan?

- What happens to your retirement benefits if you change jobs?

- Do you know how you can save for retirement even if you don't belong to an employer-sponsored retirement plan?

- Are you tracking your Social Security earnings?

- Are you entitled to a portion of your spouse's pension benefit if you and your husband divorce?

- Are you aware of the rules that govern your retirement plan and the retirement plan of your spouse if either of you dies?

2. Learn more about women and retirement by checking the information at the Choose to Save website at http:// www.choosetosave.org/brochures/index.cfm?fa=women.

3. Become familiar with more facts and figures about Women and Social Security by reading the Social Security Administration's Fact Sheet, Social Security Is Important to Women, at http://www.ssa.gov/pressoffice/factsheets/ women-alt.pdf.

4. Obtain more information from the Internal Revenue Service about life events that can affect retirement savings at http ://www.irs.gov /retirement/article/0, .id=211119 .OO .html.

Real Life, Real Money: Courtney Wants to Be a Millionaire

Even with the recent economic uncertainty, Courtney was inspired after reading the millionaire book2 and wanted to know whether it was in the realm of her possibilities to achieve a million-dollar goal. At 32, she was making a good salary. She made regular contributions to her 401(k) plan at work, and she recently started contributing to a Roth IRA. She liked the idea of a Roth IRA- it meant that her money would be growing tax-free and that when she eventually withdrew it, she would owe no further income tax on it. She now has amassed $50,000 between her 401(k) and her Roth IRA- a nice sum for a person her age. Courtney visited the website, www.womensmoney.org to calculate her future worth.

Time Value Question: How fast does money grow?

There is a simple "rule of thumb" to use in estimating how fast money will double. It is called the Rule of 72. Using $10,000 as our example and the rule of 72, we can estimate how fast our money will double to $20,000. All we need to do is to divide 72 by the interest rate. If money is growing at 3 percent per year, it will double in 24 years (72 divided by 3 = 24 years). The doubling time is not exact, but this is a good estimate. The Rule of 72 is both instructive and a handy tool. It helps us understand how important it is to search for the highest Annual Percentage Rate we can find for our savings, because even a few percentage points can make a big difference. There is an almost 10 year difference in doubling time between money earning 3 percent and money earning 5 percent a year, 24 years compared to 14.4 years. The Rule of 72 is a tool for which no calculator is needed! Just remember to divide "72" by the APR of the savings option under consideration.

What Will It Take to Become a Millionaire?

Few topics fascinate us as much as "becoming a millionaire." It is possible to build millionaire wealth through consistent saving and investing over a lifetime. For some people, it is motivating to "see the money math."

Here's what Courtney (see the Real Life, Real Money sidebar) found out. If she invests $50,000 now (the current value of what she already has), continues to save $850 per month, and earns an annual return of 6 percent, she will have $1,000,000 by the time she is 60. The combined contributions to her 401(k) and her Roth IRA already exceed $850 per month. Over the next 34 years, Courtney's salary will rise and so will the dollar amount she contributes towards retirement, so reaching her "millionaire" status will probably happen at an even earlier age. In today's world, $1,000,000 sounds like a lot of money, but adjusted for inflation, her money will be worth much less at age 60. In fact, adjusted for 2 percent annual inflation, at age 60 her million dollars would be worth $570,545.

Don't be misled by Courtney's example. Saving money for retirement is crucial; Chapter 7 will discuss this topic more thoroughly. But there are no guarantees for Courtney that she will realize a consistent rate of return of 6 percent per year, that her salary will increase each year, or that she will always contribute to her retirement fund. The economy will have its ups and downs over the next 30 years, and the value of her future retirement portfolio may be different from what she calculated at age 32.

Time Value of Money Rule of 72		
Amount of Savings	Percent Interest Per	Number of Years to
$10,000	3%	24.0
$10,000	5%	14.4
$10,000	8%	9.0
$10,000	11%	6.5

The studies about millionaires (see Stanley and Danka's book 2) suggest that many achieved millionaire status through entrepreneurship and small business ownership, and because they tended to "live beneath their means," choosing to save and invest money along life's path instead of overspending.

Time Value Question: What Are Financial "What If" questions? Whenever we ask ourselves, "What happens if?" we are asking a "what if" question. Financial questions often have a time value basis, so it is important to know how to get answers to our questions. As previously discussed in Chapter 2, Money Math, financial calculator websites designed to answer key "what if" questions are a good way to find answers to our own questions.

Developing a Comprehensive Financial Plan

This Guidebook has emphasized financial tasks and strategies you can do yourself. But there may be special situations for which you need outside professional advice and there are also a growing number of resources in the Women's Money Program One Mentoring Portal (available to Program One Member). You can go to WomensMoney.org to sign up for Program One:

● **Organize and manage your finances**. A financial planner can help you organize financial facts (your overall net worth and financial statements) and recommend specific strategies to maximize your resources and help you achieve your life goals.

● **Marriage and children.** A financial planner can help when money personalities differ between spouses or when there were previous marriages.

● **Divorce.** The impact of divorce can be financially devastating. A financial planner can help you design an equitable property settlement prior to divorce and can also assist in post-divorce planning. Women need to seek the best advice they can find.

● **Receiving a financial windfall**. Sudden income from an inheritance (or even the lottery), especially if it is a substantial sum, can present a decision- making dilemma. A financial planner can help identify alternatives and eliminate inappropriate "deals" before you make an expensive mistake.

● **Retirement planning**. A financial planner can help you understand and design your retirement plan's investment and retirement choices, and for withdrawing money from your retirement nest egg once you are ready to retire.

● **Funding for college.** A financial planner can help you understand funding choices, financial aid, and tax implications. A financial planner can also help you see the trade-offs between funding college and funding your own retirement.

● **Facing a financial crisis**. You may need professional financial advice or planning assistance when faced with a crisis, such as job loss, serious illness, natural disaster, or legal problems.

● **Career advice.** A financial planner can assess the financial consequences of a career change, compensation package, separation/severance package, and retirement plans like 401(k)s and deferred compensation plans.

● **Running a business.** Consulting a financial planner when buying a business will help in setting up retirement plans and other benefits for owners and employees and in establishing a business succession plan.

● **Buying and selling a home.** A home purchase has many financial ramifications and triggers questions for which you may need answers from a financial planner: housing affordability, type/length of mortgage, and size of down payment and tax implications.

● **Death of a spouse.** This is one of the times when you may most need objective; outside advice concerning insurance, investments, and retirement plans. A financial planner can help.

● **Charitable giving.** A financial planner can advise individuals and families who are financially able and interested to make charitable donations in ways that minimize taxes and maximize contributions.

● **Insurance.** A financial planner can help you assess all of your insurance needs in relation to your overall financial situation and your financial goals. Ask the planner if they make money on the insurance products recommended.

● **Estate planning.** Consulting a financial planner as well as an attorney will help put together the estate planning documents in a way that reflects your financial circumstances and wishes.

Check Out the Professionals

The Financial Industry Regulatory Authority (FINRA) advises consumers to check out the professional designations used by contacting the issuing organization and determining whether the individual is currently authorized to use the designation and whether the individual is the subject of any disciplinary action. Consult FINRA's database, Understanding Professional Designations (http://apps.finra.org/DataDirectory/1/prodesignations.aspx). The database lists over 100 acronyms used by professionals and provides a starting point for consumer understanding. FINRA also provides the FINRA BrokerCheck ®, which is a free tool to help investors research the professional backgrounds of current and former-registered brokerage firms and brokers. FINRA advises consumers to check this resource first when dealing with a particular broker or brokerage firm (http://www.finra.org/Investors/ToolsCalculators/BrokerCheck/index.htm).

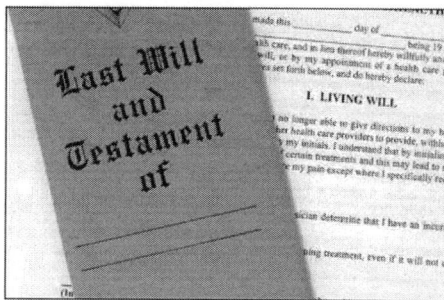

Estate Planning Basics

We have left the topic of "estate planning" to the very end, just like most people do! No one wants to think about it, yet we must. You probably know someone who died unexpectedly, before he/she had a chance to make an estate plan.

In effect, we all have an estate plan already. That's because state law determines how our assets are to be distributed upon our death. The problem is, your state's plan may not (and usually does not) meet your particular needs. You can avoid this problem entirely by developing your own plan. You will need four basic estate-planning tools: a will, durable power of attorney, living will, and medical durable power of attorney in addition to a letter of last instruction. You will need the help of an attorney and possibly a financial planner.

In Chapter 10, you learned the questions to ask when you are seeking a financial planner. Be sure you understand how the planner you hire is paid and whether that form of compensation is the right one for you. Planners may be paid in one or more ways:

Commission. The planner is paid a certain percentage by the financial institution for each financial product sold to the client.

Fees for assets under management. The planner charges an annual fee based on the total value of the client's invested assets under management.

Fees for total client assets. Some planners may charge for invested assets under management plus non-investment assets, on the assumption that the planner also provides advice on assets he/she does not directly manage.

Hourly fee. For those seeking limited advice, planners commonly charge an hourly fee ranging from $150 to $250 or more per hour.

Retainer fee. A newer trend is to charge a flat annual fee based on the size and complexity of a client's finances.

Fee and commission combination, or fee-offset. The planner may charge a fee for developing a comprehensive financial plan and receive commissions on financial products bought by the client to implement the plan. Some planners might off-set the commission by crediting the amount against the client's future fees.

Salary. A small percentage of planners who work for financial institutions, such as banks, are paid a salary that may be derived from fees or commission generated by the sale of financial products.

Real Life, Real Money

Kate married Kenneth after he divorced Marilyn. Both Kate and Kenneth drew up new wills, leaving everything to each other. Just before their fifth anniversary, Kenneth died. That's when Kate found out that the will does not supersede everything else. Although Kenneth's will left "everything" to Kate, Kate did not receive any life insurance or retirement account proceeds. Why? Kenneth had never gotten around to changing the beneficiary designation on his life insurance and retirement account, so it went to his ex-wife, Marilyn.

• **Will.** This legal document names someone you have designated as executor of your estate, specifies how you want the assets of your estate to be distributed after any debts and taxes are paid, and states who will care for your minor children. People with few assets think they do not need a will, but if they have minor children, a will is an absolute necessity unless they are comfortable in allowing the courts to decide who should raise their children. But something else about a will is very important, too, as Kate found out (see the Real Life, Real Money sidebar).

• **Durable Power of Attorney.** Unlike a will, which governs what happens after death, a power of attorney governs what happens during your lifetime. With it, you can designate someone to perform certain actions for you if you should become incapacitated or otherwise unable to manage your financial affairs or make financial decisions. A power of attorney can be either broad or narrow in scope. Without such a document, your next of kin would have to obtain court approval to carry out necessary financial transactions.

• **A Living Will.** This document is an individual's written declaration of what life-sustaining medical treatments are allowable in case of incapacitation or terminal illness.

• **Medical Durable Power of Attorney**. This document authorizes your representative to make medical decisions based on what you have specified in your living will. Sometimes, despite the fact that you have made your intentions clearly known and have had the proper documents created (living wills, medical durable power of attorney), family members or medical institutions may challenge their validity.

• **Letter of Last Instruction**. This letter includes information about your funeral plans/preferences, obituary information, insurance policy contact information, a list of your financial accounts and debts, the location of important papers, keys/combinations for lockboxes and other locked containers, and a list of persons to be contacted. We often assume that our survivors "know everything," but most of the time this is simply not true. By preparing a letter of last instruction, we will relieve at least a little stress at an emotionally difficult time.

Other types of estate-planning tools, including trusts, may be developed in accordance with the size and complexity of the estate. Your attorney will be able to advise you about the appropriateness of trusts and other planning tools for your situation. A trust is sometimes established to provide for the needs of minor children or other family members, to avoid probate, or to be able to have assets transferred to beneficiaries immediately upon death. A financial planner will be able to help you assess the appropriateness of insurance for estate-planning purposes.

Philanthropy, Service and Your "Bucket List"

Following the movie of the same name, the term "bucket list" has made its way into our vocabulary. A "bucket list" is the final "wish list" of the most important things we want to accomplish, see, or do before we die. What we put on our "bucket list" is unique because we are all unique individuals with different life goals, needs, resources, and perspectives on what is important. Women's Money has emphasized the importance of financial planning for achieving life goals. We could even say that bucket lists and life goals are synonymous.

Two items that may make it onto your bucket list are philanthropy and service. A recent report has found that women play a prominent role within their households and their communities when it comes to philanthropy. 9 As women are able to create their own wealth, they are incorporating charitable giving into their financial plans. Because of their greater longevity, many women are the beneficiaries of wealth transfers that make it possible for them to be more philanthropic. Data from the IRS suggest that women donate more of their wealth than do men. When women are in the 20s and 30s, they are likely to contribute more time than money, but in later life, both the service and financial contributions of women influence the outcomes of philanthropic efforts. To evaluate the soundness of charitable organizations you may wish to donate to, consult the following resources:

Critical Steps for Financial Security

If you have children, begin developing a plan to help them achieve education and training beyond high school. Think about how to do this and what is affordable for you. For ideas, refer back to the section on financing college costs. List the action steps you will take to make this dream a reality.

List three ways you can help enhance your child's financial literacy:

1._____

2. _____

3. _____

In which of the following areas would professional planning advice be beneficial to you?

☐ Overall financial planning
☐ Money in your marriage
☐ Divorce issues
☐ Financial windfalls
☐ Retirement planning
☐ College finances
☐ Career advice
☐ Financial crisis situation
☐ Business issues
☐ Buying/selling a home
☐ Death of a spouse or close family member
☐ Charitable giving
☐ Estate planning

Do you presently have the four basic estate-planning tools? If you do not, set a deadline for consulting with an attorney and getting any of the needed documents prepared. Be sure to ask your attorney if your financial situation warrants the establishment of a trust.

Estate-Planning Tools	My Deadline
Consult an attorney about my needs	
Will	
Durable power of attorney	
Living will	
Medical durable power of attorney	

Chapter Twelve: Record Your Accomplishments!

Possible Action Items for this Chapter:

- ☐ Interviewed and consulted with Financial Planners/Advisers
- ☐ Discussing my plans with my spouse or family (if   applicable)
- ☐ Discussed my findings and questions with my Women's Money Mentoring Group.
- ☐ Increasing my knowledge about retirement planning
- ☐ Developing an action plan
- ☐ Estimating how much I should be saving for retirement
- ☐ Projecting my future sources of retirement income
- ☐ Participating in a retirement plan at work
- ☐ Increasing my retirement contributions at work
- ☐ Meeting with an attorney to identify my estate-planning needs
- ☐ Checked Out Organizations that I can give back to with money or time.
- ☐ Opening or adding to a Roth or Traditional IRA
- ☐ Learning more about my Social Security   benefits

Accomplishment Tracker

Date _____Year_____ My Name_____ My Mentor is_____

Results from last month's action step(s) or Where I'm at right now...

_____

_____

_____

_____

Challenge(s) I overcame to achieve these results

_____

_____

_____

This is what I would like to accomplish in the next 30 days.

_____

_____

Notes, Thoughts and Inspirations:

Chapter Notes and Questions

Congratulations!

What Now?

Check into your Mentoring Portal. Take the Financial Freedom Evaluators and submit your progress.

We'll reply with next steps...

Glossary of Financial Terms

401(k) Plan – A tax deferred retirement plan that some private corporations offer their employees. Contributions to the plan may be made through payroll deduction. The money you place into the account lowers your taxable income. The employer usually matches a portion of your contribution. See definition of "Defined Contribution (Pension) Plan."

403(b) Plan – A retirement plan similar to a 401(k) plan that is offered by certain tax-exempt organizations; public schools, such as universities; certain ministers; and some charitable organizations rather than corporations. See definition of "Defined Contribution (Pension) Plan."

529 Plan – A Qualified Tuition Program (QTP), also called a "529 Plan," is a program established and maintained by a state or agency or instrumentality of a state to allow either prepaying or contributing to an account established for paying a student's qualified higher education expenses at an eligible educational institution.

A

Account Theft – Occurs when thieves use stolen personal information to access an individual's existing accounts, such as bank and credit card accounts.

Accumulation Period – The time prior to a deferred annuity's payout period when money builds up in the annuity contract.

Adjustable Rate Mortgage (ARM) – A mortgage loan that does not have a fixed interest rate. During the life of the loan, the interest rate will change based on the index rate. Also referred to as adjustable mortgage loans (AMLs) or variable-rate mortgages.

Adjusted Balance Method – A calculation used by the credit card company to determine finance charges. They take the balance at the beginning of the current billing period and subtract any payments and credits received during the current billing period. The resulting total is used to compute any finance charges.

Alimony – Court-ordered support paid by one spouse to another after they are separated.

Amortization – The process of fully paying off indebtedness by installments of principal and earned interest over a definite time.

Annual Fee – An amount charged to a credit card holder regardless of whether the card is used or not. Not all credit card companies charge an annual fee.

Annual Percentage Rate (APR) – A measure of the cost of credit, expressed as a yearly rate. It includes interest as well as other charges. Because all lenders, by federal law, follow the same rules to ensure the accuracy of the annual percentage rate, it provides consumers with a good basis for comparing the cost of loans, including mortgage plans. APR is a higher rate than the simple interest of the mortgage.

Annuity – When you pay money to an insurance company in return for its agreement to pay either a regular fixed amount when you retire or an amount based on how much your investment earns.

Asset Allocation – Involves dividing an investment portfolio among different asset categories, such as stocks, bonds, and cash.

Assets – Refers to everything that you OWN. Assets include cash and cash equivalents, invested assets, and use assets. Cash or cash equivalents include checking accounts, savings accounts, money market accounts, and the cash value of life insurance.

ATM (Automated Teller Machine) – An unattended, self-service electronic machine that enables consumers to withdraw paper money or conduct other banking procedures upon insertion of an encoded plastic card, such as a debit or credit card, and entry of a personal identification number (PIN).

Automatic Enrollment 401(k) Plan – A 401(k) defined contribution pension plan whereby employees are automatically enrolled in the plan and a specific percentage is deducted from each participant's salary unless the participant opts out or chooses a different percentage.

Automobile Collision Protection – Insurance coverage that covers damage to your car from a collision or roll over, regardless of who is at fault.

Automobile Comprehensive Coverage – Insurance coverage for damage/loss to your vehicle caused by something other than a collision or roll over. It could include fire, theft, vandalism, windshield cracking, or hail damage.

Automobile Liability Coverage – Insurance that pays for someone else's financial loss when you are held responsible for damage to someone else's vehicle.

Average Daily Balance Method – A calculation used by credit card companies to determine finance charges. The total unpaid balance for each day in a billing period is divided by the number of days in the billing period. The finance charge is figured on this average balance.

B

Bad Debt – Credit used to purchase items that lose value or are no longer around when the bill arrives. These items include clothing, food, gasoline, and other goods or services that do not retain their value.

Balance Sheet – A financial statement showing a "snapshot" of the assets, liabilities, and net worth of an individual or organization on a given date.

Balloon Loan or Mortgage – A mortgage that typically offers low rates for an initial period of time (usually 5, 7, or 10 years), after which the balance is due or is refinanced by the borrower.

Balloon Payment – A large extra payment that may be charged at the end of a loan or lease.

Ballpark E$timate® – An on-line calculator found at **www.choosetosave.org/.** The Ballpark E$timate takes complicated issues like projected Social Security benefits and earnings assumptions on savings and turns them into language and mathematics that are easy to understand.

Bankruptcy (Personal) – A legal proceeding declaring that an individual is unable to pay debts. Chapters 7 and 13 of the federal bankruptcy code govern personal bankruptcy.

- Assets may be liquidated to pay creditors, depending on the type of bankruptcy filed. Both types of bankruptcy may remove unsecured debts and stop foreclosures, repossessions, garnishments, utility shut-offs, and debt collection activities. Both types provide exemptions that vary by state and allow people to keep certain assets. Generally considered the option of last resort, a bankruptcy stays on an individual's credit report for 10 years.

- Chapter 7 Bankruptcy – Liquidation of all assets that are not exempt. Exempt property may include automobiles, work-related tools, and basic household furnishings. Some of the property may be sold by a court-appointed official – a trustee – or turned over to creditors. Debts can be discharged through Chapter 7 only once every six years. Also known as straight bankruptcy.

- Chapter 13 Bankruptcy – The court approves a repayment plan that allows the individual to pay off a default during a three-to-five year period, rather than surrender any property.

Beneficiary – The person or financial entity (for instance, a trust fund) named in a life insurance policy or annuity contract as the recipient of policy proceeds in the event of the policyholder's death.

Benefits – Nonwage compensation provided to employees. The National Compensation Survey groups benefits into five categories: paid leave (vacations, holidays, sick leave); supplementary pay (premium pay for overtime and work on holidays and weekends, shift differentials, nonproduction bonuses); retirement (defined benefit and defined contribution plans); insurance (life insurance, health benefits, short-term disability, and long-term disability insurance); and legally required benefits (Social Security and Medicare, Federal and State unemployment insurance taxes, and workers' compensation).

Bond – A debt instrument or IOU issued by corporations or units of government.

Bond Funds – A term, along with "income funds," that is used to describe a type of investment company (mutual fund, closed-end fund, or unit investment trust [UIT]) that invests primarily in bonds or other types of debt securities. Depending on its investment objectives and policies, a bond fund may concentrate its investments in a particular type of bond or debt security – such as government bonds, municipal bonds, corporate bonds, convertible bonds, mortgage-backed securities, zero-coupon bonds – or a mixture of types. The securities that bond funds hold will vary in terms of risk, return, duration, volatility, and other features.

Budget – A plan developed by an individual for directing and controlling his or her money.

C

Capital Gain – The profit received based on the difference between the original purchase price and the total sale price.

Cash Balance Plan – A new type of defined benefit plan that has become more prevalent in recent years. Under this type of plan, benefits are computed as a percentage of each employee's account balance. Employers specify a contribution – usually based on a percentage of the employee's earnings – and a rate of interest on that contribution that will provide a predetermined amount at retirement, usually in the form of a lump sum.

Cash Flow – Money coming to an individual or business less the money being paid out during a given period.

Cash Surrender Value – The amount available in cash upon surrender of a permanent life insurance policy. Also known as cash surrender value.

Caveat Emptor – Let the buyer beware.

Certificate of Deposit (CD) – A special type of deposit account with a bank or thrift institution that typically offers a higher rate of interest than a regular savings account. Unlike other investments, CDs feature federal deposit insurance up to $250,000. When you purchase a CD, you invest a fixed sum of money for fixed periods of time – six months, one year, five years, or more – and, in exchange, the issuing bank pays you interest, typically at regular intervals. When you cash in or redeem your CD, you receive the money you originally invested plus any accrued interest.

A CD bears a maturity date and can be issued in any denomination. The term of a CD generally ranges from one month to five years. There is generally a penalty for early withdrawal. At one time, most CDs paid a fixed interest rate until they reached maturity. But, like many other products in today's markets, CDs have become more complicated. Investors may now choose among variable rate CDs, long-term CDs, and CDs with other special features. Some long-term, high-yield CDs have "call" features, meaning that the issuing bank may choose to terminate – or call
– the CD after only one year or some other fixed period of time.

Checkbook Method – A method that works well for people who make most transactions by check or debit card. The checkbook register is the primary data-entry tool. Code each transaction for the budget expense category to which it belongs. Each week or at the end of the month, tally up the results by budget category.

Checking Account – An account that allows the holder to write checks against deposited funds. Some checking accounts pay interest.

Civil Service Retirement System (CSRS) – A defined benefit, contributory retirement system for certain Federal employees. Employees share in the expense of the annuities to which they become entitled. CSRS-covered employees contribute 7, 7.5, or 8 percent of their pay to CSRS. While they generally pay no Social Security retirement or survivor and disability (OASDI) tax, they must pay the Medicare tax (currently 1.45 percent of pay). The employing agency matches the employee's CSRS contributions.

Civil Service Retirement System Offset – If you are covered by CSRS Offset, you pay into the CSRS retirement fund and Social Security. Your contribution to the retirement system is very little – .80 percent – when compared to that of employees covered under regular CSRS who pay 7 percent. The Social Security Amendments Act of 1983 mandated that Federal employees first hired after December 31, 1983, be subject to Social Security. Employees who are rehired after that date who meet certain conditions remain in the Civil Service Retirement System (CSRS) but are also subject to Social Security. We now have the Federal Employees Retirement System (FERS), CSRS Offset, and the old CSRS system.

Your CSRS Offset annuity is reduced by the portion of your total Social Security benefit that is payable based on federal service performed after 1983 while covered by both the CSRS and Social Security. Your annuity will not be reduced by any portion of your Social Security benefit that is based on service other than CSRS Offset employment.

COBRA (Consolidated Omnibus Budget Reconciliation Act of 1985) – A federal law that lets you extend your job-based health coverage if you lose your job or run into other qualifying events that cause you to lose your health insurance.

Co-insurance – A co-sharing agreement between the insured and the insurer under a health insurance policy that provides that the insured will cover a set percentage of the covered costs after the deductible has been paid. It is similar to co-pay insurance plans except co-pays require the insured to pay a set dollar amount at the time the service is rendered.

Collateral – Property that is offered to secure a loan or other credit and that becomes subject to seizure on default. Also called security.

Commercial Bank – A bank that offers a broad range of deposit accounts, including checking, savings, and time deposits and extends loans to individuals and businesses. Commercial banks can be contrasted with investment banking firms, such as brokerage firms, which generally are involved in arranging for the sale of corporate or municipal securities.

Common Stock – A security that provides voting rights in a corporation and pays a dividend after preferred stock holders have been paid. It is the most common form of stock held within a company.

Compensation – A term used to encompass the entire range of wages and benefits, both current and deferred, that employees receive in return for their work.

Compound Interest – Interest computed on the sum of the original principal and accrued interest.

Computerized Financial Recordkeeping Systems – Systems used by individuals to tailor their income and expense categories to meet the person's needs and can effortlessly produce summary reports. Some people prefer the commercial software packages; others who know how to use electronic spreadsheets create their own financial recordkeeping systems. Others keep their financial information at special financial recordkeeping websites. The latest innovations involve web-based systems that bring together all of your financial transactions and allow access by computer, cell phone, or personal digital assistants (PDAs).

Consumer Price Index (CPI) – A measure of the average change over time in the prices paid by urban consumers for a market basket of consumer goods and services. The CPI is developed from detailed expenditure information provided to the Bureau of Labor Statistics, U.S. Department of Labor, by families and individuals on what they actually bought.

Co-signer – A person, other than the principal borrower, who signs for a loan. The co-signer(s) assumes equal liability for the loan.

Cost of Living Index – A measure of differences in the price of goods and services that allows for substitutions to other items as prices change.

Coverdell Education Savings Account – Named after Senator Paul Coverdell (GA), this account allows parents to make a contribution into the account with an annual limit. The contributions are taxed, but the earnings used to pay education expenses are not. Internal Revenue rules and guidelines apply to this account.

Credit – The ability of a person to borrow money or buy goods by paying over time. Credit is extended based on a lender's opinion of the person's financial situation and reliability, among other factors.

Credit Bureau – Most credit-reporting agencies are credit bureaus that gather and sell credit-related information about individuals to creditors, employers, landlords, and other businesses. The information includes whether the individual pays bills on time or has filed bankruptcy.

Credit Counseling Service – An organization that administers debt repayment plans for individuals seeking assistance with their credit. Credit counseling services may charge a fee that can range from nominal to high and may be either not-for-profit or for-profit organizations.

Credit File Disclosure (Credit Report) – A credit file disclosure, commonly called a credit report, provides you with all of the information in your credit file maintained by a consumer-reporting company that could be provided by the consumer-reporting company in a consumer report about you to a third party, such as a lender. A credit file disclosure also includes a record of everyone who has received a consumer report about you from the consumer-reporting company within a certain period of time ("inquiries"). The credit file disclosure includes certain information that is not included in a consumer report about you to a third party, such as the inquiries of companies for pre-approved offers of credit or insurance and account reviews, and any medical account information, which is suppressed for third party users of consumer reports. You are entitled to receive a disclosure copy of your credit file from a consumer-reporting company under Federal law and the laws of various states.

Credit History – An individual's record of paying loans, credit cards, and other bills.

Credit Report – A record of an individual's credit history that is compiled by credit-reporting agencies. The history contains a listing of debts, bills submitted to collection agencies, bills paid late, public information such as tax liens and bankruptcies, and a listing of who has requested a copy of the credit report. Negative information can remain in a credit report for seven years, except for bankruptcy, which remains for 10 years.

Credit-Reporting Agency (CRA) – Organization that collects information for credit reports and in turn sells the reports to people with a legitimate business need as defined by the Fair Credit Reporting Act. Examples of legitimate business needs are applications for employment, insurance, or to rent an apartment. Companies that lend money and issue credit regularly report payment behaviors to credit-reporting agencies.

Credit Score – Computer-generated number indicating the likelihood an individual will repay credit received. The most common credit scores are developed by the Fair, Isaac and Company and are referred to as FICO scores. Scores range from 300 to 850. Higher scores indicate a higher likelihood of repaying debt.

Credit Union – A non-profit financial institution federally regulated and owned by the members or people who use their services. Credit unions serve groups that hold a common interest, and you have to become a member to use the available services.

Creditor – A person who extends credit and to whom you owe money.

Creditworthiness – A creditor's measure of a consumer's past and future ability and willingness to repay debts.

D

Debit Card – Cards issued to pay for goods and services or to make transactions at an automated teller machine (ATM) and for which the cardholder is accessing funds from a personal checking or savings account rather than drawing on credit. As such, they are a "pay-as-you-go" function (compared to credit cards, which are a "pay later" function).

Debt – Money owed from one person or institution to another person or institution.

Debt Repayment Plans – Plans that are often set up by a credit counseling service. You deposit money each month with the credit counseling service. Your deposits are used to pay your creditors according to a payment schedule developed by the counselor.

Debt Service – Periodic payment of the principal and interest on a loan.

Debt Settlement Company – Among the many different kinds of services that claim to help people with debt problems. These [for-profit] companies negotiate with your creditors to reduce the amount you owe.

Debt-to-Income Ratio – The percentage of net income that pays for non-mortgage debt such as auto loans, student loans, and credit cards.

Deductible – With regard to insurance, the amount of loss paid by the policyholder. A deductible may be either a specified dollar amount, a percentage of the claim amount, or a specified amount of time that must elapse before benefits are paid. The larger the deductible, the lower the premium charged for the same coverage.

Default – Failure to meet the terms of a credit agreement.

Deficit – The amount each year by which government spending is greater than government income.

Defined Benefit (Pension) Plan – A plan that uses a specific, predetermined formula to calculate the amount of an employee's future benefit. The most common type of formula is based on the employee's terminal earnings. Under this formula, benefits are based on a percentage of average earnings during a specified number of years at the end of a worker's career – for example, the highest 5 out of the last 10 years – multiplied by the maximum number of years of credited service under the plan. In the private sector, defined benefit plans are typically funded exclusively by employer contributions. In the public sector, defined benefit plans often require employee contributions.

Defined Contribution (Pension) Plan – A retirement plan in which the amount of the employer's annual contribution is specified. Individual accounts are set up for participants, and benefits are based on the amounts credited to these accounts (through employer contributions and, if applicable, employee contributions) plus any investment earnings on the money in the account. Only employer contributions to the account are guaranteed, not the future benefits. In defined contribution plans, future benefits fluctuate on the basis of investment earnings. The most common type of defined contribution plan is a savings and thrift plan. Under this type of plan, the employee contributes a predetermined portion of his or her earnings (usually pretax) to an individual account, all or part of which is matched by the employer.

Delinquency – The failure to make timely payments under a loan or other credit agreement.

Depository Institution – A financial institution that obtains its funds mainly through deposits from the public. This includes commercial banks, savings and loan associations, savings banks, and credit unions.

Direct Deposit – A method of payment that electronically credits your checking or savings account.
Direct Stock Purchase Plans (DPPs) – Allows you to buy stock directly from a company.

Disability Insurance – Insurance that provides a weekly or monthly income benefit if you are disabled due to a covered injury or sickness.

Discharge – For people who follow the bankruptcy rules, a court order that says they do not have to repay certain debts. An individual who has sought bankruptcy receives a discharge of their debts after they have made all the payments under the repayment plan.

Diversification – The practice of spreading money among different investments to reduce risk.

Dividend – A share of profits paid to a stockholder.

Dividend Reinvestment Plans (DRIPS) – Dividends are reinvested to buy more company stock instead of being issued to you as a dividend check.

Dollar-Cost-Averaging – A strategy where a fixed dollar amount is invested at regular intervals, resulting in more shares purchased when the price per share is low and fewer shares when the price is high.

Down Payment – A portion of the price of a home, usually between 3 and 20 percent, not borrowed and paid up front in cash. Some loans are offered with a zero down payment.

E

Earned Income Tax Credit (EITC) – A tax credit for certain people who work and have low wages. A tax credit usually means more money in your pocket. It reduces the amount of tax you owe. The EITC may also give you a refund.

Electronic Banking – Conducted by automated teller machines (ATMs), telephones, or debit cards.

Electronic Funds Transfer – Transfer of funds electronically rather than by check or cash.

Electronic Fund Transfer Act – Provides consumer protection for all transactions using a debit card or electronic means to debit or credit an account. It also limits a consumer's liability for unauthorized electronic fund transfers.

Employee Benefits Security Administration (EBSA) – An agency of the U.S. Department of Labor (DOL) whose mission is to assure the security of the retirement, health, and other workplace-related benefits of American workers and their families. EBSA accomplishes its mission by developing effective regulations; assisting and educating workers, plan sponsors, fiduciaries, and service providers; and vigorously enforcing the law.

Entrepreneur – A person who organizes and manages an enterprise, especially a business, usually with considerable initiative.

Equity – Anything of value earned through the provision or investment of something of value. In real estate, equity is the interest or value an owner has in real estate over and above the mortgage against it.1

Estate – The sum total of all property, real and personal, owned by a person.

Estate Plan – A plan for the disposition of resources and property after death or during crisis. A will is one component of an estate plan. Although necessary to direct the distribution of assets after death, almost 70 percent of U.S. adults do not have wills. Many people think they do not need a will because they do not have many assets, or they think that preparing a will costs too much. Dying without a will is called dying "intestate" and means that state and federal regulations will determine the distribution of assets. A carefully written legal will, however, provides for family and others in a manner consistent with a person's desires.   In addition, a variety of other important legal documents make up an estate plan and can protect assets and ensure that financial strategies and health-care decisions are made prior to death. These documents include: General Durable Power of Attorney, Health Care Power of Attorney, and a Living Will. These documents are best completed before a crisis occurs.

F

Face Value- The amount stated on the face of a life insurance policy that will be paid upon death or policy maturity. The amount excludes dividend additions or additional amounts payable under accidental death or other special provisions.

Fair Credit Billing Act- Establishes procedures for resolving billing errors on your credit card accounts. It also limits a consumer's liability for fraudulent credit card charges.

Fair Credit Reporting Act (FCRA) - Establishes procedures for correcting mistakes on your credit record and requires that your record only be provided for legitimate business needs.

Fair Debt Collection Practices Act- Prohibits debt collectors from using unfair or deceptive practices to collect overdue bills that your creditor has forwarded for collection.

Fair Market Value- The price a use asset would fetch if sold on the market today. Homes and real estate typically increase in value while automobiles and some personal property, such as computers and appliances, usually decrease in value over time.

Federal Deposit Insurance Corporation (FDIC) -An independent agency of the U.S. government that protects the funds depositors place in banks and savings associations. FDIC insurance is backed by the full faith and credit of the United

States government. Since the FDIC was established in 1933, no depositor has ever lost a single penny of FDIC- insured funds. The standard insurance amount currently is $250,000 per depositor, per insured bank.

FICO Score- The most commonly known and used credit bureau scores. FICO scores stem from modeling pioneered by Fair, Isaac and Company (now known as Fair Isaac Corporation) (Fair Isaac), hence the label "FICO" score. Fair Isaac devised mathematical modeling to predict the credit risk of consumers based on information in the consumer's credit report.

Finance Charge -The sum of cardholder interest charges, annual membership fees, cash advance fees, transaction fees, and any other fees charged or incurred by the cardholders in connection with their use of the credit cards.

Financial Industry Regulatory Authority (FINRA)- Created in July 2007 and is the largest independent regulator for all securities firms doing business in the U.S. All told, FINRA oversees nearly 4,700 brokerage firms, about 167,000 branch offices, and approximately 635,000 registered securities representatives. FINRA is dedicated to investor protection and market integrity through effective and efficient regulation and complementary compliance and technology-based services.

Fixed Annual Percentage Rate (APR) -Traditional approach to determining the finance charge payable on an extension of credit. A predetermined and certain rate of interest is applied to the principal.

Fixed Expenses- A cost that remains relatively constant. Examples include savings, investments, retirement contributions, taxes, mortgage or rent, debt payments, and insurance.

Fixed Rate (Mortgage) Loan- Generally has repayment terms of 15, 20, or 30 years. Both the interest rate and the monthly payments (for principal and interest) stay the same during the life of the loan.

Flexible Benefits -A type of plan under Section 125 of the Internal Revenue Code that provides employees a choice between permissible taxable benefits, including cash, and nontaxable benefits, such as life and health insurance, vacations, retirement plans, and child care. Although a common core of benefits may be required, the employee can determine how his or her remaining benefit dollars are to be allocated for each type of benefit from the total amount promised by the employer.

Flexible Expenses- Expenses that are flexible because they vary in amount, such as food. Or they are "discretionary," that is, what you spend for them is at your discretion, in contrast to fixed expenses that must be paid and are usually the same amount each month.

Flexible Spending Arrangements (FSA) -A health FSA allows employees to be reimbursed for medical expenses. FSAs are usually funded through voluntary salary reduction agreements with your employer. No employment or federal income taxes are deducted from your contribution. The employer may also contribute.

Foreclosure- A legal action that ends all ownership rights in a home when the homebuyer fails to make the mortgage payments or is otherwise in default under the terms of the mortgage.

Front-end Load – An upfront sales charge investors pay when they purchase mutual fund shares, generally used by the fund to compensate brokers. A front-end load reduces the amount available to purchase fund shares.

Fund Prospectus – Describes a mutual fund to prospective investors. Every mutual fund has a prospectus. The prospectus contains information about the mutual fund's costs, investment objectives, risks, and performance. You can get a prospectus from the mutual fund company (through its website or by phone or mail). Your financial professional or broker can also provide you with a copy.

G

Garnishments – Money withheld from an individual's paycheck and remitted to another party – usually a creditor.
Good Credit Risk – People with a high credit score who are very likely to pay back their debts in a timely fashion.

Good Debt – Credit used to purchase items that retain or increase in value over time. These items include homes, education loans, and cars. Purchases that gain value over time are viewed as an investment (e.g., a car enables one to get to school or work).

Government Pension Offset (GPO) – If you receive a pension from a federal, state, or local government based on work where you did not pay Social Security taxes, your Social Security spouse's or widow's/widower's benefits may be reduced. Benefits paid to wives, husbands, widows, and widowers are "dependent's" benefits. These benefits were established in the 1930s to compensate spouses who stayed home to raise a family and who were financially dependent on the working spouse. But as it has become more common for both spouses in a married couple to work, each earned his or her own Social Security retirement benefit. The law has always required that a person's benefit as a spouse, widow, or widower be offset dollar for dollar by the amount of his or her own retirement benefit.

Government Securities – Securities issued by the U.S. Treasury or federal agencies.

Government Thrift Savings Plan (TSP) – Congress established the TSP in the Federal Employees' Retirement System Act of 1986. The purpose of the TSP is to provide retirement income.

Grace Period – The time between the billing date and when finance charges will begin to accrue. Grace periods now range from 15 to 25 days. Under most credit card plans, the grace period applies only if you pay your balance in full each month. The grace period does not apply if you carry a balance forward, nor does it apply to cash advances.

Gross Income – Money earned before taxes and other deductions. Sometimes it may include income from self-employment, rental property, alimony, child support, public assistance payments, and retirement benefits.

H

Health Insurance – Offers protection from financial losses that could result from injury, illness, or disability.

Health Maintenance Organization (HMO) – A form of health insurance. An HMO is an organization of health-care professionals that provide health-care services to members on a prepaid basis. Some HMOs have their own clinic and hospital facilities; others contract with doctors and hospitals to provide care to members.

Hedge Funds – Like mutual funds, hedge funds pool investors' money and invest those funds in financial instruments in an effort to make a positive return. Many hedge funds seek to profit in all kinds of markets by pursuing leveraging and other speculative investment practices that may increase the risk of investment loss. Unlike mutual funds, however, hedge funds are not required to register with the U.S. Securities and Exchange Commission (SEC). Hedge funds typically issue securities in "private offerings" that are not registered with the SEC under the Securities Act of 1933. In addition, hedge funds are not required to make periodic reports under the Securities Exchange Act of 1934. But hedge funds are subject to the same prohibitions against fraud as are other market participants, and their managers have the same fiduciary duties as other investment advisers.

High-deductible Health Plan – A health insurance policy that requires the policyholder to pay more out-of-pocket medical expenses but usually has lower premiums than traditional health insurance plans.

High Risk Investments – Investments where your entire principal is potentially at risk. Examples of high-risk investments are futures contracts and collectibles.

High Risk Pool – Subsidized health insurance pools that are organized by some states. High risk pools offer health insurance to individuals who have been denied health insurance because of a medical condition or to individuals whose premiums are rated significantly higher than average due to health status or claims experience.

Home Equity Line of Credit – A mortgage loan, usually in a second mortgage, allowing a borrower to obtain cash against the equity of a home, up to a predetermined amount.

Home Equity Loan – A loan backed by the value of a home (real estate). If the borrower defaults or does not pay the loan, the lender has some rights to the property. The borrower can usually claim a home equity loan as a tax deduction.

Homeowner's Insurance – A policy that protects you and the lender from fire or flood, which damages the structure of the house; a liability, such as an injury to a visitor to your home; or damage to your personal property, such as your furniture, clothes, or appliances.

I

Identity Theft – An individual's personal information is used by another person without permission to open fraudulent accounts or commit other crimes.

Index Fund – A type of mutual fund or Unit Investment Trust (UIT) whose investment objective typically is to achieve the same return as a particular market index, such as the S&P 500 Composite Stock Price Index, the Russell 2000 Index, or the Wilshire 5000 Total Market Index.

Individual Development Account – A type of savings account, offered in some communities, for people whose income is below a certain level.

Individual Health Plan – An individual policy for a single person or family. This coverage is usually provided under a contract purchased through an insurance company, agent, or broker. It is not health insurance provided through a company or union.

Individual Retirement Account (IRA) – A retirement plan offered by banks, brokerage firms, and insurance companies to which individuals can contribute each year on a tax-deferred basis.

Inflation – A process of continuously rising prices, or equivalently, of a continuously falling value of money.

Inflation Assumption – How much you think the cost of living will rise each year, on average (see also "Cost of Living Index").

Inflation Rate – The rate at which prices of goods and services rise or fall.

Inheritance Tax – A tax on the right to receive property by inheritance; to be distinguished from an estate tax.

Installment Plan – A plan requiring a borrower to make payments at specified intervals over the life of a loan. Insurance – The management of risks that have financial consequences. A promise of compensation for specific potential future losses in exchange for a periodic payment. Insurance is designed to protect the financial well being of an individual, company, or other entity in the case of unexpected loss.

Insurance Premium – The payment you or your employer makes for insurance coverage.

Insured Deposit – Deposit in a Federal Deposit Insurance Corporation (FDIC)-insured commercial bank, savings bank, or savings association that is fully protected by FDIC deposit insurance. Savings, checking, and other deposit accounts, when combined, are generally insured up to $250,000 per depositor in each financial institution insured by the FDIC. Deposits held in different ownership categories, such as single or joint accounts, are separately insured. Also, separate $250,000 coverage is usually provided for retirement accounts, such as individual retirement accounts.

Interest – A fee charged for the use of borrowed money. Also, money earned on a savings account.

Interest Rate – The rate charged to borrow funds, usually from banks or other lending institutions.

Internet Banking – Usually conducted through a personal computer (PC) that connects to a banking website via the Internet. Internet banking can also be conducted via wireless technology through both personal digital assistants (PDAs) and cellular phones.

Investment – The act of investing means to place money into stocks, bonds, mutual funds, real estate, or other choices with the expectation that the value of the money invested will grow beyond the original amount invested.

Investment Clubs – A group of people who pool their money to make investments. Usually, investment clubs are organized as partnerships and, after the members study different investments, the group decides to buy or sell based on a majority vote of the members. Club meetings may be educational, and each member may actively participate in investment decisions.

Investment clubs have existed in the United States for nearly 100 years and are generally developed by a group of people who share social interests plus a desire to learn more about investing. The investment club is not for those who want to get rich quick but for those who want to be better off financially in five to 10 years and also learn the basics of investing in the stock market. Investment clubs encourage you to invest regularly and knowledgeably and to understand the various associated risks.

IRA (Individual Retirement Account) – A tax-deferred retirement account for an individual that permits individuals to set aside a set income amount per year, with earnings tax-deferred until withdrawals begin at age 59½ or later. Investors withdrawing money earlier than age 59½ may be subject to penalties for early withdrawals.

J

Joint Tenancy (with Rights of Survivorship) – Two or more owners share equal ownership and rights to the property. If a joint owner dies, his or her share of the property passes to the other owners, without probate. In joint tenancy, ownership of the property cannot be willed to someone who is not a joint owner.

Junk Bond – High-yield, high-risk debt that, in many cases, was issued to finance corporate takeovers.

L

Letter of Last Instruction – A letter that includes information about your funeral plans/preferences, obituary information, insurance policy contact information, a list of your financial accounts and debts, the location of important papers, keys/combinations for lockboxes and other locked containers, and a list of persons to be contacted in the event of death.

Liabilities – Anything that an individual owes. It includes credit card balances, college loan balances, automobile note balances, mortgage balances, and any other type of personal loan.

Lien – A creditor's claim against a property, which may entitle the creditor to seize the property if a debt is not repaid.

Life Insurance – A contract that pays the beneficiary a set sum of money upon the death of the policyholder. These plans usually pay benefits in the form of a lump sum, but they may be distributed as an annuity.

Liquid Assets – A cash asset or an asset that is easily converted into cash.

Liquidation – The process of converting securities or assets (property) into cash.

Living Will – An individual's written declaration of what life-sustaining medical treatments are allowable in case of incapacitation or terminal illness.

Long-term Care (LTC) Insurance – Provides for your "long-term care" if you become unable to take care of yourself because of the loss of functional capacity or cognitive impairment.

Long-term Disability Insurance – Provides a monthly benefit to employees who, due to a non-work-related injury or illness, are unable to perform the duties of their normal occupation or any other, for periods of time extending beyond their short-term disability or sickness and accident insurance.

Low Risk Investments – Investments, such as government savings bonds, where your principal – the money you invested – has a low potential of being at risk.

M

Margin – Borrowing money from your broker to buy a stock and using your investment as collateral. Investors generally use margin to increase their purchasing power so that they can own more stock without fully paying for it. However, margin exposes investors to the potential for higher losses.

Market Value – The amount a seller can expect to receive on the open market for merchandise, services, or securities.

Medicaid – Provides health coverage for low-income people who cannot afford it. Each state operates its own Medicaid program and, therefore, determines who is eligible and the scope of health services offered.

Medical Durable Power of Attorney – Authorizes your representative to make medical decisions based on what you have specified in your living will.

Medical Payments Coverage – Insurance that covers all injured occupants of your car, regardless of fault. It also covers members of your family if they are pedestrians struck by a car.

Medicare – A health insurance program for people age 65 or older, people under age 65 with certain disabilities, and people of all ages with end-stage renal disease (permanent kidney failure requiring dialysis or a kidney transplant).

Medium Risk – Your principal investment has a medium potential of being at risk. Examples of medium risk investments include high-quality stocks, bonds, and mutual funds; real estate; and aggressive growth stocks, bonds, and mutual funds.

Money Market Deposit Account – A type of savings account offered by a financial institution. The Federal government insures money market deposit accounts. They are liquid investments with a rate of interest that is lower than most other investments.

Money Market Mutual Fund – A highly liquid mutual fund that invests in short-term obligations such as commercial paper, government securities, and certificates of deposit.

Mortgage-backed Security (MBS) – An ordinary bond backed by an interest in a pool of mortgages or trust deeds. The interest and principal payments collected on the underlying mortgages are the source of income to the bondholders. The Resolution Trust Corporation (RTC), which began issuing one-to-four family residential mortgage- backed securities in June 1991, was instrumental in developing the MBS market in the early 1990s. Most mortgage- backed securities have AA or AAA bond ratings.

Mortgage Insurance – A policy that protects lenders against some or most of the losses that can occur when a borrower defaults on a mortgage loan. Mortgage insurance is required primarily for borrowers with a down payment of less than 20 percent of the home's purchase price. The cost of mortgage insurance is usually added to the monthly payment. Mortgage insurance is maintained on conventional loans until the outstanding amount of the loan is less than 80 percent of the value of the house or for a set period of time (7 years is common). Mortgage insurance also is available through a government agency, such as the Federal Housing Administration (FHA) or through companies (Private Mortgage Insurance or PMI).

Mortgage Loan – A temporary and conditional pledge of property to a creditor as security for the repayment of debt.

Municipal Bond – A bond issued by cities, counties, states, and local governmental agencies to finance public projects, such as construction of bridges, schools, and highways. Municipal bonds are exempt from federal taxes and from most state and local taxes, especially if you live in the state in which the bond is issued. "Munis" are bought for their favorable tax implications and are popular with people in high income tax brackets.

Mutual Fund – A pool of money managed by an investment company. The funds are invested in a variety of securities, including stocks, bonds, and money market securities.

N

Negative Amortization – An increase in the principal of a loan, when the loan payments are insufficient to pay the interest due. The unpaid interest is added to the outstanding loan balance, causing the principal to increase rather than decrease as payments are made. This situation typically occurs in an adjustable mortgage with an annual cap limiting any increases in the interest rate, and also in a graduated payment mortgage, which has low initial payments so moderate-income borrowers can afford to make the loan payments.

Net Asset Value (NAV) – The value of a fund's assets minus its liabilities. To calculate the NAV per share, simply subtract the fund's liabilities from its assets and then divide the result by the number of shares outstanding.

Net Income – Amount of money remaining after income taxes, Social Security, Medicare, insurance (health, life, disability, etc.), flexible spending plan contributions, retirement savings, and other items have been deducted. Also known as take-home pay.

Net Worth – The difference between the total assets and total liabilities of an individual.
Net Worth Statement – See "Statement of Financial Position."

No Load Mutual Fund – A mutual fund whose shares are sold without a commission or sales charge. The shares are distributed directly by the investment company.

O

Office of the Comptroller of the Currency (OCC) – A bureau within the U.S. Department of the Treasury, established in 1863. The OCC charters, regulates, and supervises national banks, which can usually be identified because they have the word "national" or "national association" in their names. The OCC also supervises and regulates the federally licensed branches and agencies of foreign banks doing business in the United States.

The Comptroller of the Currency, who is appointed by the president of the United States, with Senate confirmation, and who is one of the Federal Deposit Insurance Corporation's (FDIC's) five directors, heads the OCC.

Office of Thrift Supervision (OTS) – An organization within the U.S. Department of the Treasury, established on August 9, 1989. The OTS, with five regional offices located in Jersey City, Atlanta, Chicago, Dallas, and San Francisco, is the primary regulator of all federal and many state chartered thrift institutions. A director, who is appointed by the president, with Senate confirmation, for a five-year term and who is one of the five FDIC directors, heads the OTS.

On-line Banking – Access by personal computer or terminal to bank information, accounts, and certain transactions via the financial institution's website on the Internet.

P

Passbook Savings Account – An account that a bank or savings institution issues to keep record of deposits, withdrawals, and interest earned in the savings account. Usually pays a very low interest rate.

Payday Loan – A transaction in which a short-term cash advance is made to a consumer in exchange for a customer's post-dated check in the amount of the advance plus a fee, or in exchange for a consumer's authorization to debit a transaction account in the amount of the advance plus a fee at a designated future date.

Payroll Deduction Plan – A plan in which an employee authorizes an employer to deduct a specified amount from the employee's pay and put the funds toward insurance, health care, or an investment account. For example, it is common for employees to deduct a set percentage of income and contribute it to their Traditional or Roth IRAs.

Perils – For homeowner's insurance, an event that can damage the property. Homeowner's insurance may cover the property for a wide variety of perils caused by accidents, nature, or people.

Personal Income – The dollar value of income received from all sources by individuals.

PITI – The four elements of a monthly mortgage payment (principal, interest, taxes, and insurance). Payments of principal and interest go directly towards repaying the loan, while the portion that covers property taxes and insurance (homeowner's and mortgage [see "Private Mortgage Insurance" for further explanation], if applicable) goes into an escrow account to cover the fees when they are due.

Points – In reference to a loan, points consist of a lump sum payment made by the borrower at the outset of the loan period. Generally, each point equals 1 percent of the loan amount.

Portfolio – An individual's or entity's combined holdings of stocks, bonds, or other securities and assets.

Predatory Lending – Targeting loans to elderly, low-income, and other people to take advantage of their financial status or lack of financial knowledge.

Preexisting Condition – Any physical or mental condition that an individual has before health coverage begins.

Preferred Provider Organization (PPO) – A form of health insurance. A PPO is made up of a group of medical care providers (doctors, hospitals, etc.) who contract with a health insurance company to provide services at an agreed upon discounted price.

Preferred Stock – A form of ownership interest in a bank or other company that entitles its holders to some preference or priority over the owners of common stock, usually with respect to dividends or asset distributions in a liquidation.

Premium – The payment, or one of the regular periodic payments, that a policyholder makes to own an insurance policy or annuity.
Prepayment Penalty – A provision in some loans that charge a fee to a borrower who pays off a loan before it is due.
Principal – The unpaid balance on a loan, not including interest; the amount of money invested.

Private Mortgage Insurance (PMI) – Insurance purchased by a buyer to protect the lender in the event of default. The cost of mortgage insurance is usually added to the monthly payment. Mortgage insurance is generally maintained until over 20 percent of the outstanding amount of the loan is paid or for a set period of time – seven years is normal. Mortgage insurance may be available through a government agency, such as the Federal Housing Administration (FHA) or the Veterans Administration (VA), or through private mortgage insurance companies (PMI).

Prospectus – See "Fund Prospectus."

Q

Qualified Tuition Program – See "529 Plan."

R

Redlining – A practice in which certain areas of a community are eliminated from eligibility for mortgages or other loans, either intentionally or unintentionally, allegedly because the area is considered a poor investment risk.

Refinancing – Paying off one loan by obtaining another; generally done to secure better loan terms (like a lower interest rate).

Replacement Level – The percentage of your income you wish to replace at retirement. One rule of thumb frequently used in projecting retirement income needs is an easy one to remember: plan to replace about 70 to 90 percent of your pre- retirement income to maintain your same pre-retirement level of living. Some experts suggest a replacement level close to 100 percent, while others may suggest different levels.

Replacement Rate – The percentage of total salary you will need to save from now until retirement age to achieve your desired income during retirement.

Repossession – To reclaim possession of goods or property, for failure to pay installments due.

Retirement Confidence Survey (RCS) – The country's most established and comprehensive study of the attitudes and behavior of American workers and retirees towards all aspects of saving, retirement planning, and long-term financial security. Sponsored by the Employee Benefit Research Institute (EBRI), the American Savings Education Council (ASEC), and Mathew Greenwald & Associates (Greenwald), the annual RCS is a random, nationally representative survey of 1,000 individuals age 25 and over.

Retirement Plan – A plan for setting aside funds from current income in appropriate investments with the expectation that money will accumulate and grow so that period withdrawals may be made during retirement. The term can also refer to the individual investment options offered to employees by employers.

Retirement Portfolio – See "Retirement Plan" and "Portfolio."

Reverse Mortgage – A type of mortgage used by senior homeowners age 62 and older to convert the equity in their home into monthly streams of income and/or a line of credit to be repaid when they no longer occupy the home.

Roth IRA – Unlike a traditional IRA, you cannot deduct contributions to a Roth IRA from your taxes; however, if you satisfy the requirements, qualified distributions are tax-free. Contributions can be made to your Roth IRA after you reach age 70½, and you can leave amounts in your Roth IRA as long as you live.

Rule of 72 – Used to determine how many years it will take your money to double. Divide 72 by the annual interest rate.

S

Savers [Tax] Credit (formally known as the Retirement Savings Contributions Credit) – Low and moderate-income workers who contributed to a retirement plan, such as an IRA or 401(k) may be able to take the savers credit.

Savings and Loan Association – A state or federally chartered financial institution that accepts savings and checkable deposits from the public and invests them primarily in mortgage loans. A savings and loan association may be either a mutual or capital stock institution and may also make loans to businesses and consumers.

Savings Bank – Depository institution historically engaged primarily in accepting consumer savings deposits and in originating and investing in securities and residential mortgage loans; now may offer checking-type deposits and make a wider range of loans.

Savings Bond – Non-marketable, registered securities issued by the U.S. Treasury Department. Non-marketable means they cannot be sold to or bought from anyone except an issuing and paying agent authorized by the Treasury Department. Registered means they are owned exclusively by the person or persons named on them. Savings bonds are backed by the full faith and credit of the United States.

SCHIP (State Children's Health Insurance Program) – Administered by the Federal Centers for Medicare and Medicaid Services, SCHIP makes funds available to states that have programs providing health insurance coverage to uninsured children. Each state sets its own guidelines for eligibility and services.

Section 8 – A program of the Department of Housing and Urban Development (HUD) that provides rental assistance to low- and very low-income families. HUD pays the difference between the market rent of a unit and the amount that the tenant is able to pay.

Secured Debt – Debt backed or secured by collateral to reduce the risk associated with lending.

Securities – Paper certificates (definitive securities) or electronic records (book-entry securities) evidencing ownership of equity (stocks) or debt obligations (bonds).

Series EE/E Savings Bond – A secure savings product that pays interest based on current market rates for up to 30 years on Treasury securities. Interest is calculated semiannually but paid at maturity and is exempt from state and local taxes.

Series I Savings Bonds – A low-risk, liquid savings product that while you own them, earn interest and help protect your savings from inflation. They pay a fixed rate that is lower than traditional savings bonds, but they also pay a variable rate that increases with inflation.

Set-Aside Account – A place to put money that you know you will need for expenses that occur periodically.

Short-Term Disability Insurance – Provides short-term (typically 26 weeks) income protection to employees who are unable to work due to a non-work-related accident or illness.

Simple Interest – Interest that is paid only on the original amount borrowed for the length of time the borrower has use of the credit. The amount borrowed is referred to as the principal. In the simple interest rate calculation, interest is calculated only on that portion of the original principal still owed.

SIMPLE Plan – A tax-favored retirement plan that certain small employers (including self-employed individuals) can set up for the benefit of their employees. A SIMPLE plan is a written agreement (salary reduction agreement) between you and your employer that allows you, if you are an eligible employee (including a self-employed individual), to choose to reduce your compensation (salary) by a certain percentage each pay period and have your employer contribute the salary reductions to a SIMPLE IRA on your behalf. These contributions are called salary reduction contributions.

Simplified Employee Pension (SEP) Plan – Provides a simplified method for small businesses to make contributions to a retirement plan for themselves and their employees. Instead of setting up a profit sharing or money purchase plan with a trust, they can adopt a SEP agreement and make contributions directly to a traditional individual retirement account or a traditional individual retirement annuity (SEP-IRA) set up for themselves and each eligible employee.

Social Security – A United States government program of social insurance and benefits enacted in 1935. The Social Security program's benefits include retirement income, disability income, Medicare and Medicaid, and death and survivorship benefits. Social Security is one of the largest government programs in the world, paying out hundreds of billions of dollars per year.

Based on the year someone was born, retirement benefits may begin as early as age 62 and as late as age 67. The amount of income received is based on the average wages earned over the worker's lifetime, with a maximum calculable amount of $102,000 as of 2008.

Spouses are also eligible to receive Social Security benefits, even if they have limited or non-existent work histories. If your spouse is eligible for retirement benefits on his or her own earnings record, Social Security will pay that amount first. But if the benefit on your record is a higher amount, he or she will get a combination of benefits that equals that higher amount (reduced for age).

Social Security Number (SSN) – A federal taxpayer identification number for Americans. An SSN number is required to get a job and claim taxes or other tax benefits.

Speculation – The practice of buying or selling stocks, commodities, land, or other types of assets hoping to take advantage of an expected rise or fall in price.

Statement of Financial Position – An inventory of an individual's assets and liabilities at a particular moment in time. Record includes a net worth calculation, which subtracts the liabilities from the assets. Also known as a Net Worth Statement.

Statement of Income and Expense – A time-specific document that summarizes income received and expenses paid for a full, 12-month year. The overall format is flexible. Expenses are categorized as fixed or variable.

Stock – Security or instrument that represents a unit of ownership in a corporation.
Stockholder – A person who owns stock in a company and is eligible to share in profits and losses; same as shareholder.

Sub-Prime Loan – An industry term used to describe loans with less stringent lending and underwriting terms and conditions. Due to the higher risk, sub-prime loans charge higher interest rates and fees.

Supplemental Security Income (SSI) – A Federal income supplement program funded by general tax revenues (not Social Security taxes). It is designed to help aged, blind, and disabled people, who have little or no income; and it provides cash to meet basic needs for food, clothing, and shelter.

T

Take-home Pay – See "Net Income."

Temporary Assistance for Needy Families (TANF) – A program that is designed to help needy families achieve self-sufficiency. It replaced the welfare programs known as Aid to Families with Dependent Children (AFDC), the Job Opportunities and Basic Skills Training (JOBS) program, and the Emergency Assistance (EA) program. The TANF Bureau within the U.S. Department of Health and Human Services provides assistance and work opportunities to needy families by granting states, territories, and tribes the federal funds and wide flexibility to develop and implement their own welfare programs. The assistance is time-limited and promotes work, responsibility, and self-sufficiency.

Term – The period from when a loan is made until it is fully paid.

Term Life – A type of life insurance that provides insurance protection for a set period of time. Term policies are written for 1, 5, 10, or 20 years. If you die before the time period ends, your beneficiaries receive the death benefit.

Thrift Institution (Bank) – A financial institution that ordinarily possesses the same depository, credit, financial intermediary, and account transactional functions as a bank but that is chiefly organized and primarily operates to promote savings and home mortgage lending rather than commercial lending. Also known as a savings bank, a savings association, a savings and loan association, or an S & L.

Thrift Savings Plan (TSP) – A retirement plan similar to a 401(k) plan that is offered to federal government employees.

Time Value of Money – The idea that a dollar now is worth more than a dollar in the future, even after adjusting for inflation, because a dollar now can earn interest or other appreciation until the time the dollar in the future would be received.

Total Disability – The definitions of "total" disability vary from policy to policy. Some define it as being unable to perform your own occupation, while a more comprehensive definition would require that you are unable to perform any occupation.

Traditional IRA – An individual retirement account (IRA) that allows individuals to direct pretax income, up to specific annual limits, toward investments that can grow tax-deferred (no capital gains or dividend income is taxed). Individual taxpayers are allowed to contribute 100 percent of compensation up to a specified maximum dollar amount to their Traditional IRA. Contributions to the Traditional IRA may be tax-deductible depending on the taxpayer's income, tax-filing status, and other factors.

Treasury Bill (T-Bill) – Short-term U.S. Treasury security having a maturity of up to one year and issued in denominations of $10,000 to $1 million. T-bills are sold at a discount. Investors purchase a bill at a price lower than the face value (for example, the investor might buy a $10,000 bill for $9,700). The return is the difference between the price paid and the amount received when the bill is sold or it matures (if held to maturity, the return on the T-bill in the example would be $300).

Treasury Bond – Long-term security having a maturity of 10 years or longer, issued in denominations of $1,000 or more. Treasury bonds pay interest semiannually, and the principal is payable at maturity.

Treasury Inflation-Protected Securities (TIPS) – Marketable U.S. Treasury securities whose principal is adjusted by changes in the Consumer Price Index. TIPS pay interest every six months and are issued with maturities of 5, 10, and 30 years.

Treasury Note – Intermediate-term security having a maturity of 1 to 10 years and issued in denominations of $1,000 or more. Notes pay interest semiannually, and the principal is payable at maturity. When you purchase a treasury note, you are lending money to the government. Treasury notes are backed by the full faith and credit of the U. S. government.

Treasury Securities – Interest-bearing obligations of the U.S. government issued by the Treasury as a means of borrowing; money to meet government expenditures not covered by tax revenues. Marketable Treasury securities fall into three categories: bills, notes, and bonds.

Trust – A fiduciary relationship in which one person (the trustee) is the holder of the legal title to property (the trust property) subject to an equitable obligation (an obligation enforceable in a court of equity) to keep or use the property for the benefit of another person (the beneficiary).

Two-cycle Daily Balance Method – A calculation used by a credit card company to determine finance charges using two months of credit transactions. An average daily balance is calculated for the current billing period and the previous billing period, with the total being divided by the total number of days in both billing periods.

U

Unemployment Insurance – In general, the Federal-State Unemployment Insurance Program provides unemployment benefits to eligible workers who are unemployed through no fault of their own (as determined under State law) and meet other eligibility requirements of State law. Each State administers a separate unemployment insurance program within the guidelines established by Federal law. Eligibility for unemployment insurance, benefit amounts, and the length of time benefits are available is determined by the State law under which unemployment insurance claims are established.

Unsecured Debt – Debt issued and supported only by the borrower's creditworthiness rather than by some sort of collateral.

U.S. Securities and Exchange Commission (SEC) – The mission of the U.S. Securities and Exchange Commission is to protect investors; maintain fair, orderly, and efficient markets; and facilitate capital formation. It is the responsibility of the Commission to: interpret federal securities laws; issue new rules and amend existing rules; oversee the inspection of securities firms, brokers, investment advisers, and ratings agencies; oversee private regulatory organizations in the securities, accounting, and auditing fields; and coordinate U.S. securities regulation with federal, state, and foreign authorities.

V

Variable Annuities – With a variable annuity, money is placed in subaccounts invested in stock and bond funds. Overall, the return on a variable annuity is subject to market fluctuation. Total value depends on how much risk the annuity owner assumes, performance of the subaccounts, and what charges and fees are deducted. Over the long term, variable annuities reflect performance and growth in the economy and can serve as an effective hedge against inflation. However, it is possible to lose money in a variable annuity.

Variable Expenses – Costs that change in proportion to an activity or use. Examples include food, transportation, clothing, education, medical, and utilities.

Vested – The amount of time you must work before earning a non-forfeitable right to your accrued pension benefit funded by employer contributions. When you are fully "vested," your accrued benefit will be yours, even if you leave the company before reaching retirement age. Employees always have a non-forfeitable right to their own contributions. There are changes to the two basic vesting schedules. Under the three-year schedule, workers are 100 percent vested after five years of service under the plan. The six-year graduated schedule allows workers to become 20 percent vested after two years and to vest at a rate of 20 percent each year thereafter until they are 100 percent vested after six years of service. Plans may have faster vesting schedules.

W

Wage Growth Assumption – How much you think your paycheck will increase each year, on average.

Whole Life Insurance – The most common type of permanent life insurance. Generally, the premiums remain constant over the life of the policy. The cash value grows based on a fixed interest rate.

Will – A legal document that names the person you have designated as executor of your estate, specifies how you want the assets of your estate to be distributed after any debts and taxes are paid, and states who will care for your minor children. The will goes into effect upon the death of the signer.

Windfall Elimination Provision – Affects how the amount of your retirement or disability benefit is calculated if you receive a pension from work where Social Security taxes were not taken out of your pay. A modified formula is used to calculate your benefit amount, resulting in a lower Social Security benefit than you otherwise would receive.

Wraparound – A financing device that permits an existing loan to be refinanced and new money to be advanced at an interest rate between the rate charged on the old loan and the current market interest rate. The creditor combines or "wraps" the remainder of the old loan with the new loan at the intermediate rate.

Y

Yield – The effective annual rate of return on an investment expressed as a percentage.

Made in the USA
San Bernardino, CA
08 February 2015